GREAT WESTERNER

KIT CARSON

GREAT WESTERNER

THE STORY OF KIT CARSON

By

BERNICE BLACKWELDER

Time is pursued by a pitiless, cruel oblivion,
Following fast and near.

EUGENE F. WARE

THE CAXTON PRINTERS, LTD.
CALDWELL, IDAHO
1962

First printing, February 1962
Second printing, October 1962

©1962 BY
THE CAXTON PRINTERS, LTD.
CALDWELL, IDAHO

Library of Congress Catalog Card No. 62-8186

Printed, lithographed, and bound in the United States of America by
The CAXTON PRINTERS, Ltd.
Caldwell, Idaho
95700

Acknowledgments

IT HAS BEEN a rare privilege to search through the legacy left by writers of a century or more ago as well as works of contemporary historians. I have helped myself liberally not only from their store of information but have used their colorful phrasings and expressions as well.

I am deeply indebted to many persons who have been generous with their time and effort in directing me toward material and data for this book. My thanks to the excellent staff of the Thomas Jefferson Reading Room of The Library of Congress and those who assisted me at The Department of Old Army, The Department of the Interior, and The Bureau of Indian Affairs of The National Archives, particularly Marshall Moody, who directed my search of records there.

The sympathetic encouragement of Dr. Jonathan T. Dorris, Professor Emeritus of History, Eastern Kentucky State College, Richmond, Kentucky, and the late Dr. Frederick A. Culmer, Professor Emeritus of History, Central College, Fayette, Missouri, must be mentioned. Also Nancy Elliott of Wellesley, Massachusetts, for her assistance in typing and correlating the material; Major Jack K. Boyer, director of The Carson Museum, Taos, New Mexico, for supplying the Carson photograph and for his continuing cooperation; Quantrille D. McClung, of Denver, Colorado, whose book, *The Carson, Bent and Boggs Genealogy* is currently being prepared for publication by The Colorado State Library of Denver, for her invaluable support; and especially R. Lynn Martin, trustee of The Winnifred Martin Memorial Library of Western Reference Works, Brookville, Kansas, without whose editorial help, guidance, and encouragement this book would not have reached completion.

My deepest gratitude must go to the late John J. McCurdy, veteran Kansas lawyer, historian, and family friend who first aroused my curiosity about Kit Carson and urged me to write this book. After visiting Carson's unkempt grave in 1924, John J. McCurdy organized The Kit Carson Memorial Foundation and devoted the remainder of his life to reviving interest in the history of The Great Westerner.

Table of Contents

Border Boy (1809-1828)

The thoughts of youth are long, long thoughts.

HENRY WADSWORTH LONGFELLOW

MISSOURI's hardwoods were tingeing, bittersweet pulsed languorously in the underbrush, and September waited quietly, expectantly.

There was stepped-up activity on Franklin common as there always was before the take-off of the annual wagon freight and Workman's saddlery was a hub of excitement. The saddler's apprentice, working steadily at his bench repairing harness, laid down his awl to gaze out the open door. He was a rather ordinary-looking youth, clothed like any border boy in nettle shirt and linsey-woolsey from his mother's loom, quiet and undersized, likely to be overlooked among his tall brothers. Certainly no one in the village would have suspected great dreams of adventure to stir within this mild, unprepossessing sixteen-year-old.

Kit Carson looked toward the west as all Carson men had since the first one left Dumfriesshire, Scotland, to find greater freedom in North Ireland. His grandfather, William—first to cross to America—settled in North Carolina with a grant from Lord Grenville and died one hot day before the Revolution from "an over-draught of water from the church pump." The eldest son, Lindsey, with Wade Hampton's Brigade, turned away from an inheritance of many acres on the Yadkin to follow Daniel Boone down the Wilderness Road to Kentucky when the lands west of the Alleghenies were first open to settlement.[1]

Choosing a heavily wooded tract in Madison County,
Lindsey Carson and his older sons began a logging
business, binding the logs into rafts to be floated by
creek and river to New Orleans. A double-roomed
house of ash and poplar logs with a solid rock chimney was built at the edge of the clearing by Tate's
Creek. Here, on Christmas Eve of 1809, Lindsey's
second wife, Rebecca, presented him with his ninth
child. The son was named Christopher Houston, for
a patriot friend in North Carolina, but affectionately
called Kit throughout his lifetime.

As the land began to fill up, Daniel Boone, disgusted at finding himself practically landless for having failed to file the proper claim papers, decided to
move on beyond the Mississippi River, where there
was more elbowroom, and to mark a site for a new
settlement on the Missouri. Kit was not yet two years
old when he was lifted out of Kentucky to follow
Boone's trail to Missouri.[2]

Taking their goods and livestock down the pike,
the Carsons passed the little cabin on Knob Creek
where Thomas Lincoln lived with his wife and small
son, eleven months older than Kit Carson. The families were acquainted, for Thomas Lincoln's father had
also come to Kentucky with Boone and settled not
far from the Carson homestead. The journey was a
safe one, Rebecca riding the tiresome miles horseback
and holding her little son in front of her between the
reins.

In the new settlement—later to be named Franklin
—in the territory designated as Missouri, North Loui-
siana, three picket forts, Hempstead, Kincaid, and
Cooper, were hastily put up, for the country was again
at war with England and the peril of Indian attack
had become more acute. The zealously patriotic Lind-

sey Carson and his older sons served in the militia on frontier duty while the families lived close together in the forts and, under guard, made the clearings, put in crops, and built their homes.

The crude fort was the first home Kit Carson could remember. The sturdy stockade seemed secure enough but most of the cattle and horses were stolen. An Indian crawled in from the forest during a thunderstorm, picked a hole in the chinking between the logs, and killed Captain Sarshall Cooper as he sat before the fire holding his youngest child. Kit's father lost a finger, shot off in a surprise attack.[3]

The pioneer children were not to be denied "book learning" and Kit was among the first pupils in the tiny log hut schoolroom built behind the stockade with a floor of poles laid on the ground. Daniel Boone himself took a load of skins down river to St. Louis to trade for textbooks and brought back a young schoolmaster, John Savage, who saw Kit through the primary grades, the extent of his formal education.[4] Lindsey Carson had hopes of making a lawyer of this quickwitted son who apparently was to be the runt of the family, even though an extra fee was required for such subjects as history and geography; but tragedy was to change these plans. (In later years, Kit jokingly explained the early end of his schooling thus: "I was a young boy in the schoolhouse when the cry came: 'Indians!' I jumped to my rifle and threw down my spelling book and there it lies!")

After four years the families felt safe enough to come out of the stockade. The Carsons moved into a sturdy farmhouse a few miles from the village. It was near the spot where Lewis and Clark had camped a decade before on Bonne Femme Creek. The children rode horseback to and from school, sometimes two and three to a horse. One morning, after heavy rains had brought up the creek, one of the horses bolted at the flooded ford, throwing Mary Ann and one of the Calloway girls into the water. Kit, following closely, urged his pony into the rushing stream in time to pull the girls up on his horse, acting with surprisingly mature calm for so young a lad.[5]

Like any border boy, Kit spent every extra hour hunting in the woods and participating in shooting matches. His marksmanship was becoming incredible. When he was nine, his father was killed by a falling limb while fighting a brush fire on a neighboring farm. Soon after this tragedy, the family was increased to fifteen children with the birth of Lindsey, Jr.

The town of Franklin, growing steadily from the start, was a transplanted bit of Kentucky rather than a typically raw frontier settlement. By 1820 there was a one-room library; a newspaper, the *Missouri Intelligencer and Boon's Lick Advertiser;* a meeting-house warmed by an open fire in the middle of the floor under a chimney; a dozen or more stores and taverns and about 120 houses—some with a second story of brick.[6] Daniel Boone died that year without realizing his ambition to reach Santa Fe. Only a few daredevils had crossed the Great Plains to that far-off Spanish city and no one yet had taken a wagon there and returned to tell the tale—every attempt ending in disaster or oblivion. In May of 1819, Kit Carson and his brothers had witnessed a great event that would put Franklin on the map—the arrival of the first steamboat, the *Independence,* which puffed past the snags and sand bars from St. Louis to Franklin in seven "sailing days," to be greeted by a wildly cheering crowd and a federal salute.[7] Two years later, William Beck-

nell, a Franklin man, took three wagons filled with
everything from pig iron to luxurious feminine ap-
parel and made it to Santa Fe and back to show a
huge profit. Incidentally, Becknell brought back to
Franklin several jacks that were the progenitors of
the famous Missouri mules.[8]
Franklin, the tip of the wedge of the settled area,
soon became known as the Cradle of the Trade link-
ing the East to the Spanish Southwest, a busy terminal where trappers unloaded their winter's catch and
wagons assembled to lay in supplies for the overland
journey. The huge freight wagons, loaded with skins
and furs, began arriving late in the spring, having
left New Mexico as soon as winter was over and the
new grasses high enough for forage. The teamsters
—many of them French-Canadian *engagés* who had
worked their way down from Montreal by boat—went
on to St. Louis for a taste of civilized living while the
traders rested a few weeks and stocked the wagons for
the return trip, planning to leave as late in the summer as possible to avoid the heat but still be assured
grass enough for the animals.

Four years after his father's tragic death, Kit's mother
married Joseph Martin, a widower neighbor with several children. The stepfather did not share the family's high plans for Kit's education but arranged for
him to be apprenticed to David Workman, an English-
born saddler, so that he could contribute to the support of the family which now included a half brother,
John Martin. In the busy saddle shop, in an atmosphere of acrid tanning vats, crisp new leather, and old
harness, Kit Carson learned a useful trade though he
later confessed that the only use he had for a saddle
was on a horse's back. After two years at his bench,

listening to exciting tales of adventure, Kit became restless. When the wagons were being prepared for the trek west in September, 1826, the saddler's assistant asked to be taken along.

The older Carson brothers, all veteran teamsters of the Santa Fe Trail, thought Kit too young. His employer, "a tall, hard-featured man, and most determined,"[9] did not take the request seriously. Only his mother listened sympathetically, promising he might go the next year, but now was bound to Davy Workman.

On the morning the great wagon freight was to pull out, Kit stood with the crowd gathered at sun-up to watch the departure. The wagons were ready —twenty-six carefully loaded Pittsburghs covered with double heavy white sailcloth drawn tightly over six-foot iron hoops; the bottoms caulked with tar so the wagons could be floated if necessary; extra lumber for broken tongues and spokes strapped underneath and the sleek, well-fed mules hitched in the harness Kit had helped repair.

At last there came the wagon master's loud shout, "All set!" followed shortly by a resounding "Stretch out!" At this signal, the "navigator," sitting astride a rear mule, whipped out a sixteen-foot lash and with a great clamor of clanking chains and creaking wheels, the bulging wagons started. Kit's heart was pounding before the last of the billowing whitetops had disappeared into the enveloping dust. He made a quick decision to go along no matter what the consequences —the first of many instant though momentous decisions that would guide his adventuresome life.

After the crowd broke up, Kit went back to his bench. He worked throughout the day but after a sleepless night he picked up his father's old rifle and

slipped quietly down the outside ladder leading from
the loft where he slept. On a mule left grazing un-
claimed on the commons, Kit rode off to overtake the
caravan.[10]

The sight of a solitary rider caught the eye of the
traders, and they thought it might be the bearer of
news. When Kit galloped in shouting for his brothers,
they insisted that he be sent home. Next morning he
started dutifully back but after riding a mile, turned
the mule loose to find its way to Franklin, then walked
back to the wagon camp. The wagon master hired
the plucky boy to herd the loose stock at fifty cents a
day and board.[11]

Kit's disappearance was noted in Franklin but Davy
Workman knew well enough what had happened. He
waited a few days, then, as required by law, inserted
the famous notice in the *Missouri Intelligencer,* October 12, 1826:

> *Notice is hereby given to all persons,* That Chris-
> topher Carson, a boy about 16 years old, small of his
> age, but thick set; light hair, ran away from the sub-
> scriber, living in Franklin, Howard county, Missouri,
> to whom he had been bound to learn the saddler's
> trade, on or before the first of September last. He is
> supposed to have made his way towards the upper
> part of the state. All persons are notified not to har-
> bor, support or assist said boy under the penalty of
> the law. One cent reward will be given to any person
> who will bring back the said boy.
>
> DAVID WORKMAN
>
> Franklin, Oct. 6, 1826.   16-3w

Fortunately, the ruse worked; the reward was never
claimed. No doubt David Workman was sympathetic
to his apprentice. The following year he went to Santa
Fe with the wagons himself.

✕ By 1826 the frontier had not yet reached halfway across the continent. Except for the freight road, the country was but slightly traced with crossing trails of buffalo and Indian. The land west of the border states, while officially United States territory for a quarter of a century, was still possessed by the Indians of the Plains: the Pawnee, Osage, Comanche, Sioux and Kanzas. Not even Missouri's powerful Senator Benton, who was completely and uncompromisingly dedicated to the development of the West, could envision expansion beyond the Rockies which he called "a convenient, natural and everlasting boundary." Plans were being drawn to build a small military post, Fort Leavenworth, the following year just beyond the Missouri River, this to be the sole protection for these endless miles and empty acres.

The last link with civilization was only an oak woods, given the name Council Grove the year before by George Sibley, the leader of a surveying party, to designate the spot where a treaty had been made with the chiefs of the Osage tribe. Kit's brothers, Andrew and Robert, were with Sibley's expedition to mark the road to "St. Afee" and legend holds that one of them nailed a buffalo hide carved with the name COUNCIL GROVE to an oak that still remains. This was the last big stand of timber that would be seen for hundreds of miles.[12]

When young Carson joined the great trade caravan, he became part of a well-planned, capable organization with the wagon master in full command. The men, working for a dollar a day and rations, were divided into messes with one of them cook and firewood gatherer for his group. Each man was his own dishwasher. The teamsters were responsible for the mules. Scouts and hunters, hired especially for the job, rode ahead but everyone was expected to bag game if he could—prairie chicken, rabbit, fish.

The trees gradually thinned until they were seen only along the streams. Grassy hills folded into an ever-widening horizon and rolled down to a flat prairie land. Days, slowly marked off, fell into a monotonous pattern—wagons rolling by sunup, a leisurely nooning with the men stretched out on the ground to rest while the animals grazed, the camp site reached by late afternoon. The wagons, carrying as much as three tons each with eight or ten mules, could make scarcely more than twelve miles a day in good weather. They were drawn into a protective circle with tongues pointing out and wheels linked with heavy log chains to form a corral with an opening left at one end for a gate. Beans and sowbelly was the staple food and bed, a blanket under the open sky.

The lush long-stemmed grass gave way to short grama grass that spread like an inch-thick sponge until the plains slip into the foothills of the Rockies. This was the buffalo range. Hump meat roasting on sticks over the fire helped revive sagging spirits.

The trail cut deep and dusty grooves across the drab gray-green face of the prairie. Occasional bright patches of sunflowers and purple verbena grew profusely "where there were no hands to pick and few eyes to admire."[13] Sudden storms ripped open the sky to flood the fords and mire down the mules. Lightning sometimes struck the iron wheel rims and stunned the animals within the enclosure while the men sought protection under the wagons. Moving day to weary day, through storms and blasting midday sun, the string of dusty wagons crawled across a deserted land—often the only living, moving thing to be seen in all the emptiness.

There was a constant dread of sickness and accident. A thunderstorm could start a stampede or a
rattlesnake cause a runaway with overturned wagons,
dumped loads, splintered spokes and broken wagon
tongues. Kit Carson was early initiated into firsthand knowledge of the hazards of the trail when he
played an important part in what probably was the
first operation ever performed on the Plains.

One of the teamsters, Andrew Broaddus, accidentally picked up his rifle by the barrel, discharging the
load into his forearm. After several days of extreme
suffering and near death from gangrene, he finally
consented to an amputation. Young Kit volunteered
to give whatever help he could. As the only instrument available was a handsaw too coarse to be used,
one of the men filed a set of teeth along the smooth
edge of the saw. Another removed the kingbolt from
one of the wagons and heated it white hot for a cau-
tery. With these instruments and a razor, the operation was successfully accomplished "by a hunter who
had attained some celebrity in cutting out hump meat.
A small cord was twisted around the limb for a tourni-
quet and the operation was concluded by an appli-
cation from the nearest tar bucket. Not a groan or
a sigh was uttered."[14]

Bands of Indians were occasionally seen riding far
on either side above the low horizon. All were not
hostile and "friendlies" sometimes visited the camp
seeking trinkets the traders brought along for good
will. None were trusted too far. Considered the most
dangerous point on the trail was a dark sandstone
promontory that jutted out on the prairie like a ready-
made fortress. This remnant rock that had withstood
ages of wind and weather was used as a signboard by
both red and white men and as a hideout for the

brigands of the prairie. This famous landmark near the Great Bend of the Arkansas was to be known as Pawnee Rock after a later caravan survived a savage attack from that fearsome tribe.

At the rock the journey was about half over and from this point there was a choice of routes. The longer—with more grass and water—followed the river to within sight of the mountains, then turned directly south at a spot called La Junta (The Junction). The alternate route crossed the Arkansas at the Great Bend directly into Mexican territory, following a southwesterly direction to the Cimarron River—a stretch of dry sand hills so formidable that Sibley had called it "the big bugbear of Benton's damned road to Santa Fe." However, many miles could be saved without too great risk if a two-day supply of water was carried along and most of the traveling done at night. Always the great concern of the pioneer was the welfare of the animals on which life itself depended. Grass and water . . . grass and water . . . the lack of it more to be dreaded than hostile Indians.[15]

Kit's train followed the Cimarron Cutoff. It was a veritable slice of hell deceptively overgrown with rank grass. For miles on end the mules sank to the fetlock or treaded thorny cactus. When they finally pulled up to the river, they found the channel stained white with alkali. There was not a trace of dew and no relief from the clouds. Past this waterscrape, the trail ran along a high ridge divided into three spurs called the Point of Rocks—another scene of ambuscade. From this landmark could be seen the first faint glimpse of the Rockies. The Mexican teamsters shouted and shot off their carbines in salute.

As the train wound through the hills nearing Santa Fe, excitement mounted. Several of the traders rode

ahead to announce the arrival of the wagons while
the teamsters put on new shirts and tied gay streamers
to their whips as they urged the mules over the last
of nearly eight hundred miles.

Santa Fe, built upon a high plateau against purple-
red mountains, had been a thriving commercial center long before the *Mayflower* reached Plymouth Rock.
Now free of Spanish domination, it welcomed trade
with *los Americanos*. The buildings were squat and
ugly, low-built of a sun-dried clay brick stuck together
with mud. Strings of bright red chilies, hanging from
the roofs to dry, added a gay note of color. Crude ox-
drawn *carretas* with solid wooden wheels lumbered
through the narrow, crooked streets and strings of
tiny gray burros wandered about unbridled, weighted
down with curved wine kegs, fodder, and firewood
brought down from the mountains.

As the wagons pulled into the plaza, the market
place suddenly woke up, for the arrival of the caravan brought the year's greatest excitement and silver
for the city treasury. The grimy teamsters, cracking
their beribboned whips, invited the girls to ride behind them on the mules while the traders mingled
with the Mexican rancheros, elegant in their wide sombreros and serapes, and sought their favorite *señoritas*
from the crowd of waiting beauties. Bells were rung,
wine casks opened, confections brought out, guitars
tuned, and the streets watered down for dancing. Kit
Carson, in his worn homespun, watched with wide-
eyed amazement while "young and old, rich and poor,
saint and sinner," danced till dawn.

Now at the end of the trail, jobless, with no chance
of returning home until spring, Kit decided to put
up for the winter with an old trapper named Kincaid. The old man "holed in" at Fernandez de Taos,

a trappers' snuggery about seventy miles from Santa
Fe. Though it was the second city in New Mexico,
Taos was only a treeless village of crude flat-topped
mud huts, most of them windowless, with the naked
earth, hardened with ox blood, for floor. Only those
of the aristocratic Spanish-Mexicans were washed with
white earth and hung with calico within, the mica-
paned windows guarded with heavy iron grills. Some
five hundred Mexicans, Indians, and Americans dwelt
there in a kind of peaceful confusion with more hundreds of dogs, chickens, burros, and oxen meandering
freely through the streets and narrow alleys. Here
young Kit Carson spent his first winter in the West
in company with his old trapper friend. He would
call Taos home for the rest of his life.

The boy was given an opportunity to learn from a
seasoned experience. Through the long winter weeks
he acquired considerable knowledge of the fur business
and earned his keep by his skill with leather. Visiting
the corrals of the Mexican *caballeros,* he learned their
tricks with a whirling rope and helped to break wild
ponies rounded up from the free-running herds of
the open country. Incidentally, Kit picked up a practical knowledge of Spanish and also the odd language
of sound and sign used by the Pueblo Indians living
in an ancient communal village near Taos.

As a Missouri boy brought up in fear of any red
man, Kit had a natural curiosity and often crossed
through the wild plum thicket north of town to visit
the two pueblos near the picturesque peak the Indians
called the Sacred Mountain. Built several stories high
of rough adobe brick, these *casas grandes* had been
lived in for centuries before Coronado. A foot-bridged
creek ran a sparkling course between them, dividing
a wide promenade where the Indians held their con-

vocations and the squaws baked their bread in outdoor ovens. Nearby stood San Geronimo Mission Church. The upper stories of the pueblos, reached by ladders, on festive days and at sunsets became a mass of startling color as the Indians gathered on the roofs and walls to worship the gods of nature and watch the spectacle of their games and dances. Kit marveled at the strange and unexpected beauty and came to realize that the Indian, so feared by the pioneer as a treacherous foe, in his own surroundings lives peaceably.

As soon as the ice crust broke on the streams, the trappers packed their mules and set off for the mountains. Old Kincaid had died and Kit reluctantly decided to return home when the wagons left for Missouri late in the spring. Hired as an extra teamster, Kit rode with the train as far as the Arkansas where he was persuaded to return with a party bound for Santa Fe. It had to be a quick decision for there was little time for more than a hurried exchange of news and some bartering for necessities before the wagons moved on; no trains ever camped together for fear of exhausting the supply of grass. Not much argument was needed and Kit—feeling almost as though he were rescued—once more faced west. The West claimed him forever.

Returning to Taos, Kit found a variety of jobs. He drove a mule team down to El Paso, the trading center of Old and New Mexico, and worked for his board as cook for a trappers' boardinghouse at Taos, operated by Ewing Young, successful trader in skins and explorer extraordinary. Finding this even more frustrating than making saddles, he resigned himself and started back to Missouri with the first wagon freight leaving in the spring. Again he got no farther than the Arkansas. Surprisingly, his knowledge of Spanish by this time was sufficient for the boy to be hired as interpreter for an outfit going to Chihuahua, the southernmost extent of all his lifetime travels. At Chihuahua, Kit met Mr. Robert McKnight, a hard-lucker. Pioneering in 1812, McKnight and ten of his men had been captured with a load of goods and thrown into the *calabozo* where they were held for nine years, to be released only after the President of the United States intervened with the king of Spain and his viceroy in Mexico. Now, in 1828, McKnight was back in business with wagons running between El Paso and the copper mines on the Gila River. He hired Kit as muleteer for several trips but any routine job was irksome and he was back in Taos when the wagons returned from Missouri.[16]

The traders brought back history — a flood had washed out the riverbanks of the Missouri. Franklin had slid into the river and oblivion. A new Franklin, yes, but Independence Landing had taken over the trade and was booming. The Independence jump-off meant a hundred less miles of trail.

NOTES FOR CHAPTER ONE

1. Cowles, "Genealogy of Five Allied Families." Manuscript, Rare Books, Library of Congress.

2. Collins, *History of Kentucky*.

3. Houck, *History of Missouri*.

4. Levens and Drake, *History of Cooper County, Missouri* (1876).

5. Levens and Drake, *History of Howard and Cooper Counties, Missouri* (1883).

6. Jonas Viles, "Old Franklin; A Frontier Town of the Twenties," *Mississippi Valley Historical Review*, Vol. IX.

7. Smith, *History of Howard and Chariton Counties, Missouri*.

8. Becknell, "Journal," *Missouri Historical Review*, January, 1910.

9. Ruxton, "A Journey Through New Mexico," Chap. VII, p. 136, in *Ruxton of the Rockies* (Porter and Hafen).

10. Cowles, "Genealogy of Five Allied Families."

11. The identity of the wagon master has not been reliably established. Charles Bent and Ceran St. Vrain, most often mentioned, were probably trapping in the mountains (Lavender, *Bent's Fort*). In his proclamation as governor of New Mexico, Bent stated that he first came to New Mexico in 1829. St. Vrain piloted a train in the spring *(Missouri Intelligencer,* April 14, 1826) and received a passport to trap in Sonora with a company of thirty-five, August 29, 1826 *(Southwestern Historical Quarterly,* January, 1916). A likely candidate was Stephen Turley who, with his brother Jesse, "crossed the plains as regular as the seasons come and go" (Smith, *History of Howard and Chariton Counties, Missouri).* The Carsons and Turleys had come to Missouri together from Kentucky and it is probable that young Kit would ask to go with someone well known to him. This is confirmed by Mrs. Anna Turley Noland, of Richmond, Kentucky, a great-niece of Stephen Turley, and Mr. Jerre Broaddus Noland, grandson of Andrew Broaddus, who was with the wagon train. Talton Turley, an intimate friend of Kit Carson, who died at Arrow Rock, Missouri, in 1925, aged ninety-three, also stated that Kit went west for the first time with his Uncle Stephen Turley (Cowles, "Genealogy"). For further information see Christopher Carson, *Kit Carson's Autobiography,* with editorial notes by Quaife.

12. Kate L. Gregg, ed., *The Road to Santa Fe; Journal and Diaries of George Champlin Sibley and Others.*

13. Ellsworth, *Washington Irving on the Prairies,* quoting John H. B. Latrobe.

14. Wetmore, "Diary," October 11, 1831 (Senate Doc. 90, 22nd Cong. 1st Sess.).

15. Sage, *Scenes in the Rocky Mountains.*

16. For a sketch of McKnight's career, see Carson, *Autobiography,* editorial note p. 8.

CHAPTER TWO

Exploring with Ewing Young (1828-1831)

Now to the Desert—once again
The gun and knife!
ALBERT PIKE (1834) [1]

BETWEEN JOBS, Kit usually drifted back to Ewing Young's place. Heretofore the eighteen-year-old had been considered too raw a hand to be hired by the trapping brigades. But after two years of jobs requiring strength and endurance, he returned to Taos that summer of 1828 radiating good health and eager to tackle anything. Young, one of the most daring and ambitious of the early Westerners, was quietly organizing a company to trap in the southwest, hoping to get away unnoticed by Mexican officials who had refused to issue hunting licenses to Americans. The previous year Young had secured a license but returned to have his furs confiscated because a change of administration during his absence had nullified the permit. Now he was preparing to take forty men to trap without license or passport and signed Kit for the expedition. Their start was delayed.[2]

As travel on the Santa Fe Trail was growing more perilous each year, President Jackson issued an order that troops from Fort Leavenworth were to escort an annual caravan as far as the Arkansas—the border of Mexico. Independent traders agreed to travel together and chose twenty-six-year-old Charles Bent to command the big train. There could not have been a better choice. Bent agreed to lead the assortment of mule-drawn wagons with Colonel Bennet Riley in command of a company of foot soldiers for escort. As an experiment, Colonel Riley had hitched some oxen to his supply wagons—the first instance of ox-drawn wagons on the trail.[3]

After a timorous journey, with the last wagon pulled safely up to the Great Bend of the Arkansas, Captain Bent was hesitant to continue on across Apache country without escort. A scouting party was sent out, among whom was Bent's younger brother William. Camp was set up across the river as it always was in anticipation of a chance flood that might cause delay. Here the traders were joined by nearly a hundred Mexican buffalo hunters who had seen Indian signal fires and were apprehensive about returning to Taos. The Americans, fatigued from vigilance to near exhaustion, were grateful to share the watch but afraid to sleep with loaded rifles for fear of shooting each other in a nightmare.

When news of the beleaguered caravan reached Taos, Ewing Young called for volunteers to ride the four-hundred-odd miles to the rescue. There was immediate response and one of the first to step up was Kit Carson. Ninety-five men rode out in two parties to be greeted with delirious shouts of gratitude from the besieged company. This, possibly, was the first meeting of Kit Carson and the Bent brothers.

William Bent had a harrowing tale to tell of outriding a band of feathered braves on his split-eared black mule. He was about the same age as Kit and, like him, short and sturdily built. William, who had spent three years in the mountain country, was tempted to accept Young's offer to join his trapping brigade. But Charles persuaded his energetic brother to stay with him and help with a partnership he was forming with another veteran trapper, handsome Ceran St. Vrain, who had acquired some wagons to go into trading. So the new friends parted, William to look for beaver in the foothills near the Spanish Peaks and Kit to start on an expedition pointed toward California.[4]

To throw both Mexicans and Indians off their track, the trappers started east, then zigzagged back west through the hills. Though young, Kit approached the wilderness with a mature regard, carefully observing the landscape, the streams, the timber lines, rock formations, and signs of wildlife and Indians. Good beaver was found along the headwaters of the Salt River with only one close encounter with hostiles. A band of Apaches appeared one evening about dusk, silhouetted along the horizon as they came over the ridge Indian file. Using an old Indian trick, Young sent most of his men into hiding. As the hundred warriors cautiously drew closer with ready bows and lances, sudden shots rang out of the darkness. The Apaches, outwitted, fled.

As the season wore on, provisions ran low. Young decided to cache the furs in an abandoned mine on the Gila and divide the company, sending all but eighteen back to Taos. The others would attempt to penetrate the region farther west. There had been scarcely any exploration of the desert barrier to California. All commerce had been directed over the Old Spanish Trail along the Green River in Utah territory. Young had led trapping parties along the Gila and the Colorado and knew of the explorations of Jedidiah Smith, the first to bring back any information from beyond the Colorado. Careful preparations were made. Three small deer were killed, the meat stripped and dried, and the skins made into watertight bags by caulking the seams with tallow. Before

leaving the Gila, the deerskins were filled with water
for both men and mules.

The explorers started hopefully across the sand.
They came, after three days under the merciless sun,
to a stream, led by the mules smelling water. Men
and mules together jumped into the cooling water.
After a two-day rest, the company was sufficiently revived to continue. Four more days of sand and sun
brought them at last to "the Colorado of the West,
below the great Cañon."[5]

A village of Mojaves was living on the brink of the
canyon in flat-topped log lodges covered with sand.
The Mojave men, many of whom were six and a half
feet tall, wore only breechclouts to display their elabo-
rately tattooed bodies; women wore but a petticoat of
fiber. On a previous expedition, Young had lost several men in a scrape with these desert Indians but
this time found them friendly, offering to share their
supply of beans and squash, and maize from their
granaries. Young bartered with the chief for an old
mare which was killed and eaten on the spot by the
hungry trappers; "even the foal was devoured."

After several days in the Indian village, the explorers started on toward California though all they
knew was that it was somewhere farther west. They
crossed the river on the Mojaves' rafts which were
simply bundles of reeds bound together with grasses
and sinews but buoyant enough to ride the rapids of
the swift river. They took a southwest course that led
to an unexpected river flowing northeast which suddenly disappeared into the sand to emerge a few miles
below.

The Mojave River intrigued the white men as it
had the red men. Its mystery had in part inspired
the ritual Rain Dance of the Desert Indian who be-

lieved the vibration of the earth, by cry of voice and stomp of foot, could open the hard crust to release subterranean streams and also bring the "long water" down from the skies.

There was no marked trail, no chart to follow. No one knew where the springs might be and when they did come upon a water hole, it had to be shared with the mules. Often the holes were rimmed with alkali and the water too bitter and brackish to be drunk. Sudden whirlwinds drove the flinty sand particles to darken the air, shifting the dunes to cover any game trail that might have led to water. Promises of green shade proved to be only mirages.

The trappers were equal to the desert. They mastered the desolation, endured the thirst and eventually escaped the emptiness. No mirage, the green fields and vineyards of San Gabriel Mission spread out before them. Kit called it "a paradise on earth." There a bountiful reception was given the half-starved, footsore explorers. The leader of the mission, who was the *jefe* as well as the padre, had authority over a few soldiers and about a thousand Indians who worked for the mission. Kit estimated there were eighty thousand cattle grazing on the hills. Young bartered for a supply of beef, trading four butcher knives for each ox.

Leaving San Gabriel, Young's company hunted in the Sacramento Valley, wandering deep into the region shadowed by the high Sierra. Kit memorized all the country. Mink and otter drew them through the tule marshes along the clear waters of the Sacramento, a virgin cousin of Kit's muddy Missouri. Traps were set along the San Joaquin where they were joined by a party of French trappers of the Hudson's Bay Company, called "Here Before Christ" by the Americans. Their leader, a great explorer by the name of Peter

Skene Ogden, had brought his company by canoe from Montreal to Oregon, a disputed area. In the lush Oregon-California country, there was game abundant for all. The two companies stayed together through the winter in the region that is the ancestral home of the Klamath tribe, each party learning much from the other and finding more safety in the greater number.

Unlike the tribes of the Plains, the Klamath were not nomadic, or were they unfriendly when unmolested in their wigwam homes. Acorns for coffee, sweet roots and berries were dried on top of the lodges with a supply of deer meat and fish, all of which they offered to share with the trappers. A favorite delicacy was grasshoppers, drowned, dried, mixed with meal, and baked in the ashes. By the time the trapping parties separated to hunt, Kit could keep up a conversation in French with any of them.

When the fur packs were as heavy as the mules could carry, Young turned south toward Ciudad de los Angeles, breaking the long journey with a stop at Mission San Rafael on San Francisco Bay. There they found a great state of excitement for unrest had spread among the Indians of the mission and many had run away to join other tribes in revolt. The padre, in desperation, asked the trappers to ride with his soldiers in an effort to bring them back. Young obliged by sending Kit, now second in command, with a dozen men to attack the hostile village. The Indians showed a very different respect toward the Americans who did not resort to the cruel tactics of the Spanish soldiers and the runaways were persuaded to return. This was Kit Carson's first command.

While at San Rafael, Ewing Young sold all the furs and purchased some good horses for the return journey to New Mexico. Soon afterwards, a band of

Indian horse raiders stole sixty of the herd. Young again called on Kit. Following the trail of hoofprints over a hundred miles of wilderness, Kit's party came upon the Indians feasting on horse meat. Eight were killed in a surprise attack and the rest fled. Carson and his men returned to San Rafael with all but the six horses that had been killed.

It had been a profitable venture. Before starting back across the desert, the company looked forward to one big spree in the city. When the trappers approached Los Angeles and Young could produce no passports, the Mexican authorities decided the best way to handle the situation was to soften the well-armed visitors with liquor, hoping to start a disturbance and then demand exorbitant fines. The plan very nearly succeeded. Realizing that the reward for all the patient work of a long year might be confiscated if the hilarity should end in a brawl, Young put Kit in charge of the three soberest men, hoping to get them out of town with the silver. Kit headed toward Cajon Pass, picking up whatever supplies he could before leaving the settlements.

In the meantime the Mexicans plied the willing young trappers with *aguardiente,* riding with them toward San Gabriel where they expected to make the arrest. As they rode along in high spirits, one of the trappers suddenly jumped from his horse and deliberately shot his companion, hoping to frighten off the Mexicans. They obligingly fled in terror, wanting no dealings with men who shot one another with no provocation. Surmounting these complications, the company was reunited next day and started toward the Rio Colorado following their previous route. With fresh horses and the benefit of experience, they reached the river in nine days.

The camp was aroused one night by a thundering herd of horses running so close there was danger of being trampled. The men quickly threw on their saddles to join the chase, believing it to be a herd stolen from one of the ranchos in Sonora by marauding Indians who prized horses above all possessions. Young's men succeeded in capturing most of the herd and after selecting as many as they could use, let the rest run free to roam the stunted hills or be captured by their owners or the thieving Indians. It was the unwritten law of that barren country for every man, red or white, to seize his opportunity where and when he found it.

The company looked for beaver all along the way and one day while most of the men were visiting the traps several Indians suddenly appeared in camp. Though they professed friendliness, Kit noticed the outline of weapons under their blankets and told them in Spanish that though they were few in number, his men did not fear them and were prepared for any kind of a fight. The intruders withdrew without molesting the camp, to the amazement and relief of all concerned.

The trappers continued along the south bank of the Colorado to tidewater, then followed the north bank of the Gila to the copper mines where they found their hidden packs of furs undisturbed. Ewing Young was now faced with the problem of bringing the load to Taos without showing a license. He solved this simply by going to Santa Fe, securing a permit, then returning to the company waiting on the Gila. The heavy packs, two thousands pounds of choice beaver, were brought in by Kit's former employer, Robert McKnight, and sold for the high price of twelve dollars a pound, each man receiving several hundred dollars when the company disbanded. Everyone thought Ewing had made a good trade, not realizing he had been gone over a year.

Back in Taos, according to Kit's own words, the trappers "passed the time gloriously. . . . Our only idea was to get rid of the dross as soon as possible but at the same time have as much pleasure and enjoyment as the country could afford."[6] He later confided to friends that he was much wiser after this experience, realizing the folly of extravagance and loose living without a thing to show for it. For the rest of his life he followed a temperate but not intolerant course.

In 1830, business in New Mexico was in a slump. The new partnership of Bent and St. Vrain was hurting. Records show that Kit's brother Andrew, who was driving for the company for fifty cents a day, was sent to square an account with a St. Louis merchant for "a wagon, eleven mules, one horse and 653 beaver."[7] Meanwhile, things were going well for Kit's young friend, William Bent, who had put up a small stockade fort where the Arkansas meets the mountains and was carrying on trade with the friendly Cheyennes. Impressed by William's success, Charles Bent and St. Vrain offered to take him into their partnership and build a large trading post a hundred and fifty miles downstream at La Junta, where they could catch the overland trade as well as the Indian and fur business. The Bent brothers offered to put Kit in charge of the logging camp on Short Timber Creek, five miles from the site of the fort.

That fall, after the trading season was finished, all the company's horses and mules were turned loose at the logging camp to browse on the bark and branches of the felled cottonwoods, believing there was little chance that marauding Indians would be about so late in the season. Kit welcomed visits from the Cheyennes, who did not resent this intrusion into their domain because William had gained their confidence by fair trading.

One wintry afternoon, two horsemen rode into the logging camp. Black Whiteman, a former slave employed as a cook by the Bents, and a Cheyenne brave, Little Turtle, had come to hide from the deserted husband of Otter Woman, who had eloped with the Negro. Later that same day, a large band of the Crow tribe, quite by chance, saw the camp while passing through the country and waited for darkness to steal most of the horse herd. The camp was left with only a few stragglers and the visitors' horses which had been tied. This was a calamitous blow to Kit and he was determined to recover the herd entrusted to him. A snowstorm was threatening.

The Cheyenne, riding out to pick up the trail, returned to report that the horses had been run up the creek. Everyone in camp was ordered to mold bullets and prepare for a long snow trek. Kit started about noon with eleven loggers, trailing along the creek and out on the open prairie. After forty miles of heavy going, slowed by migratory buffalo herds, they discovered the Crow camp hidden in a willow thicket, its position revealed by smoke and sparks rising into the clear cold air. Leaving their horses tied, Kit and his men, spreading out in a wide circle, crawled toward the Indian camp where a big celebration was going on in honor of the successful robbery. They remained hidden and numb with cold until the singing and dancing quieted, then worked their way over the soft snow toward the stolen horses, cut the ropes, and threw snowballs to herd the animals toward the place where their mounts were tied.

A dog's sharp bark was heard and instantly a little puff of steam rose above the trees. Kit knew by this sign that the Indians were aware of their presence and had doused their campfire with snow. He drew the men together for an attack. Stepping up their advance, the loggers were within a few feet of the camp when about sixty screaming Crows ran out and almost surrounded them. Instantly, Kit ordered his men to fire a volley which so startled the warriors that they turned and ran back into the cover of the woods. Surprised to find the horses gone, they kept on running through the grove and out on the open plain. Carson's men, satisfied to have recaptured the herd, were too tired from the fight and the long pull through the snow to pursue them farther. Two dead Crows lay on the ground—a scalp for Black Whiteman and one for Little Turtle. Later, Cheyenne Chief Yellow Wolf honored Kit with the title Vih-hiu-nis, Little Chief, in recognition of Carson's courage and command of a difficult situation.[8]

NOTES ON CHAPTER TWO

1. Albert Pike, *Prose Sketches and Poems, Written in the Western Country*. Albert Pike, future Confederate general and author of "Dixie," came to New Mexico with Charles Bent in 1831. Josiah Gregg was also with that train.

2. For a sketch of Ewing Young's career, see Christopher Carson, *Kit Carson's Autobiography*, edited by Milo Milton Quaife (Chicago, 1935), editorial note by Quaife, p. 7.

3. Young, *First Military Escort on the Santa Fe Trail, 1829.* Letter from Thomas Forsythe, Indian agent, to Secretary of War, October 24, 1831 (Senate Doc. 90, 22nd Cong. 1st Sess., p. 77).

4. Lavender, *Bent's Fort.* See also William Waldo, "Recall of a Septuagenarian," paper printed by the Missouri Historical Society, 1880. Reprinted in *Glimpses of the Past*, Vol. V (1938).

5. Carson, *Autobiography*, editorial note by Quaife, p. 12.

6. Carson, *Autobiography*, editorial note by Quaife, p. 21.

7. Lavender, *Bent's Fort*, p. 123. Letter from St. Vrain to Messrs. B. Pratte & Co., September 14, 1830.

8. Grinnell, *Bent's Old Fort and Its Builders (Kansas Historical Society Collections*, XV, 36); Carson, *Autobiography*, p. 24, editorial note by Quaife, p. 28.

Trapping with Broken Hand's Brigade (1831-1832)

Have a good hat; the secret of your looks
Lives with the beaver in Canadian brooks.
OLIVER WENDELL HOLMES

NEWS MANAGED TO circulate throughout the West. Early in the summer of 1831, Kit heard that the newly organized Rocky Mountain Fur Company was recruiting men for the fall hunt. So far, the high mountains had been to Kit only an enthralling land-scape—the scene of trappers' adventurous tales. He longed to go into them and straightway hurried to Ewing Young's place where Thomas Fitzpatrick was filling out his list of trappers. Fitzpatrick, a hardy Irishman with a better education than most moun-taineers, had heard of him. Kit signed the record book and for the next ten years he was to trap and hunt along the multitude of streams between the Rio Grande and the Canadian border.

Fitzpatrick, who some years before had injured his hand in a gun explosion, was generally referred to as Broken Hand. He had come west along with several other great mountain men in answer to what has been called "the most successful want-ad of all time"—the one inserted in the *Missouri Republican* of March 20, 1822, by the Ashley-Henry Company seeking a hun-dred enterprising young men to explore the Missouri River. Jim Bridger, William Sublette, James Beck-wourth and Kit's half brother, Moses Carson, were others in that remarkable group.[1]

Broken Hand became Kit's close friend and adviser. With Bridger, they were to become famous as the

Great Triumvirate among mountain men. They knew the sign languages and the peculiarities of the various Indian tribes. They understood the red man better than anyone else ever would. They served as guides for the emigrants and the great government surveys. More remarkable, each managed to live a full quota of years.

Fitzpatrick had acquired the stock of goods left by Jedidiah Smith, whose adventurous life had come to a tragic end on the way to Taos with Broken Hand. Kit was exuberant over the fine salary of four hundred dollars for the season. Supplies were advanced to all the men—traps, blankets, ammunition, mule, and such—to be paid for out of the winter's earnings; few trappers were ever out of debt to the company after that first stake. Kit was to be initiated at once into the great fraternity of mountain men for Fitzpatrick was leaving as soon as possible to lead a pack-mule supply train to the hunters' rendezvous on the Green River. This was an annual holiday where trappers, hunters, traders, friendly Indians, and anyone else who happened to be in the West, gathered together for a few weeks each summer at a spot agreed upon the previous year, to trade skins for supplies, sign contracts for the next season, visit old friends, gamble, test their skills, and get uproariously drunk.

Though a few wagons had by this time been taken over the Continental Divide, Fitzpatrick preferred to carry his goods by pack mule. There is an Indian legend that Broken Hand lost his way and was found only after a medicine man dreamed where he was. A party of trappers took off in the direction pointed by the ancient seer and found Fitzpatrick right where the spirits had said he would be and guided him to the Green.[2]

No trading could begin until all who had agreed to attend were on hand. But as soon as the liquor kegs were uncorked, the hilarity began with all the bartering, brawling, gambling, gorging and guzzling that could be packed into a few weeks. Among the hundreds assembled on the Green could be found writers, missionaries, government officials, and even foreign correspondents. Hostiles, sworn to wipe out the white intruder, came in under truce flags to trade with the paleface enemy; friendlies set up their tepee villages nearby and wholeheartedly entered into the fun. There were contests of skill in shooting, riding, roping, and wrestling, with the Indians imitating and often bettering every accomplishment of the mountaineers who joined in the powwows and singing around the Indian campfires. One fascinating game lined up a dozen or more heavy poles, twenty-five feet apart, with a rider at full gallop required to shoot two balls into any three of the posts, changing rifles between shots.

Exhorbitant prices were demanded for groceries, tools, traps, ammunition, and whiskey sold only by the glass. A pint tin cup served as the standard measure, coffee selling for $1.25 and sugar for $2.00 a pint. Gamblers' tents, festooned with green boughs and flowers, invited the lonesome men to come in and enjoy themselves. Sometimes a whole season's earnings would be squandered in a few reckless days manipulating the horse-hide cards. The complete indifference of Old Bill Williams was typical of the mountaineer's philosophy. Bill came into rendezvous one year with a heavy pack of prize pelts but when not offered what he considered a fair price, he threw the furs on the ground, got on his mule and rode off into the mountains, not to be heard from until the next year.

Young Kit Carson seemed somewhat out of place among the rough, hairy mountain revelers. He stood only five-feet-six with a stocky frame, bronzed and bowlegged, his sandy hair shoulder-length, his eyes friendly, clear, and farseeing, and his soft voice almost feminine. Mountain men had heard about him; he was accepted at once.

After rendezvous, Fitzpatrick led his company in quest of beaver as far as the headwaters of the Salmon River. The trapping expedition was as efficiently organized as the wagon train that had brought Kit to the West. Fitzpatrick, the leader, rode in front with the bell mare carrying all the company papers, records, and contracts. Each man had charge of three mules —one to ride and two to pack. The clerk brought up the rear.

Except for their broad-brimmed hats or woolen caps, most of the mountaineers were dressed entirely in deerskin. Their long hunting shirts reached nearly to the knee; the trousers, with the hair left inside, were fringed about the ankle; and the moccasins were of parfleche. Belts of strong buffalo leather fastened by steel chains were hung with sheaths for flints, whetstone, skinning knife, and awl. Each man was issued a three-point blanket—the three woven stripes indicating the weight. All carried knives of British import with the letters *G R*, for George Rex, cut into the hilt, but to the mountain man "G R" stood for Green River. Next to his rifle his most prized possession was his razor-edged Green River knife. Bullet pouch hung on a cord from his neck; bullet mold, ball screw, and gun wiper dangled from a strap thrown over his shoulder. Thus equipped, the trapper picked up his rifle and gunstick, lit a shuck, and headed for the hills.

No greenhorn at the business, Kit embraced the trappers' life with eagerness and became a hivernan (winterer) his first year in the mountains. Fitzpatrick's company wintered with the Nez Perces, a tribe more peaceable and civilized than the Indians of the Plains. They looked upon the fair-haired young trapper as a great curiosity. Kit felt a response to the country not unlike that shown by the Indians themselves. He put to good use his training at the saddler's bench as through the long winter the trappers repaired their gear, replaced their worn and greasy deerskins, and tanned a supply of leather. Even while sitting around the fire swapping yarns and listening to Indian legends, the time was well spent making bullets, boats, and packsaddles, oiling their guns and sharpening tools for the coming season.

After the spring hunt, when Fitzpatrick left for another trading trip, Kit went with the company of Captain John Gantt. One night, soon after Kit had joined the brigade, two men disappeared with four of the company's best horses and the first thought of everyone was the rich cache of furs on the Arkansas. Thinking this might be exciting as well as helpful to Gantt, Kit volunteered to ride with another trapper to track down the thieves, though there was little hope for success.

It was a hazardous undertaking through a country that had heard the sound of war drums. Futile, too, for when the riders arrived at the river, they found the cache torn open and empty. The scoundrels had piled the loot into a pirogue left hidden near the site and started downstream, leaving the exhausted horses behind. Kit and his partner, after following along the riverbank for a day without any luck, stopped for the night in an old hut Gantt's company had built. Next morning the trappers found themselves completely surrounded by Indians. Their only hope of escape was to remain where they were until Gantt would send a searching party to find them. The thieves who had caused all the trouble were never heard from again. Theirs was a foolhardy attempt as the river was too treacherous to navigate at night and anyone in an open boat by day would be asking for Indian flint.

Kit and his companion had almost given up hope of being rescued when Gantt's partner, Jefferson Blackwell, quite by chance stopped at the old hut with fifteen men. A few days later, when Gantt's searching party arrived, the trappers started for their home camp at Salt Springs, harassed all the way by hostiles. Early one morning one of the guards spotted several Indians creeping into the corral. As he fired to bring down one of them, the others fled—one lucky brave cutting a hobble and riding off before the guard could reload.

Expecting no further trouble, Kit and a small party rode out to look for beaver sign. Noticing four braves riding in the shadow of a low ridge, Kit decided to charge and rode straight into a neat trap. Instead of four lone Indians, they found themselves facing a long line of warriors rising out of hiding. Here was a case of ride or lose your hair! The trappers dug in their spurs, pressed their bodies flat against their ponies and were through and away before the startled Indians could believe their eyes. "The Redskins made a good attempt," Kit told Gantt, "but Thank God, failed."[3]

Kit soon left Gantt's company to strike out for

himself. Believing there would be less Indian trouble
with a small company, young Carson started out that
fall of 1832 with two towering giants: Richens "Dick"
Wootton and Valentine "Rube" Herring, both newly
arrived in the West. They followed the tributaries
of the Yellowstone into the region of the Blackfoot.
That tribe looked on all white men as intruders, encouraged in this by Kenneth McKenzie of the American Fur Company, who held a treaty for their ex-
clusive trade. The canny McKenzie surreptitiously
furnished his Indian customers liquor by the barrel,
as well as rifles and ammunition, to protect his interests.

The young trappers waited until the Blackfeet had
moved out on the plains for their winter buffalo hunt,
then set their beaver traps. In this fresh territory
which even the American Fur Company had feared
to invade except for trade, Kit and his partners found
fine furs which they packed by mule to Taos. Among
mountain men, Kit Carson was now considered as expert as any trapper in the mountains. The Pueblos
called him Na Chi Gaime, "Successful Hunter."[4]

Kit was now determined to have his own outfit
and work as a free trapper. He did not linger long
in Taos but joined Captain Stephen Lee, a trader
with Bent and St. Vrain, about to set out for Robidoux's Fort on the Uinta.

Antoine Robidoux, one of six brothers who had
exchanged lace stocks for buckskin, came down from
Canada early in the century to become famous as the
kingpin of the fur trade. He chose a spot sheltered
by a natural wall of limestone, called White Rocks,
as the site for a trading post. This first white man's
dwelling in the region known as Utah was nothing
more than a semicircular row of log huts without the
usual stockade. Robidoux made little effort to fol-

low anything like the civilized life he had known.
Large chips of wood served as plates with butcher
knives the only cutlery. The post had become notorious for gambling and traffic in squaws. Trade was
primarily with the Snakes and Utes who brought in
stacks of fine sheepskins and deerskins to be sold for
a pittance—a large antelope hide, "snowy white and
soft as velvet and big enough for a pair of panta-
loons," bringing possibly ten rounds of ammunition
or two or three awls.[5]

Before winter set in, Lee and Carson had put up
a small adobe fort about a mile from the confluence
of the Uinta and the Green. Here Lee set out his
wares: bright calicoes, bells, mirrors, abalone shells,
tools, knives, beads and other glittering geegaws to
attract the Indian trade.

One morning Robidoux, in a great state of excitement, rode out to the little trading post to ask Kit's
help in finding an Indian in his employ who had
run off with six of his best horses. Soon Kit was again
on the trail of horseflesh in company with one of the
Utes. They followed the tracks along the Green for
about a hundred miles when the Indian's horse suddenly went lame. Kit rode on alone thirty miles farther before catching sight of the thief who turned
into the woods when he realized he was being trailed.
Both rifles cracked at the same instant. Kit's aim was
good, the Indian's bad. Barricading himself as well
as he could, Kit rested overnight before leading the
horses leisurely back to the post. Robidoux, sardonic,
moody, not too well liked, never forgot this favor.[6]

In the spring, when news was brought in that Bridger
and Fitzpatrick were camped with a large company
about fifteen days away, Captain Lee and Kit left
their sturdy little fort to join that brigade. Fort Kit

Carson, as it came to be called, was later occupied
by the Hudson's Bay Company who held it successfully against all attempts by other fur companies to
take it over.[7]

Kit was startled to see that Fitzpatrick's hair had
turned completely white after a harrowing escape from
a band of Gros Ventres. Lee exchanged his stock of
goods for pelts and headed toward Taos. Kit and three
of Bridger's men took off for the Laramie. Keeping
to the safer timber-line country, they trapped and
hunted through the summer without much success.
On the way to rejoin Bridger, Kit came almost too
close to a pair of grizzlies.

This encounter, which Kit considered his "worst
difficult" in all his years in the mountains, happened
late one afternoon when he was alone hunting game
for supper. He had just emptied his gun, bringing
down an elk, when the bears charged out of the forest
toward him. Dropping the useless rifle, Kit ran for
the nearest tree, a not too sturdy sapling. He stayed
in the tree several hours, whipping down the bears
with a branch as they reached for him and desperately
afraid the slender aspen trunk might break under the
weight. He managed to hold on until dark, when
the bears, howling with rage, gave up the siege and
lumbered off. Picking up his old muzzle-loader, Kit
wearily got back to camp. That night the prairie
wolves feasted on elk while the hungry trappers endured another meal of stewed beaver.

The disconsolate trappers rejoined Bridger and
stayed through the winter with his company. Kit had
now stepped up from the status of hired trapper to
skin trapper, free to go wherever he chose with an
agreement to sell his catch to Bridger. For his first
company, Kit chose five men about his own age of

twenty-five. In the little company, besides Kit, there were Bill Mitchell, an eccentric daredevil who had lived with the Comanches; Joe Meek, a Virginian, just back from Joe Walker's expedition to California; and three Delaware Indians who were accorded equal consideration in everything. These were the original Carson men, the nucleus of a band that would grow to number more than a hundred. They were lucky to survive their first hunt.

Through the winter they got an outfit together, planning to set their traps along the far reaches of the Laramie. Well equipped with a pack mule apiece and full provisions and paraphernalia for the season, Carson & Company rode confidently out from their winter hole in the foothills. Stringing along across a treeless stretch of prairie, Mitchell suddenly drew up his mule, pointing to a distant whirl of dust which to his keen eye, signified but one thing—Indian spy!

It was the war season and this was the region of the Comanches, the most feared of all the Plains Indians. An attack came almost at once as a savage horde swept down from the bald hills, shrieking out their murderous threats. There was only one thing to do. Kit ordered each man to kill his mule, jerking back the head and slitting the throat with his Green River blade. In a matter of seconds, the trappers were lying on the ground with their rifles pointed over the still-quivering bodies of the mules. Every shot must count. Three were to shoot while the others reloaded.

The Chief Medicine Man, resplendent in eagle-feather bonnet, led the attack. Three rifles spoke and the proud man fell from his saddle, his pony dragging him across the grass. The charging Comanches rushed by the mule fort sending in a sheet of arrows. Carson's men reversed their position while the Indians wheeled to charge again. They were superb riders, swinging completely out of sight by holding horsehair ropes. The trappers withstood the second charge and the warriors rode off a distance to hold council.

The loss of the Medicine Man was an ill omen. As a squaw dashed out to claim the body of the fallen chieftain, Kit pushed aside one of the Delawares who pointed his rifle toward her. Women and children were to be respected by Carson men.

Unwilling to believe six men could hold off their great number, the Indians rode up for another attack. By this time the trappers had dug into the ground for better entrenchment and were ready for them. No better luck for the Comanches, though they turned sharply before Carson's men could reload. Then the unbelievable happened. As the Indians rode up for what might have been the crushing blow, their horses began to rear up and became unmanageable—they would not come near the dead mules! The smell of blood ended the charge better than gunfire. The frightened horses turned what seemed an inescapable Comanche victory into a rout. Near exhaustion under the vertical sun, the trappers cheered and wept as they watched the warriors ride off to their village beyond the hills.

The bodies of the mules were stuck full of arrows but none of the men received a wound. They came out of their cramped quarters grateful to be alive though disheartened over their severe losses. After sundown they started in a dog-trot toward Bent's Fort, seventy-five miles away, leaving their valuable equipment on the prairie—spoils of war for the Comanches. The young men had the resilience of old-timers. Hardship and good luck were only part of the business of keeping alive.

NOTES ON CHAPTER THREE

1. Morgan, *The Great Salt Lake.*

2. Hafen and Ghent, *Broken Hand, the Life Story of Thomas Fitzpatrick.*

3. Carson, *Autobiography.*

4. Cheetham, "Kit Carson" (*New Mexico Historical Review*, Vol. I, No. 4).

5. Sage, *Scenes in the Rocky Mountains* (1847).

6. For a sketch of Robidoux's career see Carson, *Autobiography* (ed. by Quaife), editorial note p. 35.

7. Reagan, "Forts Robidoux and Kit Carson" (*New Mexico Historical Review*, X, 121-32).

Mountain Man (1832-1840)

We find them accordingly, lithe, vigorous and active:
extravagant in word, in thought, in deed: heedless of
hardship; daring of danger; prodigal of the present
and thoughtless of the future.

WASHINGTON IRVING

RENDEZVOUS, THAT began as a fur-trade meeting and summer vacation, had grown into an annual festival fair attracting not only the mountain trappers and their business associates but artists and writers eager to catch the color of the great holiday of the West. In the summer of 1834, Kit arrived at Ham's Fork on the Green to find many old friends and that year met Captain Sir William Drummond Stewart, a Scotsman on half pay from the King's Hussars.

Stewart, who was writing a novel set in the Western scene, had spent several seasons in the mountains following a rigorous life without sacrificing all the civilities he had known. At first a subject for ridicule in his European-cut clothes topped with a fine panama and carrying an ancient fowling-piece for a weapon in the wilderness, the nobleman soon won the respect of the mountaineers with his shooting skill, fine horsemanship, and courage equal to any of them. Stewart carried with him a cartload of tinned foods, vintage wines, sugar and flour by the barrel, and of course tea. All of this he shared generously with whomever he chanced to meet. He could be seen, his pocket full of quills, writing on a portable desk of "the kenions, mosquetos and grisely bears." His accounts of the exploits of the Western heroes were popular reading in this country and abroad.[1]

Carson and his men joined Bridger's company of

fifty going into Blackfoot territory, still an almost
untouched beaver country. Finding the Blackfeet no
more hospitable, the trapping company moved on
after losing five of their number and set up winter
quarters on the Big Snake. All through that bitter
winter, the Blackfeet continued to annoy them. Finding eighteen horses missing from the corral one morning, Carson and eleven men trailed the animals through
waist-high drifts to a hillside blown free of snow, within sight of an Indian village. Making no attempt
to recapture their horses, the trappers cautiously approached the chief's lodge to ask the return of their
animals. The crafty Blackfoot feigned innocence. His
braves, he said, had no intention of stealing from
the white man and had taken the horses from their
enemies, the Snakes.

Kit asked for a smoke. After both parties had stacked
their weapons, the long-stemmed stone pipe was passed.
The chief started with two puffs, adding a puff each
time the pipe came to him. There were puffs to the
sky, the earth, the winds and waters—an unhurried
ritual exasperating to men who were desperately hoping to recover the animals their very existence might
depend upon.

The Blackfeet continued to "talk crooked" but finally brought up five worn-out nags, though the trappers could see their own ponies hobbled nearby. No
amount of argument could accomplish more. The
Indians, outnumbering the white men three to one,
needed to make no concessions. Kit decided on a bold
step. Jumping to his feet, he shouted for his men to
seize their rifles. After a shuffle for arms, all sought
shelter behind rock and tree.

The fight was a bloody one and that day, Kit received the only serious wound he was to suffer in a

lifetime of Indian scrapes. He might have escaped if he had not shifted his fire to save the life of Markhead, one of the Delawares, who had carelessly exposed himself. Markhead and Carson had fired at the same instant. In this dangerous position with an unloaded gun, Kit turned to see an Indian sighting for his heart. He tried dodging behind trees and rocks but the Blackfoot's bullet felled him, grazing his neck and passing through the shoulder.

All through that brutally cold night, Kit lay on a blanket in the snow with a wad of beaver fur in the wound to stanch the bleeding. It was too dangerous to build a fire but the very cold itself congealed the blood and saved Kit's life when no one expected him to survive.

Next morning the Blackfeet were waiting to take up the fight but the trappers, acknowledging defeat, returned to camp with the five disreputable horses the Indians had given them. Bridger took off with a larger force but was not able to locate the wily Blackfeet who grew more bold with each success. Fortunately for the trapping company, the Nez Perce had good horses for sale.

Horses were of special importance to Kit Carson because of a pretty Arapaho girl he had seen at the last rendezvous. Wanibe — Singing Grass — had been trailed by the eye of more than one mountain man but had shown favor to Kit in the Sundown Dance. Her father, Chief Running Around, demanded several fine horses from any man eligible to ask for this favorite, well-guarded daughter. Trailing along the lonely beaver creeks, Kit was warmed by the thought of her inviting smile, singling him out from the company of rough men for her attention.

When the company had worked its way down the

Green to rendezvous, Kit set out at once to find the Arapaho village and the bronze-skinned beauty. Now in a position to barter with Wanibe's father and brothers, Kit found them stone-faced and unrelenting. After much wrangling in sign language, he learned the reason. A burly Frenchman with Andy Drips' company had accosted Wanibe and attempted to pull her away from a group of Indian girls walking along the river as they often did at sundown. The terrified girl ran to her father's lodge and the men of her family informed Kit that there would be no white man for Singing Grass.

Kit had heard of this ruffian who was heartily disliked by everyone but respected for his quick trigger and savage fists. He did not know of Shunar's boast that he would take the Indian girl without respect to any tribal custom. The Frenchman held some particular grudge against Americans and fired by Taos lightning, became intolerably insulting.

Kit took off in a whirl of dust to look for Shunar. He did not have long to wait for as he dismounted to talk with some men of his company, the Frenchman rode up brandishing his pistols and challenging any man of any nation to meet him. Kit stepped out almost into the path of his horse, shouting in his high-pitched voice that he was only a trifling American but if Shunar wanted to die, he was his man. An incredulous look spread over the ruffian's face when he saw the youthful trapper mount and ride up to him. The two men faced each other, their horses nose to nose, then turned and rode off a short distance. At a signal, both wheeled and fired almost instantaneously. Shunar's shot scraped Kit's collarbone and barely grazed his temple above the left eye. Kit firing from the belt, shattered the bully's forearm, the ball entering the wrist and lodging in the elbow. Swinging down from his mount, Shunar begged for mercy, all the contemptuous bravado gone from his voice. Later, Kit admitted that the Frenchman was the only man he was glad to kill.[2]

"Such scenes, sometimes for passion and sometimes for amusement, make the pastime of their wild and wandering life," wrote the Rev. Samuel Parker. His book, *Journal of an Exploring Tour Beyond the Rocky Mountains,* published in 1838, contained an account of the duel. It was the first mention in print of the name, "Kit" Carson.

The Rev. Mr. Parker was visiting the rendezvous as a foreign missionary. The men gave polite attention to his sermons but grabbed their rifles and rushed off in a body when a herd of buffalo came into view on the distant prairie. Mr. Parker kept right on with his discourse, pausing only to berate the men for their discourtesy in not waiting for the benediction. It was noted, however, that preacher Parker did not refuse a portion of succulent hump roast the next day. "The men conducted themselves with great propriety," wrote the good man in his report. "I did not feel any disposition to upbraid them for their sins, but endeavored to show them they were unfit for heaven. . . ."[3]

More to the liking of the mountain men was the discreet and understanding Dr. Marcus Whitman, on his way to establish a mission school in Oregon territory. He was constantly called to administer to the ills of both white and red men and successfully removed an arrowhead that had been imbedded in Bridger's shoulder for three years. "With self possession and perseverance" the doctor cut away the cartilage that had held it fast. Bridger "manifested equal firmness" with a stiff drink of liquor to sustain him and a piece of wood to bite on. "The Indians looked on in wonder at the skill."[4]

Captain Stewart was on hand again and wrote the duel between Carson and Shunar into an episode in his novel *Edward Warren*. His description of Kit is probably the best written of him at this time:

> The light of the fire now showed me the face of my new friend, who was much shorter and slighter of stature than myself; his head without other covering than waving locks of light brown hair, was occasionally turned to me as he carolled some of the stanzas of the air of Bruce's March, then much in fashion among American boys, and showed a pleasant open countenance, with blue eyes.[5]

Stewart carried away as an interesting souvenir of that rendezvous the arrowhead that had been "butchered out" of Old Gabe's shoulder. Curious about the operation, Sir William asked Bridger why the wound had not become infected. Squinting up at him, Bridger replied: "In the mountains meat never spoils."

Stewart and Carson became close friends. There seemed to be a special affinity between the aristocratic Scotsman and the young trapper because of their common Scotch ancestry. Kit questioned him eagerly about the land of his forefathers. Stewart brought out a copy of *Scottish Chiefs* for campfire reading. Joe Meek was so fascinated by one of the tales he later named one of his daughters Helen Mar for the heroine.

When Kit left the rendezvous of 1835, Singing Grass rode beside him to be his companion in the wilderness, his wife, his warmth and comfort. According to the custom of her tribe, she was given a new white tepee, decorated with the symbols of her people, and

all she would need for her housekeeping. Kit called
his pretty squaw Alice and, unlike many Indian women
who refused to work after marrying a white man, Alice
Singing Grass became a capable trapper's wife. Kit
never denied his happiness with her.

Carson's growing band of trappers covered the tawny
country of the Yellowstone, wandered along the Big
Horn, crossed to the Three Forks of the Missouri, and
set their winter camp on the Big Snake. The Indian
wives went everywhere with the trappers through the
sublime high country. Their skill in curing skins con-
tributed greatly to the success of the company. All
shared equally in the food whether it be a saddle of
black-tail deer or stewed beaver. All were expected
to add to the store. The native women knew where
to find nourishing roots and greens so necessary to
vary the all-meat diet and avoid the resulting "cow-
sickness." The general health was remarkably good
though there were times of real hunger. Joe Meek
told of putting his hands into an anthill and greedily
licking the ants from his fingers. Crickets, crisped
over the fire, were stored for dire emergencies and
sometimes blood was drawn from the horses' ears to
add to the soup. Following the custom of their people,
the Indian women practiced the fast as a religious rite
to withstand famine.

Hearing there was an untapped supply of beaver
on Mary's River, Kit left Wanibe and his company
at Fort Hall on the Snake and joined four men of
the Hudson's Bay Company. Exploring far into the
desert region now called Nevada, they found sparse
pickings. After nearly starving to death, the men
managed to get back to the fort only to have a guard
leave the corral open for the Blackfeet to steal all
their horses. At this low point, Thomas McKay, a

giant of the Hudson's Bay Company, luckily arrived with horses enough to get the company to rendezvous, held that summer (1836) on Horse Creek, a tributary of the Green.

Warned of trouble with hostiles, Kit and some of his men rode out to meet Fitzpatrick's supply train. Stopping for a few hours' sleep before daylight, the men turned their horses out to graze. Only Kit and Joe Meek kept theirs saddled with the picket ropes tied to their bodies and next morning, theirs were the only horses to be seen. Reluctantly leaving their companions to get back to rendezvous any way they could, Carson and Meek rode on to meet the train. "Every man for himself and God for all of us." All got back safely and Doc Newell beheld an incredible sight —his own horse peacefully grazing by Horse Creek![6]

Meanwhile, Kit and Joe, joined by a band of friendly Nez Perces, loped across the sage to greet their old friend Broken Hand "with a whoop and a holler and a rifle salute." The trappers blinked their red-rimmed eyes when they beheld two white women riding side-saddle alongside an overloaded farm wagon drawn by a span of four. These first white women to cross the Divide—Narcissa Whitman, the attractive bride of Dr. Marcus Whitman, and Eliza Spalding, the dour-faced wife of the Rev. Henry Spalding—were on the way to the missions founded the year before in Oregon.

William Gray, a mechanic with the missionary party, gave this vivid account of the trappers' welcome:

Two days before we arrived at our rendezvous, some two hours before we reached camp, the whole caravan was alarmed by the arrival of some ten Indians and four or five white men whose dress and appearance could scarcely be distinguished from that of the Indians. As they came into sight over the hills, they gave a yell such as hunters and Indians can only give; whiz came their balls over our heads, and on they came in less time than it will take you to read this account. The alarm was but for a moment. Our guide had seen a white cloth on one of the guns, and said, "Don't be alarmed, they are our friends," and sure enough, in a moment they were. It was difficult to tell which was the more crazy, the horse or the rider; such hopping, hooting, running, jumping over sagebrush, whirling around for they could not stop to reload their guns, but all of us as they came on gave them a salute from ours, as they passed to the rear of our line and back again hardly stopping to give a hand to anyone.[7]

There were more than a hundred persons in the cavalcade, including the ubiquitous Captain Stewart, traveling by buggy with several servants and an immense amount of baggage. Also the fur trader, Milton Sublette, who was returning with a new rubber leg for a last visit to the country he loved. Joe Meek had saved Milton's life several years before when his trapping party had left him for dead after a knifing by a Bannock chief. Remembering that great favor, Milton had decided to reward Joe by giving him his pretty Shoshone wife, Mountain Lamb, whom Joe had greatly admired.[8]

The presence of white women threw a minor bombshell into the revels of the rendezvous. The mountaineers softened their oaths and gambled, drank, and sought favors from the Indian maidens less openly. Probably no westering woman was ever more greedily admired than the lovely auburn-haired Narcissa, while Eliza, with grim disapproval of all things Western and masculine, recorded in her journal what she thought of the whole iniquitous debauch.

The squaws stood about watching these first white women they had ever seen, admiring their dexterity with rolling pin and thimble, tasting their biscuits and endeavoring to imitate their prayers. Several hundred braves, in full ceremonial finery, put on a spectacular exhibition of their skills for the ladies. Leading the procession was the chief wearing "an American hat and coat and carrying an American flag and an enormous calumet, the great pipe of peace." Then followed closely the men of the tribes riding without saddles on wolf and panther skins with buffalo horns on their heads and silver foxtails tied to their heels. All carried human bones decorated with human scalps and chanted plaintively. Behind them, in a long column, rode the young women, "their wonderfully sweet voices keeping excellent time, floating far through the air."[9] The sunlight caught the brilliance of cut-glass beads, silver bands, and iridescent shells decorating their white deerskins. Tiny hawk bells and strings of elks' teeth, hanging from the blue and scarlet breast bands of their ponies, jingled and rattled as they pranced by. It was an amazing revelation to the Easterners who had expected only savagery to find this Indian artistry and love of music. Long after rendezvous, the red men could be heard singing the Doxology high in the Rockies.[10]

Fitzpatrick still favored pack mules as the best means of transporting supplies. He always left his heavy wagons at Fort Laramie, William Sublette's trading post on the Platte, and urged the missionaries to do the same. Dr. Whitman, however, was determined to take at least one of his wagons to prove that travel by wagon was possible through the mountains. He also had a herd of seventeen milk cows, the first the Indians had ever seen.

After the missionary party started on toward the Columbia, escorted by McKay's brigade, the Carson men, numbering nearly a hundred—many with Indian wives and several children—moved once again into the region of the upper Yellowstone. They were joined there by a village of Crows, a tribe noted for their handsome lodges, some housing as many as fifty persons. Altogether it was the largest settlement, temporary as it was, that had yet been assembled in the West.

A daugher was born to the Carsons that year, named Adaline for Kit's niece, Adaline Cooper. Alice Singing Grass carried her baby on a backboard with deerskin wrappings, filled with a delicate plant covered with little white blossoms called babies'-bed, and padded with cattail down. Kit, an affectionate man, was devoted to his first-born, a healthy child who resembled her mother.

Spreading along the high-up streams, Carson's men found a wealth of beaver, then at the high price of six dollars a plew. The silken furs, packed by calloused hands into bales, were taken to the trading posts of the various fur companies: Fort Hall on the Snake, Fort Clark on the Little Missouri, Fort Cass—formerly Fort Benton—at the fork of the Yellowstone and Big Horn, and the largest, Fort Union, where the Yellowstone joins the Missouri. All were in ruthless competition, cheating trapper and Indian alike.[8]

The winter of 1836 was a cruel one for Carson's company, holed in on Powder River. The snow so completely possessed the land that the animals almost died of starvation. Willow twigs were gathered and the tender inner bark peeled off to feed them. The buffalo came in from the range to fight with the horses for the meager supply of food, arriving in such numbers that huge fires were built of the scarce timber to keep them from overrunning the camp.

When the snowbound company was at last freed, the spring hunt began. Retracing the trail of the previous season, Carson's company joined Bridger, following the Twenty-Five-Yard River and the Missouri back into Blackfoot country.

There had been no hint of trouble from that sullen tribe all winter but they were soon to be heard from. Carson, reconnoitering with several scouts, found positive sign that a large village was moving just ahead. Leading their horses to a ridge, the trappers could see the Indians breaking camp, the squaws taking down the lodges, the young boys catching up the animals, the men putting on paint and feathers for a war dance. With extreme care not to be discovered, Kit and his men raced back to alert the camp. Forty crack shots were delegated to ride with Carson for an attack. Strike first and strike hard was the first principle of Indian warfare. Taken completely by surprise, the Blackfeet men, women, and children scattered in all directions. For three hours the Indians cannily drew the white man's fire without too much danger to themselves. When confident that their attackers were running low on ammunition, they made a sudden charge, driving the weary trappers back toward the hills. After a short distance, Kit ordered the men to turn quickly to attack their pursuers. The give-and-take battle lasted for hours.

Kit had another hair's-breadth escape while running to help Cotton Mansfield, who was pinned under when his horse fell. Seeing half a dozen Indians starting for his scalp, Cotton cried out: "Tell Old Gabe that Old Cotton's gone." Kit, shouting for the others to surround the helpless man, jumped from his horse in time to save him. Four warriors were shot from their mounts as the trappers converged around Mansfield. Doc Newell swung down from his saddle to filch another top-knot but the touch of his knife brought

the "dead" Blackfoot to his feet, slashing wildly. The
two fought a close hair-pulling duel with Doc's fingers
caught in the Indian's hair ornaments. Newell saved
his scalp. The Blackfoot was not as lucky.

Left with an empty rifle and no mount, Kit's predicament looked hopeless until one of his men raced
by and pulled him up behind him on his horse. By
sheer luck and faultless aim, all the trappers escaped
alive. "The prettiest fight I ever saw," said Kit, but
a stunning defeat for the Blackfeet who had decorated
their largest lodge for a Victory Scalp Dance.[11]

When the American Fur Company's boat, the *St.
Peter,* steamed up the Missouri in the spring of 1837,
bringing merchandise for the posts and presents for
the Indians, it carried, hidden in the goods, the curse
of smallpox. The devastating disease ran like prairie
fire through the tribes and no chanting, drumming,
sacrifice, or secret magic could stay the spreading death.
The plague did not reach the camps of the fur gather-
ers, scattered in remote valleys, but the traders, their
families and *engagés,* were not spared. The Indians
boycotted the trading posts and the fur companies
were faced with bankruptcy.

That spring Kit joined the hunting party of Captain Stewart, along with mountain men Bill Williams,
Lucien Fontenelle, and Isaac Rose. While he had
great admiration for Stewart himself, Kit could not
condone the ruthless killing of wildlife which the
Britishers seemed to relish and soon rejoined his company. They worked up to the headwaters of the Green
where news was brought by express rider that rendezvous would be held that summer on Wind River, an
eight-day journey away.

Kit and Joe Meek rode in, proud of their handsome squaws dressed in the finest broadcloth out of

St. Louis and bedecked with all the trinkets they loved best. Wanibe was as eager as any young mother to show her bright-eyed baby to the people of her tribe. Mountain Lamb, belle of the pale Shoshones (Snakes), rode astride a dappled gray fitted with beaded bridle and silver trappings. A tomahawk hung from one side of her saddle and a peace pipe from the other. In her bright dress, scarlet leggings, and richly embroidered moccasins, she was well aware of the fine picture she made.

The campground was thrown into confusion when a band of Bannocks rode in demanding payment for horses they claimed had been stolen by a party of white trappers. The Indians had, in fact, taken the animals from one of the brigades on the way to rendezvous and the trappers had retaken their own horses. The Bannock chief demanded restitution or trouble. During the argument, one of the braves, starting toward the disputed animals, was promptly leveled by Bridger's rifle. When the shooting ended, twelve of the thirty Bannock warriors lay dead, and in the skirmish Joe Meek's Mountain Lamb fell with an arrow piercing her heart. This was the first and only attack ever made by the Bannocks, who promised to be peaceful if allowed to stay and trade.[12]

This year Captain Stewart had brought with him a young artist, Alfred Miller, of Baltimore, to sketch the holiday scene. In Stewart's amazing collection of baggage carried by ship, train, wagon, and pack mule, there was a complete suit of heavy armor for Jim Bridger. Sir William had followed Old Gabe over many tangled trails and enjoyed listening to his improbable yarns. While Miller worked at his easel, Bridger rode about the grounds, an incongruous knight

strangely set in a mountain scene among half-clad
natives and bearded trappers.[13]

After three weeks of rendezvous, saddened by the
loss of happy-spirited Mountain Lamb, Kit and Wanibe sought the quiet of beaver creeks, trapping with
a small party along the fingers of the Green and into
the narrow gulch known as Brown's Hole. There,
where Colorado meets Utah and Wyoming, Fort Davy
Crockett was built in 1837. Kit and seven of his men
decided to leave their families at the fort while they
joined the factors, Thompson and Sinclair, on a trading trip to Navajo country.

Kit knew and loved every mile of the trappers' trail
to Taos. It was a long trek, edging along, winding
around and between towering rocky peaks topped with
perpetual snow. Every stream, spring, gorge, and sheltered rock were part of his mountain home. Following the Arkansas from headwaters to the Great Bend,
the traders found a caravan of nearly two hundred
wagons camped on the far side, afraid to attempt the
Cimarron Cutoff where the Kiowas were on the warpath. Kit's company volunteered to ride escort. On
the third day, after the wagons had rolled past the
worst of the stretch, the escort dismounted, tied their
horses to the rear wagon, and climbed under the canvas to ride. Kit had anticipated an attack that was
not long in coming. The Kiowas, forced back by sharp
rifle fire from the rear wagon, fled to their hills without damaging the train.

Kit took a great liking to one of the cavvy boys,
fifteen-year-old Oliver Wiggins, a runaway like Kit
himself had been a little over a decade before. When
the train reached Taos, Oliver decided to stay with
Carson though it meant forfeiting his wages for the

entire trip. The boy had every qualification necessary to become a first-rate mountain man.

Their trading done, Kit's party returned to Crockett's Fort with thirty mules and a fine supply of Navajo
blankets which were greatly desired by other tribes.
Kit spent the winter at the fort, hired as hunter to
provide meat for twenty men and their families. The
fort, a low three-winged adobe structure without a
stockade, was known among mountaineers as Fort
Misery, the meanest fort in the West. Soon to out-
live its usefulness, it was abandoned a few years later.

The remaining years of Carson's sojourn in the
mountain country were spent for the most part in
company with Jim Bridger. Old Gabe loved the Yellowstone region, the land of the pale Shoshones, who
had adopted him into their tribe. He joined enthusiastically in their ritual dances, sang their strange chants,
and took one of their daughters for his devoted wife.

This weather-worn hivernan could tell the best tall
tales in the West, tales of petrified valleys echoing
petrified bird song and a crystal mountain that could
magnify an elk twenty miles away to appear to be
within twenty feet. "It was so cold one winter," said
Bridger, "that all the buffalo froze and when they began to thaw, all I had to do was to tumble them into
the Great Salt Lake to have enough pickled buffalo
for myself and all the Ute nation for a year."[14] He
knew where there was an echo so perfect that he used
it for an alarm clock. Before rolling into his blanket
at night, he would say: "Time to get up!" and the
echo never failed to answer at the right moment next
morning. The mountaineers were so used to hearing
these yarns that when Bridger brought back reports
of what he had seen in the valley of the Yellowstone,

no one believed his stories of boiling springs, painted mud, and fire holes spouting on the hour.

Carson and Bridger were men of the same stripe who took an unashamed delight in the grandeur of their hunting grounds. Together they withdrew to the solitude of far valleys tracing through incredible beauty. A demanding curiosity led them through seemingly impenetrable forests and over hitherto impassable mountains to break the westward path, and not always where the beaver was most abundant. Few men have reached such fullness of freedom.

With their companies they followed the lesser tributaries of the Yellowstone, the Big Horn, the Wind, the Sweetwater, the Popo Agie, the Seedeskeedee, and myriad other waters with rhythmic Indian names. Bridger led Kit to the bottomless Hell's Canyon of the Snake; he pointed out the spectacular Shoshone Falls. To the eyes of a man who had known the desert, this was "the grandest water" Kit had ever seen. They zigzagged along the folds of the Snake, probing the breaks in the glazed rock in search of hidden nooks where beaver might be found, and skirted the bastions of the Grand Tetons to visit Davy Jackson's Hole, then threaded their way to Pierre's Hole on the far side. In all this traveling, the only map was memory.

The Blackfeet were still undaunted in their determination to stay the paleface encroachment of their ancestral domain. Far up the Missouri, Carson and Bridger came upon a camp site recently vacated by another trapping party. Taking fifteen men, Kit rode ahead to investigate and found the company of Joseph Gale, of Fort Hall, in a destitute condition after a foray with the Blackfeet. Among the wounded was Richard Owens, a most resourceful and energetic young man, later to be closely associated with Kit Carson. Rather than risk returning through a broken country where danger lurked behind every rock and stump, Kit decided to wait for Bridger and the main company to catch up.

Two of Kit's men, riding out to set some traps a few miles from the camp, were fired upon by Blackfoot scouts. At the sound of rifle fire, Carson ordered Gale's men, who were without ammunition, to hold the horses in the brush while his men made ready for a certain attack. The trappers lay face down at the edge of the thicket, almost completely out of sight. Soon down from the hills came the Blackfoot warriors in one great wave of color toward an enemy they could not see. As they charged the open stretch before the woods, they were shot like clay pigeons from their saddles. When repeated attacks failed to rout the white men, the Indians set fire to the grass hoping to stampede the horses and force the trappers from hiding.

The fire quickly licked across the sere plain, sending in dense smoke fanned by a rising wind. It came so close the trappers could feel the heat on their faces and the smoke in their throats. Several times the impatient red men attempted to rush their ponies through the fire only to be repelled by the heat and smoke. In dire emergencies, Kit's coolness had been his salvation but this time there seemed to be no possible escape. The animals must be released before the fire came much closer yet he hesitated to give the order. As the flames reached the edge of the brush and the men drew back to run for their lives, the miracle happened. The wood was too green to burn! The fire died out, the smoke swirled away and the unbelieving Blackfeet raced back to their hideout behind the red buttes, certain that Kit Carson possessed some magic medicine. Kit called it "the protecting hand of Providence." Bridger, hearing the gunfire as he approached with the rest of the company, arrived after all danger had passed. So the legend grew among the superstitious that Kit Carson's life was charmed.

Veteran mountain men puzzled over the fame that had come to the scrappy little leader. Many of them had comparable skill in trapping, shooting, riding, and exploring, yet it was shy and unassuming Kit Carson, in direct contrast to the rough men and wild country, who became symbolic of the indomitable spirit of the West.

The last all-out attempt of the Blackfeet to repulse the interloper came unexpectedly in dead of winter. Kit, with several men hunting game for the camp on the Yellowstone, quite by accident discovered a large war party moving toward them. Bridger agreed that the best strategy was to anticipate them. With forty of his best horsemen, Kit closed in on a party of Blackfoot scouts, forcing them to take refuge on one of the large islands in the river. The trappers continued the attack from shore until nightfall expecting to rout the Indians in the morning. Sunrise revealed a deserted island. The Blackfeet had disappeared completely, leaving only a bloody trail to a hole in the ice where they evidently had disposed of their dead.

Bridger warned that the Blackfoot village could not be far away and predicted that before many days had passed their warriors would be out in force to avenge their slain braves. A lookout was posted on a nearby ridge. "When there are no Indians, that's the time to look for them," cautioned Old Gabe. The whole company, about sixty, hurriedly threw up a strong fort of logs, brush, and stone, then waited fifteen days without a sign of a skulking Indian. "Keep your scalps

by thinking about them," Bridger warned the trappers, restless for action as they huddled together for
warmth. Looking through his spyglass "for a squall,"
the sharp-eyed Bridger noticed a far distant line of
moving specks. On they came until there were over
a thousand Blackfeet gathered beyond the buttes, with
more hundreds streaming in from the hills. The Indians took a position on the island and put up breast-
works for a siege. When the last of their number
arrived—about fifteen hundred in all—they began the
dismal chants and drumming usually preceding a sunrise attack.

The trappers prepared to battle for their lives against
what seemed insuperable odds. In the "dry cracking
cold night," blood-red streaks appeared in the sky and
the slowly moving streamers of the aurora borealis began to weave above. A roseate glow, spreading over
half the sky, lasted several hours and appeared as a
sign for the Blackfeet to delay their attack. The trappers, eager for action, were forced to wait, cramped
in the tiny fortress through another interminable day
and night.

With dawn of the second day, a whooping drove of
warriors came charging out. Cautioned by the warning from the skies, they rode only close enough to see
the strength of the white man's position, fired a few
shots into the air, and withdrew a mile to sit in council. After unhurried deliberation, the Indians separated into two bands and rode off in opposite directions leaving the white man in possession of their lands.
The trappers could scarcely believe their good fortune but Carson and Bridger, after years of intimate
contact with many tribes, understood the Blackfoot
decision to accept the inevitable with dignity and without useless bloodshed.[15]

Except for the hatred shown by the Blackfeet, there was generally a spirit of friendliness between the Indian and the early trapper, each showing a common respect for the land and sharing feast and famine. Veteran mountain men who loved the friendlies foresaw an end to their unparalleled freedom in the beautiful and unspoiled region that was their hunting ground. Soon from the East would move a stream of prairie schooners bringing settlers with plows to tear the sod and break the cherished quietness and determined to exterminate as many red men as possible. In all the great space, there would not be room enough for two peoples to live in peace.

"For some time clouds of misgivings had appeared to darken the trappers' free and happy horizon." With the big trading companies almost bankrupt from disease and deceit, many struck out for themselves to find the beaver not only worth little but the supply almost exhausted. The rendezvous of 1838 was a cheerless gathering poorly attended by men soon to be out of business. The crushing blow fell when the traders announced they could not afford to bring supplies another year.

Captain Andy Drips appeared that summer at Wind River with a string of pack mules escorting the missionary party of the Rev. Cushing Eells. Accompanying them was none other than the visionary Swiss, Johann Augustus Suter, who had settled for a while in Missouri, simplified his name to John Sutter, and begun running wagons on the Santa Fe Trail. After three years of this, Sutter, hearing reports that California offered a new field for enterprise, sold his trade wagons and took the Oregon Trail with Drips. At rendezvous, Sutter could not persuade a single man to join his party but did obtain the services of a bright twelve-year-old Indian boy in Carson's employ. Since the boy knew both Spanish and English as well as his native tongue and signs, he would be invaluable as an interpreter but Kit did not want to part with him. Impressed by Sutter, Kit relented and agreed to accept an order for a hundred beaver drawn on the Hudson's Bay Company for the boy's release. As the season was getting late, Kit advised Sutter to go on to Oregon and wait until spring before trying to get to California, a course wisely followed by the energetic Sutter.[16]

At first thought it seems remote that a change of fashion in New York could affect the mountaineer in the Western wilderness. However, when men of distinction in the East began replacing their high beaver hats with stylish silk toppers, the price of beaver began to slide. From eight dollars a plew it dropped to a dollar and hit bottom at twenty-five cents a bale. When the slump eventually reached the mountains, many trappers, Kit among them, decided to leave the beaver for the Indians and reluctantly turned toward the settlements. It was not easy for Kit, who usually kept his feelings to himself, to part company with the men who had been close to him and faithful to his leadership. There was an especially strong tie between Kit and the effervescent Joe Meek. Joe and Doc Newell undertook and successfully accomplished the job of piloting the first wagons to Oregon. Four years before, Dr. Whitman's farm wagon had broken down at the ford of the Snake beyond Fort Boise.

There was a semblance of a trappers' meeting during the next two summers. The final gathering marked the appearance of the beloved Jesuit, Fr. Pierre-Jean de Smet, who celebrated the first mass held in "the shining stony mountains." He baptized forty or more children of the trappers and Indians, probably among them Kit's small daughter Adaline. Kit expressed great admiration for the courageous churchman. "If ever there was a man who wished to do good, it was de Smet."[17]

NOTES ON CHAPTER FOUR

1. DeVoto, *Across the Wide Missouri;* Stewart, *Altowan* (1846).
2. Jessie Benton Fremont in *Land of Sunshine,* Vol. VI, No. 2 (1897).
3. Parker, *A Journey Beyond the Rocky Mountains* (1841).
4. Parker, *A Journey Beyond the Rocky Mountains* (1841).
5. Stewart, *Edward Warren* (1854).
6. Victor, *The River of the West* (1870). Biography of Joe Meek.
7. Gray, *A History of Oregon* (1871).
8. Victor, *The River of the West.*
9. Rev. Henry Spalding, report to the American Board of Foreign Missions, 1836. Mentioned in Myron Eells' biography, *Marcus Whitman.*
10. Eells, *Father Eells.*
11. Carson, *Autobiography.*
12. Victor, *The River of the West.*
13. DeVoto, *Across the Wide Missouri.*
14. Inman, *The Great Salt Lake Trail;* Chittenden, *Yellowstone Park.*
15. Russell, *Journal of a Trapper.*
16. Dana, Julian. *The Sacramento.*
17. Carson, *Autobiography.*
18. A second Fort Benton was later established at the Great Falls of the Missouri.

Hunter for Bent's Fort (1841-1842)

The man who bestrides a horse must be essentially different from the man who cowers in a canoe.

WASHINGTON IRVING

KIT CARSON was not one to act impulsively except in emergency when he moved with sharp primitive instinct at lightning speed and almost without fail in the right direction. To give up the free life in the mountains that he loved was a decision to come by gradually. Convinced at last that there was no future in the dwindling fur business for a family man, Kit disposed of his pelts for a discouraging price at Robidoux's post in the spring of 1841 and started toward Bent's Fort along with Bill Mitchell, Bill New, and Old Bill Williams. Alice and four-year-old Adaline rode one of the pack mules. Bronzed by the sun and clothed in fringed deerskin, Kit might have been mistaken for an Indian himself except for his fall of fine sandy hair. Even his countenance, more stern and determined, bore an Indian resemblance belying his gentle manner.

Old Bill Williams, shaggy red-haired ex-preacher from Missouri, usually traveled alone and was known throughout the mountain country as its most eccentric character. He knew the terrain as well as any living man and liked to appear in the most unlikely places with enviable packs of the heaviest beaver from his secret haunts. The religious beliefs and superstitions of the Indians interested the master trapper tremendously. He translated long passages from the Bible into various Indian languages and would tell other mountaineers in high-flung oratory that he believed in the transmigration of the soul, warning them to be exceedingly careful not to kill an elk with certain well-defined peculiarities lest they disturb their old friend William Sherley Williams.

Old Bill put all persons into two classes: "them that spits and them that has no cause to," referring to the Indian custom of spitting in a hole, then covering it with earth to bury revenge and hate. Almost a caricature of a man, Old Bill rode a small mule fitted with a high-pommeled Spanish saddle with short stirrups that drew his bony knees almost to his chin; his trouser legs were split and flapping, and six-inch spurs jangled at his heels. Unlike most mountaineers, Williams did not wear deerskin and spurned a hat. In frigid weather the old hivernan would kill and rip the hide from a timber wolf and pull the warm skin down over his ears.

This strange company was about a hundred miles above Bent's when Mitchell and New, still unwilling to give up, decided to stay and put out some traps. Kit could not be persuaded to join them for he had made up his mind that the mountain roam was over. Arriving at Bent's, Carson eagerly accepted the job of hunter for the fort, offered to him by his long-time friend, William Bent. He moved his family into one of the lodges built within the walls of the great prairie fortress that had become the most important commercial establishment in the West. Ten days later, Mitchell and New came dragging in nearly naked but glad to be alive after the Indians had stolen everything they possessed.

In a few years' time, the Bents, Charles and William, with their younger brothers George and Robert, had grown rich in the commerce of the plains and ruled

like kings over a great, untamed empire. Standing
about a hundred yards from the Arkansas, their mud-
brick castle was an impressive structure on the otherwise bare plain. The fort had been four years in building with a hundred laborers brought from Chihuahua
to make the sun-dried brick of clay mixed with wool.
Massive fifteen-foot walls with thirty-foot towers on opposite corners enclosed an immense courtyard. Loop-
holes were left in the walls for guns, and inside hung
a ready arsenal of rifles, muskets, lances, knives, and
sabres. A six-pound brass cannon, to be fired on special occasions, stood in one of the towers where a con-
tinuous watch was kept over an area seven miles in
all directions. Two bald eagles nested there, flying
freely about until one was caught by an Indian boy
for the coveted tail feathers.

Solid wooden doors studded with metal plate opened
toward the river and over the gateway a large American
flag whipped in the breeze from a sturdy ash pole.
The outer wall rose four feet above a row of two-
story houses—the second floors and roofs merely pole
platforms covered with straw and a foot-thick layer
of clay dried to the hardness of cement. With walls
so thick, the houses were cool in summer and warm in
winter, and the graveled roofs made them practically
fireproof.

Within the enclosure stood several council rooms,
an icehouse, billiard room, bar, blacksmith shop, supply depot and an immense robe press. The wagon
yard had space for a dozen big Pittsburghs. Several
large storehouses were stocked with an unusual assortment of goods. Besides the popular red and blue calicoes and fufuraw for the Indian trade, there were cut-
glass beads from Italy, knives from England, mirrors
from Germany, and even Chinese preserved ginger in

decorative boxes—all brought overland in the bulging freight wagons in exchange for the robes and peltries in great demand in Europe.

The huge corral, a short distance away, was surrounded by an eight-foot wall planted on top with spiny cacti. In case of attack (which never happened), the animals could be led through a gate into the main courtyard. *Acequias* carried river water into a large garden plot which had been abandoned after a few years because the Indians stole all the produce. Two peacocks, which the Indians called thunderbirds, strutted about the grounds unruffled by the swarm of halfbreed children frolicking with a variety of pets which included a bear cub, several dogs, a buffalo calf, and a goat hitched to a cart.[1]

William Bent, who was in command of the fort, had shown himself to be a friend and ally of the Indian by marrying the daughter of a Cheyenne chief. This was a great advantage in that savage country for Owl Woman's relatives kept the post informed of trade demands, the whereabouts of the various tribes, and where the best robes were to be found. The Cheyennes, whom William called "my people," set up their tepee village outside the wall of the great fort and were free to roam about the grounds if they returned to their lodges at night.

Nearly a hundred traders, trappers, teamsters, and laborers were employed by the company. Rosalie, the half-Indian wife of one of the traders was the housekeeper and Charlotte, a huge Negress who referred to herself as "the onliest lady on the plains," managed the kitchen with remarkable efficiency, turning out immense quantities of food daily.[2]

Bent's was more than a prairie trading post; it was the only speck of civilization on the Great Plains.

Constantly arriving visitors were welcome to stay as
guests for as long as they wished. There were travelers
of every description: writers, artists, soldiers, invalids,
politicians, promoters, tourists, and renegades. A variety of entertainment was planned for their pleasure:
cards, billiards, horse racing and dancing by the light
of buffalo-tallow candles. The squaws in brocade and
lace-trimmed ball gowns brought from St. Louis tried
to execute the intricate steps of the cotillion which
Louis Garrard, a young writer from Cincinnati, described as "a combination of the halting, irregular
march of the war dance, the slipping gallopade, the
more nice gyrations of the Frenchmen, and the boisterous pitching of the backwoodsmen."[3]

This was a scene of excitement for Kit and his squaw
after the quiet of the mountain trails. It was no small
job that Kit undertook to be responsible for the large
quantities of meat required for the great hostelry even
though the country teemed with game. The buffalo
herds were so tremendous that the supply of meat on
the Great Plains had seemed inexhaustible. Kit was
a crack shot and enjoyed the chase but his regard for
the country and the generous provision of food was
in accord with that of the Indian who killed no more
than he needed. With the coming of the white man,
the buffalo range narrowed and it required real skill
to find the food necessary for the welfare of the fort.

The first months at Bent's were happy ones for Kit
without any worry of hostiles or the sinking price of
beaver. Wanibe was near her people, who came to
trade at the fort. Kit lost much of his reticence and
enjoyed visiting with the great variety of visitors eager
to hear the tales of the mountaineers. It was, however, but a snatch of happiness, as most of Carson's
life was to hold. He returned one day from hunting

to find his wife delirious with fever. The incantations of the medicine man were to no avail and her death soon afterward ended a genuine happiness. The Arapahos claimed their daughter and according to tribal custom, burned the body with all her possessions and never again spoke her name. The women of the fort took little Adaline to care for with the same complete affection they gave their own children.[4]

During the late summer months, when there was little activity at the fort, Bill Williams persuaded Kit to ride back to Missouri with him. Old Bill had not been home since he had left with Sibley's surveying expedition sixteen years before; nor had Kit, who came West the following year. Taking a few possibles, a blanket apiece and a pocketful of nuggets they had picked up on the Platte, the two mountaineers set out on their Indian ponies to ride across the summer prairies. They found the settlements extending a considerable distance beyond the Missouri and Williams succeeded in locating his daughter's home in Kansas territory. A brother, living nearby, would claim no kinship to the bewhiskered old trapper until Bill revealed a tattoo on his arm. Reaching his old home, Wild Bill—as his family called him—spurned any show of affection as his eighty-six-year-old mother opened her arms to the son she had hopefully believed would one day return. He went on to St. Louis, never to see his family again.[5]

It was different with Kit, who had kept in touch with his family through his teamster brothers and found his fame had preceded him. All of Boone's Lick turned out to greet the returning runaway. It was a shock to find his home town of Franklin swallowed by the river. Only the cemetery, high above flood danger, had been spared. New Franklin was just another small river village.

Kit and Williams found, on returning to Bent's Fort, that the Cheyennes had taken the warpath against the other tribes of the Plains despite William Bent's earnest effort to impress upon these Indians the importance of peace among the tribes. Though his father-in-law Chief Gray Thunder, Keeper of the Sacred Arrows, had heeded William's admonitions, he was unable to restrain the headstrong youths of his tribe. The whole body of Bow String warriors was annihilated by a coalition of Comanches, Kiowas, and Apaches, leading to all-out war among the Plains Indians. The broken-hearted chief gave his life at the battle of Wolf Creek Pass by openly exposing himself to enemy arrows.

Bent sought Kit's help in negotiating a peace settlement. Representatives of all the tribes were called to gather near the fort. Carson, riding out to locate the Comanches, found in one of their villages two white men captured the previous year from a trading party. They had been well treated and one of them, Captain James Hobbs, had married the daughter of Chief Old Wolf, "a good-looking hardy squaw." The chief could not be persuaded to come to terms for the release of the captives but finally agreed to visit the fort to barter with Bent and meet the other tribes in council.

When the leading men of the tribes had gathered and set up their lodges, it was the largest Indian camp ever known to be assembled on the Plains. Kit went freely among the camps, playing with the children and talking with the chiefs who respected the sincerity of his friendliness. He found them responsive, affectionate among themselves, and full of wisdom and humor. His men patrolled the area to confiscate liquor smuggled in by the Mexicans. At length a treaty was drawn up assuring lasting peace among these nations. Guns were fired to salute the great occasion, Bent's supplies were almost entirely bought out for presents, and all joined in one magnificent powwow.

Old Wolf arrived as he had promised and was invited into the fort for royal entertainment with the best food and drink there was to offer. He appreciated his presents and the many toasts to his good health but thought the bread fit only for good smoke-fire. The old Indian nearly collapsed with fright when the tower cannon was fired to celebrate the treaty. A great throng of his people, fearing their chieftain had been the victim of treachery, gathered at the gates to demand his return. Old Wolf made an appearance on the wall at noon, every day of his visit, to show himself to his tribesmen, then returned to his luxury. William gave six yards of red flannel, a pound of tobacco and an ounce of beads for the release of Captain Hobbs. Eight yards of calico was all that was asked for the other captive, considered too lazy to be worth more. Hobbs offered to take his wife with him but Old Wolf would not be parted from this favorite daughter. She cried and wailed, refusing to be reconciled even with a red dress and many crystal beads, but did not leave her father.

Captain Hobbs joined Kit's band of hunters, who also trapped whenever they found good beaver sign. Sometimes as many as eighty beaver and a dozen otter were caught in one night. A band of Crows accidentally came upon the hunters' camp one evening while looking for an old squaw who had wandered from the tribe. Seeing the white men, the Indians turned to run but were persuaded to come back and lay down their bows when Kit waved a white handkerchief tied to his gunstick. Throwing his own rifle to the ground, Carson invited the Crows to sit with him for a smoke. As the pipe made the rounds, he learned they were in dire need of supplies but were afraid to trade at the fort for fear of meeting an enemy tribe. Kit assured them that if they would return by the next moon, the goods they needed would be waiting for them. One of the Shawnees in the company was sent back to Bent's with the order and for this deal, William, who sent five hundred dollars' worth of merchandise, received payment in furs worth three thousand dollars.[6]

By this time all Carson men carried Colt revolving pistols in addition to their trusted rifles. Kit's most prized possession was a percussion cap pistol brought from Boston for which he paid sixty dollars in gold. The repeating fire confused the Indians. One decided the white man must shoot "one time with rifle and six times with butcher-knife."[7]

By living with the Indians and trading with them, Kit had learned many of their cunning ways. Only once was he completely deceived by their tactics. While on a buffalo hunt with six men, he noticed one evening that the dogs seemed restless and were barking more than usual. Investigation showed two large timber wolves skulking along the edge of the brush. One of the men quickly raised his rifle but was ordered to hold his fire for fear of wounding the dogs. Always intuitive, Carson wondered if the "wolves" might be Indians until he saw one turn and gnash its teeth at the dogs. The Indians had fooled the white men by rattling a couple of dried bones each time they lunged at the dogs. Trusting the dogs to keep the "wolves" away from the camp, the men rolled into their blan-

kets and fell soundly asleep. A crashing sound followed by a blaze soon sent them running toward their
ponies. Three stood guard while the others fired
blindly in the direction of the disturbance. The Indians had tried unsuccessfully to start a stampede and
the entire camp might have been wiped out if they
had not fled at the first shot. One of Kit's men, "poor
Davis," was mortally wounded and one brave was
found next morning with five bullets in his body and
eight in his buffalo robe.[8]

When spring opened the snow-locked mountain
passes, Kit made a business trip to Santa Fe for William Bent. He took with him Captain Hobbs and
a character called Peg Leg Smith who was said to have
amputated his own leg and whittled out a new one
which at times served as an effective weapon. Peg
Leg headed at once for the luxurious gambling establishment of Doña Gertrudes de Barcelo, a successful
businesswoman and confidante of Governor Manuel
Armijo. The elegant *sala* stood in Burros Alley, a short
distance from the rambling adobe Palace of the Gov-
ernors.

Their business finished, Kit and Hobbs looked for
Peg Leg to join them at the fandango but found him
too liquored for dancing. After sobering up on tea,
Smith buckled on his leg and they made their way to
the plaza. Two musicians, one with a leather fiddle
and the other strumming a guitar "large enough to
float a man," supplied the music for three dollars a
night. Most of the dancers were Americans, popular
with the *señoritas*. With the dance in full swing, a
group of young Mexicans, resentful at the attention
given the *Americanos,* broke up the dance. The music
was carried on by a "half-way fiddler," George Stilts,
who years later was to marry Kit's daughter. The

brawling continued with Peg Leg in the midst of it until the Americans were forced to ask protection of the governor. Armijo not only sent a guard but, being in a dancing mood himself, brought his own musicians to keep the fandango whirling until dawn.

Later that day, four hundred troops from El Paso, escorting a pack-mule train belonging to Armijo, called on the governor for wages. When offered a draft on the Chihuahua government, they threatened violence unless they were paid in coin. On an appeal for help from Armijo, Kit and the others joined with the palace guard to form a circle around the Mexican soldiers who were rowdy drunk and fighting among themselves. Kit proposed a compromise which the governor accepted: each soldier to be advanced ration money to get back to Chihuahua and pay of 37½ cents a day for eighteen days' service. The unruly troops left the city without further disturbance, thanks to Carson's diplomacy. Armijo did not forget the quick response the Americans gave to his call for aid and afterwards often sided with the Americans against his own country.[9]

Returning to the fort, they found William recovering from a serious throat infection. A Cheyenne medicine man, called to attend the sick man, dipped a sinew strung with sandburs into hot buffalo tallow and forced it down the throat with a peeled stick. After the tallow melted, the string was jerked out to remove the infected membrane and William was saved from choking to death. Except for a siege of smallpox, there was generally good health at the fort.[10]

Through the years, the friendship of Carson, St. Vrain, and the Bents grew more solid. "I wish I were capable of doing justice for the kindness I received from their hands," Kit recorded later in his life story. "I can only say their equals were never before seen in the mountains."[11] William and his younger brothers, George and Robert, had their headquarters at the big fort on the Arkansas. Charles and Ceran St. Vrain operated a store at Taos and supervised business operations in New Mexico and the overland traffic. The company's other post, Fort St. Vrain on the Platte, was supervised by Ceran's brother Marcellin.

Probably no visitor at the fort caused more excitement than St. Vrain's sixteen-year-old niece, Felicité, the first white woman to come there. She became quite smitten with Kit Carson, whose feats of daring were well known. Ceran promptly sent the pretty girl back to St. Louis by the first stage, convinced that his aristocratic family would never accept a squaw man. The decision did not, however, end that problem for the St. Vrain family. Marcellin took two Indian wives at the same time and after fathering several children, returned home to marry a belle of St. Louis. One of the deserted wives truly loved him and every day this Poor Butterfly of the Prairies watched faithfully from a hilltop for his return. She finally gave up, married a county judge, bore him several children, and lived to a venerable age, greatly respected in the West.[12]

Charles was the most influential of the Bent brothers politically. He had attended West Point and by his marriage in 1836 to the charming and aristocratic young widow, Doña Maria Ignacia Jarmillo-Luna, of Taos, had become popular with the Spanish-Mexicans who fondly called him Don Carlos. Bent was also on intimate terms with the American consul at Santa Fe, who considered Charles an authority on inland commerce. With adroit diplomacy, Charles kept the business running smoothly without too much interference and succeeded in getting a reduction in the prohibitive Mexican tariff rates that encouraged smuggling and bribery.

Through Governor Armijo's friendliness, several prominent Americans had acquired title to vast acreage of New Mexican land. Charles was in on a million-acre deal with Charles Beaubien, a French-Canadian trader, and Guadalupe Miranda, a prominent Taoseno. The grant gave control over most of the northeastern section of the province. St. Vrain and Cornelio Vigil, an uncle of Ignacia Bent, received another enormous tract. Opposing this giveaway policy was the parish priest of Taos, Fr. Antonio Jose Martinez, a sardonic but cleverly brilliant churchman who published incendiary articles in his newspaper, *El Crepusculo,* and commanded an autocratic authority over the Pueblos. Martinez had little respect for the fat and scheming Governor Armijo and openly opposed the powerful Bents. To add to the feud, Charles had remained Protestant and dared to defy the padre who lived anything but an exemplary private life.

Doña Ignacia Bent was a handsome woman and her home one of the most attractive in Taos. Rich rugs of Eastern import and native bright-striped serapes brought color to the rough floors and heavy hand-hewn furnishings. Ornate religious articles and sconces of hammered tin reflected soft candlelight in an atmosphere of quiet serenity. Here Kit Carson met and fell in love with Ignacia's sister Maria Josefa, a fourteen-year-old dark-eyed beauty. Kit, approaching thirty-three, was a man of some importance in the West and in spite of the fact that he had spent most of his years living in a very primitive manner, possessed a natural dignity that impressed young Josefa. Her family—the Castilian Jarmillos and Vigils—made no objection to Kit's suit though he had no fortune to offer and Josefa chose to accept the gentle man whose destiny of fame appeared certain. On January 28, 1842, Christopher Carson was baptized into the Catholic faith by the controversial Padre Martinez.

As Adaline was now of school age, Kit decided to take her to live with one of his sisters in Missouri. He was fond and extremely proud of his handsome daughter, who resembled her Arapaho mother, and anxious to give her every opportunity for education. At the same time she would in this way present no problem for his bride-to-be who was only eight years her senior. When the wagons left in the spring for Missouri, Adaline rode the miles from Bent's Fort to Independence in one of the dearborn carriages that now usually accompanied the caravans to accommodate visitors—probably the first child to make that uncomfortable trip.

While less hazardous, the journey required as many weeks as ever but in spring the prairies were a delight. Writers were ecstatic in praise of the unexpected beauty of endless flowering acres where desert wasteland had been expected. "There is a charm in the loneliness, an enchantment in the solitude and a bewitching variety in the sameness," wrote Rufus B. Sage in his book *Rocky Mountain Life,* published that year. This trip was far different from Kit's first crossing of the trail sixteen years before. The runaway cavvy boy was the prospective brother-in-law of the wagon master and a man of consequence. Oxen had generally replaced mules on the trail, now a busy commercial highway. Westport Landing (Kansas City) was the terminal point. Bent and St. Vrain maintained a large farm there complete with corrals, storage houses, and crops to care for the animals between trips.

Kit decided to leave Adaline in the care of a family with whom they had spent the night at Westport while he rode on ahead to prepare his family for her visit, having some misgivings about how his half-Arapaho daughter might be received. When assured that the child would be warmly welcomed, he returned to bring her to the home of his sister, Mrs. Mary Ann Rubey, living in the vicinity where he had spent his own childhood.[13]

Kit went on to St. Louis, which he was to see for the first time. "For several consecutive years," he said, "I have never slept under the roof of a house or gazed on the face of a white woman." He did not care for the city and said he felt like the old trapper who had gone there for the first time and was found asleep in the market place. "Lost my way," he said, "because the danged brick canyons all look alike." After ten days—enough for any mountain man—Kit took passage to Kansas Landing on a river steamer, intending to return west with the first wagons.

At the time Kit was in St. Louis, Lieutenant John Charles Fremont, the personable son-in-law of Senator Benton, was also there recruiting men for a government expedition to survey the South Pass of the Rockies and acquire information concerning the advisability of extending the railroad into the mountains. The young officer discussed the venture with Charles Bent, whom he had met on a social occasion, and Charles suggested Kit Carson as the best possible man he could find to guide the expedition.

It happened that Fremont's company took the same river boat as Kit and the two men met on deck. Here began a friendship unequaled in the saga of the West.

The two men completely complemented each other. Fremont, called "the handsomest man who ever walked the streets of Washington," was twenty-nine, aggressive and scholarly. He had eloped the year before with the popular and vivacious Jessie Benton. Carson, three years older and of undistinguished appearance, was far more wise, practical, and experienced. He could converse easily in several languages including those of various Indian tribes and had noteworthy skill in everything necessary for frontier existence. Lieutenant Fremont had intended hiring Captain Andrew Drips, veteran guide of the American Fur Company, but instead offered Kit a hundred dollars a month to accompany his party as guide and interpreter. Kit, badly in need of funds, accepted at once.[14]

NOTES ON CHAPTER FIVE

1. For a description of Bent's Fort see Grinnell, *Bent's Old Fort and Its Builders;* Lavender, *Bent's Fort;* Mumey, *Old Forts and Trading Posts;* Lieut. J. W. Abert's Journal (Senate Ex. Doc. 438, 29th Cong., 1st Sess.).

2. Inman, *The Old Santa Fe Trail.*

3. Garrard, *Wah-to-yah and the Taos Trail.*

4. Vestal, *Kit Carson, the Happy Warrior of the Old West,* gives the date 1838 as the year Carson came to the fort. In his *Autobiography,* Carson mentions September, 1841. Vestal tells of another Indian wife but this was vigorously denied by Kit. See Estergreen, *The Real Kit Carson.*

5. Favour, *Old Bill Williams, Mountain Man.*

6. Hobbs, *Wild Life in the Far West.*

7. Sabin, *Kit Carson Days.*

8. Inman, *The Old Santa Fe Trail.*

9. Hobbs, *Wild Life in the Far West.*

10. See *Bent's Fort on the Arkansas,* published in 1954 by the State Historical Society of Colorado.

11. Carson, *Autobiography.*

12. Lavender, *Bent's Fort.*

13. Adaline eventually lived with Kit's niece, Mrs. Leander Amick, daughter of his sister, Elizabeth Cooper. (Sabin, *Kit Carson Days*). An article in *The Nutmeg,* official publication of the National Guard, Hartford, Conn., Vol. I, No. 12, reports an interview with Kit's sister, Mrs. Mary Ann Rubey, who states that Adaline was not sent to a convent in

St. Louis as reported in Fremont's *Memoirs,* but attended Howard **Female** Seminary at Fayette, Missouri. William Switzler (Missouri Historical Society, Vol. II, January, 1900), gives Mrs. Rubey's account of Kit's early life.

14. Material on Fremont's life and career has been taken from the following sources: Fremont, *Report of the Exploring Expedition to the Rocky Mountains* (1845), *Memoirs;* Nevins, *Fremont, Pathmarker of the West;* Goodwin, *John Charles Fremont;* Preuss, *Exploring with Fremont.*

CHAPTER SIX

Guide for Fremont's Expedition to the Rockies (1842-1843)

Wherever railroads now run and trails are followed, Kit Carson led the way and his footprints are all along the route.

AN OLD COMRADE

FREMONT'S COMPANY stayed three weeks at Cyprian Chouteau's post ten miles up the Kaw River preparing for the expedition while the animals gained strength from the spring grass. Two Delaware runners were dispatched to Taos with instructions for fifteen of Carson's men to meet the expedition at Fort Laramie, bringing supplies.

Included in the company were nineteen *voyageurs,* eight armed and mounted, the others to drive the carts and herd the loose stock; Prussian cartographer Charles Preuss, a melancholy fellow critical of Fremont's wisdom in risking lives for longitudes and latitudes; two youths out for adventure, Jessie's twelve-year-old brother Randolph and his cousin, Henry Brant, nineteen, also of St. Louis; and Kit's long-time friend and trapping confrere, Lucien Maxwell, hired as a hunter.

The expedition set out the tenth of June in fine spirits, following the Kaw over the now well-worn Santa Fe Trail as far as the site of Topeka, then along the Vermillion and the Big Blue to the unpredictable Platte. All went well for the first hundred miles. The country was beautiful, the grass thick and the weather benevolent. Though there was slight danger of Indian attack, full precaution was observed. The animals were hobbled on short tethers and every man slept with a half-cocked pistol pointing over a saddle barri-

cade. Guard was changed every two hours throughout the night. During Kit's watch from ten o'clock
till midnight, he entertained the two boys with hair-
raising accounts of Indian fury. Though completely
terrified they endured the test and were a source of
much entertainment for the company.

The first real problem came with the crossing of
the flooded Kaw which was nearly four hundred feet
wide at the ford. The mounted men swam it easily
and the stock was safely driven over—all except four
oxen that turned in midstream and swam back to
shore. Fremont, foreseeing trouble with the carts, had
included in the equipage an inflatable rubber boat
of his own design, twelve by five feet. The boat was
unpacked, pumped full of air with the bellows, and
the carts loaded on, one at a time. With three men
paddling and a swimmer towing with a rope held in
his teeth, six successful crossings were made. With
darkness coming on, Fremont impetuously decided to
take both remaining carts on the last trip. Halfway
across, the boat capsized, throwing barrels, boxes, carts,
and bales into the water. Most of the provisions were
recovered though two men were nearly drowned in
an attempt to salvage the coffee.

The unco-operative cattle were rounded up next
morning and the company rested a day to dry out
the soggy baggage. Fremont, determined to make the
most of each day, required the men to spend some
time in target practice while Preuss picked and pressed
specimens of prairie flowers.

The company, continuing westward along the shallow Platte, "the most magnificent and useless of
rivers,"[1] met a party of ragged trappers coming down
the river on the barges of the American Fur Company. They had a woeful tale to tell of one misfor-

tune after another. They had left Fort Laramie two months before and after forty days of floods and shallows had covered only 130 miles. Losing their way in the maze of small tributaries and unable to pull against the strong current, they had unloaded and carried the barges overland, then returned for their packs and supplies. Convinced at last that the Platte was unfit for commercial navigation, the trappers had decided to sink the unruly barges in the sand, cache the furs in the trees, and carry what they could on foot to the Missouri. Leading the party was Baptiste Charbonneau, son of Sacajawea, who had carried him as a babe on her back when she guided Lewis and Clark on the first expedition to the West.

Fremont recorded everything of scientific interest and wrote enthusiastically of the smiling prairies, yellow with sunflowers, of the sage glittering like silver, and of the sweet prairie roses. Preuss complained about the monotonous "same landscape day after day with not a tree in sight." Kit was in his element. He loved the flatlands and could not imagine having an easier, better-paying job.

The prairie quiet was shattered one day when a guard galloped in shouting that he had counted twenty-seven Indians riding far in the distance. In an instant Kit had straddled his pony and was off to investigate. He returned shortly with the comforting report that it was only a herd of antelope grazing peacefully on a hillside. "Kit Carson, springing on one of the hunting horses, galloped off into the opposite prairies to obtain intelligence of Indian movements," noted Fremont. "Mounted on a fine horse, without saddle and scouring bareheaded over the prairies, Kit was one of the finest pictures of a horseman I have ever seen."[2]

Maxwell brought in the usual variety of game: pigeons, antelope, squirrel, and even a large turtle, none of which was cooked to suit the taste of the finicky Preuss. Breakfast was warmed-over leavings and there was only muddy river water to drink. Some of the cattle had to be slaughtered before they walked off too much weight.

These worries were over when they reached the buffalo range where the herd spread like "a dark undulating wave" over the level land. At times the camp was completely surrounded and there was scarcely grass enough for the animals of the expedition. Dense clouds of dust rose from the loosened earth as the immense herds crossed and recrossed the prairies and scooped out great hollows for their wallowing grounds. White wolves following the herds sometimes came uncomfortably near the camp, scavenging but never attacking.

Nothing stirred the blood like riding into the herd to bring down a fat cow and no one was more expert at this than Kit and Lucien working together. One day, Kit's horse, running at full speed, stepped in a prairie dog hole and threw his rider out of the saddle. The horse sprang up and ran off following the buffalo as horses often did. Maxwell wheeled and sprinted after it intending to shoot the animal if necessary to recover Kit's fine Spanish silver bridle. Fortunately, he was able to ride close enough to bring the horse in with a lasso. In the meantime, Kit, left horseless, began skinning the buffalo he had killed when an infuriated bull suddenly charged him. His only escape was to run for the river. He jumped in just in time, leaving the angry buffalo pawing at the bank. Fremont's accounts of such adventures were to be the first Wild West stories. "The Indians and Buffalo are the poetry and life of the prairie and our camp was full of their exhilaration," wrote the enthusiastic lieutenant.

Fourth of July was celebrated at the Grand Fork of the Platte by opening a brandy keg and bringing out food saved especially for the occasion. Here Fremont decided to go with Maxwell and a small party to purchase mules at Fort St. Vrain on the south branch of the Platte which was Lucien's headquarters. Kit was to stay with the main company commanded by Clement Lambert. All were to meet at Fort Laramie, Sublette's imposing fortress of the Northern Plains. The supply of pickled pork and everything else not needed until their return was to be cached near the river.

Soon after Fremont left, Kit was happily surprised to see his old friend, Jim Bridger, come riding into camp. Bridger was serious, warning that trouble could be expected from the Sioux, Cheyenne, and Blackfeet who had united against the white man and were planning to attack the trappers' rendezvous on the Sweetwater. Carson respected Bridger's judgment enough to insist that the company break camp and move immediately on to Fort Laramie.

Meanwhile, Fremont's party was having some unexpected excitement. Some distance on the way, Lucien, scanning the shadowy hills, caught sight of some minute moving objects he thought were buffalo coming toward the river. As they came closer, there was no mistaking the fact that a band of Indians were bearing down upon them. As the only timber in sight was on the opposite bank, with water too deep to ford, the men crouched together on the ground waiting for an inevitable attack. As the Indians rode near, Maxwell recognized them as Arapahos with whom he

traded and called out to them that he was their friend
Big Nostrils. The chief explained his tribe was on
a buffalo hunt and, riding wide not to give the wind,
had accidentally spotted the explorers. The squaws,
"naked from the knees down and the hips up," followed on pack mules with a large pack of scrawny
wolflike dogs. Fremont exchanged presents for cuts
of hump meat and continued unmolested on to Fort
St. Vrain where he purchased mules and started for
Fort Laramie.

A few intrepid settlers had broken a wagon route
through to Oregon by way of Fort Laramie and the
ebullient Senator Benton now reversed his statement
calling the Rockies an everlasting boundary and envisioned "the Anglo-Saxon race planting itself firmly
on the shores of the Pacific . . . the government to
follow with its shield and spread over them."[3] Daniel
Webster did not agree. "What do we want with this
vast worthless area, this region of savages and wild
beasts, of deserts, shifting sands and whirlwinds of dust,
of cactus and prairie dogs?" he asked the Senate in
a speech in 1838. "To what use could we ever hope
to put these great deserts of endless mountain ranges,
impregnable and covered to their very base with eternal snow? What use have we for such a country? Mr.
President, I shall never vote one cent from the public
treasury to place the Pacific coast one inch nearer
Boston than it is now."

Fort Laramie, built with massive adobe walls similar to Bent's, stood on the border between the plains
and the mountains, a three-sided structure with one
side left open to the Platte. Twelve buildings stood
within the enclosure and there was a corral large
enough to hold two hundred animals. It was the half-

way stop on the Oregon Trail, a position similar to
Bent's on the Santa Fe route. The fort was now owned
by the American Fur Company and "swarmed with
women and children whose language like their complexion was mixed."[4] By its strategic location, it was
capitalizing on the misfortunes of the emigrants. Passing over country stripped of grass by the buffalo and
those who had gone before them, many arrived at
the fort with oxen too hungry and footsore to go farther. Here they either traded their good wagons and
stock for old and jaded horses that probably would
give out before they reached the high country—or
simply gave up and returned east.

An air of anxiety hung over the fort. A company
of Oregon-bound settlers had started on, July 4th,
across Sioux country against the warnings of the young
braves of the tribe that no more white wagons would
be allowed to pass unharmed. Fortunately for the
emigrant party, Thomas Fitzpatrick, who had come to
the fort with Bridger, had agreed to pilot them across
South Pass. Kit was disappointed to have missed seeing Broken Hand but relieved to see Fremont and
Maxwell arrive with extra mules and supplies. Both
Carson and Bridger advised against continuing the expedition at this time but the indomitable Fremont
would not be deterred. He had come on an army
assignment and like any other soldier, considered it
his duty to undertake the mission at any cost. He was
even eager to meet some Indians, he said, so he could
advise how a train might be protected if attacked.
Preuss noted that he felt there was no honor in going
forth to be murdered. Fremont's courage and sense
of responsibility impressed Carson but before con-
senting to go farther, he drew up a will as a not too

subtle way of reminding the headstrong lieutenant of the serious danger of the undertaking.

The two boys who had enlivened the journey so far were left, under protest, at the fort with seven of the *voyageurs* who refused to budge. Proceeding toward South Pass, Kit, well in advance of the expedition, came upon the camp site of Fitzpatrick's party near Independence Rock. A pair of blood-stained trousers with a pipe in one of the pockets, found nearby, was an ominous sign for men triggered for disaster. (The emigrant train had in fact been overtaken by a party of 350 Sioux warriors who followed closely but did not attack. Only Fitzpatrick's great personal influence with the tribe saved the settlers from what seemed certain annihilation. The one man lost had lagged behind to paint his name in axle grease on the historic rock.)

Kit, who knew this country as well as the back of his hand, pushed on eagerly into the mountains over a treacherous route ending in a tortuous climb to a mountain peak 320 miles beyond Fort Laramie. They were forced to abandon most of the carts and several footsore animals along the way. The sagebrush, though monotonous, kept the mosquitos away but grasshoppers had stripped the land of good grass. Both men and animals knew keen hunger as provisions ran dangerously low. The supply of jerked buffalo was found to be spoiled by improper curing and fresh game was scarce. Cherry-root tea substituted for coffee and breadroot, sliced thin and sprinkled with a little gunpowder for salt, tamed appetites until food could be found. An offer to share a dog feast with friendly Indians was gratefully accepted. Next to panther, dog roasted on hot stones in a pit was the favorite food of the Indians. Fremont remarked that it tasted somewhat like mutton but was difficult to enjoy with friendly puppies running about.

Though it was August, the mountains were draped with snow. Pruess sketched flowers and rocks while Fremont noted, poetically, the botanical and geological data. "After the long stretch of plains, the mountain beauty is almost overwhelming . . . a panorama of lakes, aspens, pines and snow-capped mountains, fresh air, rich undergrowth and varicolored flowers . . . a night picture of very wild beauty . . . the glow of campfires, the unknown all around . . . mountains glitter with sun that has not yet reached us . . . little lakes like gems, water crystal clear and blue flax added to the magnificent mountain garden."

By some misfortune, the big barometer had been broken shortly before they reached the ridge "where the water begins to run westward to the Pacific." After several unsuccessful attempts, Fremont ingeniously mended the invaluable instrument with a translucent buffalo horn. As they climbed the rocky ridges split with chasm and fissure, nerves were strained and tempers flared. Their smooth-soled parfleche moccasins were replaced with thinner ones that enabled them to use their toes to cling to the icy sheet rock.

With their goal in sight, Fremont became too ill to go farther. The insensitive Preuss, who had explored the Alps, was not impressed with Fremont's importance and thought his headache only an excuse to rest when he could not keep up. Fremont complained that Kit walked too fast and chose another man to guide him to the crest of the peak which he believed to be the highest in the Rocky range. There, on the fifteenth of August, 1842, he planted a flag with thirteen stripes and an eagle perched on a peace pipe.

Kit remained calm, ignoring the outbursts and conflict of personalities and held the outfit together. John
Janisse, the only Negro with the company, when sent
ahead with the barometer, became separated from
the others. Kit soon found the man and left a note
for Fremont saying they had gone ahead to the main
camp.[5] The lieutenant got down the glazed mountainside and, realizing how necessary the veteran experience was to the success of his project, managed to
curb his irritation. Kit wisely kept down any explosion of nerves and won everlasting gratitude from
the short-tempered young officer. His admiration for
Fremont grew with each demonstration of courage
and the two men shared a common appreciation for
the enchanting mountain world. Kit became intensely
interested in the scientific data, bringing in specimens
a less keen eye might have overlooked.

On the return, Fremont's rubber boat was brought
out again and loaded with the heavy equipment that
had been cached before the ascent to the peak. In
this frail craft, Fremont and five *voyageurs,* who were
masters of canoeing, attempted to run the rapids between the Red Narrows, a stream half-choked with
fallen rock. It was too much for the straining oarsmen. Guns, ammunition, instruments, and records
were swept overboard and lost. Only Fremont's two-
shoot gun was saved. All managed to survive though
one man had to be pulled out by the hair and Fremont was left with one moccasin to walk through
broken rock and cacti. In gratitude, he carved an
impression of a cross with the names of his men in
the living rock—a simple act, later to be used against
him.

Forty-two days were used in the return to Fort
Laramie. Some of the horses that had been abandoned

on the way were recovered and found to be well-fed and in surprisingly good condition. The expedition had been a complete success without any threat from warring Indians, a great personal triumph for the ambitious John Charles Fremont. In the future, his reckless decisions would not always be so happily resolved.

The Indians at the fort were first to discover Fremont's flag waving before his band of straggly explorers as they wound in from the hills. Carson's men—Oliver Wiggins among them—were waiting at the fort. They had not joined the expedition but had stayed nearby trapping in the region of the Atlantic and Pacific Springs, ready to join Kit if he needed them. At this point Carson's service to Fremont came to an end. The lieutenant retraced his route east with Kit's promise to join him if there should be a second expedition.

Kit, now considerably better off financially, continued in the employ of Bent and St. Vrain, spending the winter at the fort. On February 6, 1843, he took the lovely Josefa Jarmillo for his bride with Fr. Martinez performing the ceremony at the Plaza of Our Lady of Guadalupe in Taos. When Ceran St. Vrain married into the Beaubien family a few days later, Taos had a double celebration, one of the last happy occasions together for Kit, Ceran, and the Bent brothers.

Fremont's party returned to St. Louis a few days before the birth of the Fremonts' first child, a daughter. That winter, the lieutenant and his wife together wrote a colorful and extensive report of the summer's expedition which received great success and through it, the name of Kit Carson became famous throughout the country. Jessie's father immediately began drafting plans for a second and more extensive expedition. The Fremont report aroused great public interest in the settlement of the Far West. Many families packed their goods, pulled up stakes, and moved westward by mule and ox-drawn wagons. "Emigration poured like a torrent down upon the vale."[6]

Texas, now an independent republic, had hopes of annexing New Mexico. Several attempts to capture Santa Fe having failed, President Sam Houston sent representatives to Bent's and other frontier posts to recruit volunteers for another try. A band of nearly two hundred, organized under Colonel Jacob Snively, called themselves the Battalion of the Invincibles, their purpose "to annoy Mexicans, intercept trade and force terms of peace."

Padre Martinez stepped up his anti-American crusade, adding Texans to the list. He had tried without success to overthrow Armijo but helped to put Charles Bent behind bars with an eight-hundred-dollar fine. Money for his release, collected from his friends, was held by Ignacia in a cache beneath the floor of their home. Soon after his release, Bent left Taos along with Kit and Dick Owens to accompany a string of wagons sent to relieve St. Vrain who, for an experiment, had taken several boatloads of robes down the Arkansas and found himself grounded beyond the Great Bend. At Walnut Creek, near the site of the future Dodge City, Kansas, Bent's train came upon the camp of four companies of United States Dragoons under Captain Philip St. George Cooke, escorting a huge caravan owned by Governor Armijo. Since the troops could not go beyond the river, the Mexicans were afraid to proceed without escort for fear of meeting the Texans.

It seemed incredible good fortune that Kit Carson

should just happen along at this time. He accepted
the traders' offer of three hundred dollars to carry
a message back to Santa Fe asking protection from
Armijo. Soon, in company with Owens, Kit was racing
the 250 miles back to Bent's Fort where they were
warned that the Utes were warring. Kit decided it
would be safer to try crossing their territory alone.
With a fresh horse loaned by William Bent, he managed to skirt the hostile encampment after dark by
leading his horse. He hid in a canyon the next day,
then spurred his mount toward Taos. Too fatigued
to continue, Kit turned the message over to the alcalde
who forwarded it by rider to Santa Fe. Anticipating
trouble, the governor had already sent a hundred men
to the border and a larger party was preparing to
follow.

While their husbands were away, Josefa and Ignacia
were living together at the Bent home. With the
sudden return of her husband whom she had not expected to see for many weeks, Josefa began to realize
how unpredictable her life was to be. After four brief
days of rest, Kit started back across the hostile country with Armijo's reply, taking with him Sol Silver,
a young Mexican who knew every break and ridge
of the land. As they hurried across the deceptively
empty hills, any hope of avoiding trouble was shattered when a war party rode out of an arroyo toward
them. Sol begged Kit to make a break for safety for
the sake of the men waiting on the Arkansas. In spite
of this obligation, Kit refused to leave a lone man
to the mercy of the savage Utes. They dismounted
and stood back to back to await the inevitable attack.
When the Indians rode up, the chief, splendid in
paint and feathers, swung down from his horse offering Kit his hand in friendship, then tried to wrest

his rifle from him. In the scuffle, Kit held to his gun. Keeping it leveled on the chief, he told them in their own language that two of them would surely die if anyone moved an inch nearer. Admiring this show of genuine courage, the Utes whirled their ponies and rode away. Again, the long chance had paid off.

While Carson was streaking across the prairies, Snively's Texas Battalion, waiting at Cold Springs for Armijo's wagons to arrive, spotted the column of Mexican soldiers sent to escort it from the border. Most of them despised Armijo. Some had been sent out tied to their horses. They were given a chance to surrender to the Texans but the fifty Pueblos among them refused. Within five minutes, twenty-five were killed. Cries of *"Misericordia!"* ended the slaughter. Only two escaped, one riding off on a Texan's saddled pony to take the devastating news to Armijo camped with 600 troops on the Cimarron. The terrified governor fled back to Santa Fe without waiting to learn the fate of his valuable freight.

Before Snively's men could start after the escaping Mexican, they were surprised by a roving band of Kiowas and Comanches who had heard the gunfire and attempted to stampede their horses. The prisoners were treated kindly, given a few guns and told to return home and profit by the experience. The Texans bivouacked on the Arkansas waiting for the "carryvan" to roll up to the river. After a few days, the twenty-four richly loaded wagons came into view, flanked on either side by fifty United States cavalrymen. At Captain Cooke's demand that the Texans throw down their arms, Snively explained that his men were merely out looking for buffalo. Uncertain about the exact boundary, Cooke hesitated, anxious to avoid a border incident involving Texas, Mexico, and the United

States. Finally, he gave Snively and his men thirty minutes to surrender their arms. The Texans slyly passed over the old and out-moded guns recently taken from the Mexicans and kept their own weapons. Cooke turned back to Fort Leavenworth with Snively and fifty "Texians" in tow, leaving the traders to proceed safely to Santa Fe. President Sam Houston loudly protested but was powerless to do anything as his men had been captured on United States' soil. This was the last attempt by Texas to capture Santa Fe.[7]

Kit learned of the incident when he returned to Bent's with Sol Silver. Assured that Armijo's wagons were safely on the way, he decided to remain at the fort to await news from Fremont whom he had expected to contact in Missouri. Fremont was in fact at this time leading his second expedition into Colorado after a dramatic take-off at Kansas Landing.

NOTES ON CHAPTER SIX

1. Washington Irving's description.
2. All Fremont quotations are from his *Memoirs of My Life.*
3. Benton, *Thirty Years' View.*
4. Inman, *The Great Salt Lake Trail.*
5. Preuss, *Exploring with Fremont,* refutes the contention of some writers that Carson was unable to write.
6. Hildreth, *Dragoon Campaigns to the Rocky Mountains.*
7. Sage, *Scenes in the Rocky Mountains; Southwestern Historical Quarterly,* LIV, 261.

With Fremont's Second Expedition (1845-1846)

In vain may rocks,
   and precipices, and
wintry torrents
   oppose his progress.
      WASHINGTON IRVING

As THIS SECOND expedition was to be a more extensive and perhaps a more dangerous undertaking, Lieutenant Fremont had asked for and received from Colonel Stephen Watts Kearny, in command of Jefferson Barracks, St. Louis, sufficient arms for his company including a twelve-pound howitzer, the kind the French had found particularly well adapted for mountain warfare. The expedition party left St. Louis in May and was well on the way to Kansas Landing when the War Department dispatched an order demanding that Fremont delay his start until he had explained why it was necessary to take a cannon on a purely scientific survey.

When the letter was received and read by Fremont's energetic young wife, she decided this action by the regular army was due to jealousy caused by her husband's unprecedented acclaim. The letter expressed concern that if it became known that Fremont's company was heavily armed, trouble might arise with Mexico or even England, who had her eye on both Oregon and California. To Jessie Fremont, this was only a thinly veiled excuse to relieve her husband of command of the expedition. She hid the dispatch in her sewing basket, then dashed off a message to be carried to Fremont by Baptiste de Rosier, about to leave St. Louis to join the company. Jessie urged de Rosier to ride with all haste to reach Kansas Landing

before the riverboat, often delayed by fog and sand
bars, would have time to arrive with a duplicate letter.

"Do not delay another day. But trust and start at
once," was all that Jessie wrote and Fremont gave
marching orders within an hour after de Rosier rode
in. The company started west without knowing the
reason for the great haste and Jessie would have no
word from her husband for a year and a half, except
for his answer, "Good-bye, I trust, and go," brought
back by de Rosier's brother.

When assured that the expedition was on the way,
Jessie Fremont wrote to Colonel J. J. Abert, Chief
of the Army Topographical Corps. She confessed what
she had done in the interest of her husband and that
of her father, who was primarily concerned with the
political aspects of the venture. When the matter was
made public, Senator Benton was furious and gave
forth with some fiery oratory in defense of his daughter
and her husband. The U.S. Army surrendered to Jessie
Benton Fremont but that was not to be the end of
the incident.

Meanwhile, Kit Carson, hunting near Boiling Spring
River on July 14, learned from one of Bent's men
that Fremont and a large company were camped at
the edge of the mountains. They had taken a more
central route, bypassing Bent's Fort with the hope of
finding better grass. Eager to see the man he had
come to admire so much, Kit put the spurs to his
pony and came riding into Fremont's camp "with a
shout of glee." Nothing could have pleased Fremont
more than the sight of this "true and reliable" friend.

The party was well outfitted, numbering forty experienced men and including two Delaware Indians—
a father and son. Fitzpatrick was the guide, Maxwell
serving again as hunter, and, most surprising to Kit,

the artist Charles Preuss had joined Fremont for a second time. The howitzer was under the supervision of Louis Zindel, formerly with the Polish army. In addition to the gun carriage, there was a light wagon to carry the instruments and a dozen mule carts loaded with equipage and supplies.

Maxwell had tried unsuccessfully to buy extra mules from his father-in-law, Charles Beaubien. He found the ranch on the Cimarron plundered by Mexican outlaws and the other rancheros would not trade with *los Americanos.* Kit volunteered to ride the seventy-five miles back to Bent's, buy some mules, and meet the company at the confluence of Cherry Creek and the South Platte. He arrived there two days ahead of Fremont, though he had traveled a much greater distance, and brought with him, in addition to the mules, a supply of flour, rice, sugar, and coffee, and two small pigs to be divided among forty hungry men.

With two first-class guides in Fitzpatrick and Carson, Fremont decided to divide his company. Broken Hand was sent with the heavy equipment across the flat country to pick up the Oregon Trail at Fort Laramie. Carson and a select few with the lieutenant himself would try for a beeline across the mountains to find, if possible, a new route around Longs Peak. The plan was for the two parties to meet at Fort Hall on the Big Snake.

Kit once again in his old trapping grounds, now looked for botanical specimens with Preuss instead of beaver sign, while the exuberant Fremont recorded everything of interest and beauty. "The river bottoms were covered with radiant flowers of every hue . . . some spikes rising above our heads as we rode among them." But all was not rosy. They were pelted by incessant rain and every night built fires to dry

out the soggy baggage, only to have it soaked again
the next day. The torrential downpour brought up
the little streams and they were forced to cross the
swollen Cache la Poudre eight or nine times with
almost complete immersion each time.[1]

Traveling with the company was a young Indian
woman, the widow of a French-Canadian trapper, returning with two lively little half-breeds to her people,
the Snakes. As game was alarmingly scarce, with only
an occasional buffalo or antelope brought in, the Snake
woman's knowledge of mountain vegetation saved the
expedition from extreme hunger. Especially nourishing was a root called *yampah* which was greatly favored
by the Indians but "indescribably disgusting" to Preuss.

The explorers seemed to be in luck one day when
"a good red ox" wandered into camp, probably a stray
from some emigrant party. The prospects of a good
beef dinner brightened the spirits but by morning
the ox, evidently enjoying its freedom, had departed
and Fremont would not allow his men to look for it.

With infinite patience Kit probed into a multitude
of rocky chasms and ravines, attempting to penetrate
the granite rampart. On one day's particularly gruelling climb the carriage lamps were knocked off and
some of the equipment, including an all-important
thermometer, was broken. They wandered late into
the night, looking for a camp site, until, too tired to
go farther, they stopped in a forbidding ravine. By
the light of sagebrush fires, they cooked a midnight
supper of "buffalo meat crusted with sand and bitter
coffee tasting of sage." Daylight revealed a fine green
pasture a scant mile away and so inviting that Fremont
decided to rest there for a day to repack the equipment and jerk some buffalo meat.

The pleasure of a day of rest was suddenly interrupted when one of the guards caught a glimpse of an Indian's head peeking over a crag. The camp was "thrown into a tumult by a charge of seventy mounted Indians coming over the low hills." Luckily there was sufficient time to roll out the howitzer. At the sight of the cannon, the Indians—a combination of Cheyennes and Arapahos—immediately became friendly, explaining they had mistaken the Americans for a hostile tribe. The stone pipe was passed around, presents given, and the intruders rode off.

With time wearing away, Fremont reluctantly gave up his hope of finding a better route through the Rockies and turned toward the Sweetwater Valley, arriving at South Pass a week ahead of Fitzpatrick and the rest of the company. The ascent over the pass, Fremont noted, was "as easy as that of the hill on which the capitol stands."[2] His expedition became part of the great ox-drawn, canvas-covered procession rolling in mile-long trains toward Oregon. The wagons had crushed the sage and so pulverized the sod that clouds of fine dust rose with every wheel turning in the deepening ruts—a thousand miles of slow turnings from South Pass to The Dalles on the Columbia, the end of the trail.

Fremont was fully aware that the report of his previous expedition had been largely responsible for many decisions to go to Oregon. With Carson his constant companion, he visited the encampments and noted that "they seemed strangely civilized with an air of quiet security in that remote wilderness," sitting by their campfires "to forget the perplexities, fatigue and hardship and build up future hope."[3]

Since the defeat of the Blackfeet by the trappers, the danger of Indian attack had greatly lessened. There were only a few scattered trappers left in the

mountains and the big fur companies had almost entirely disappeared. The herds of antelope and buffalo had noticeably decreased and both Carson and
Fremont decried the useless slaughter that was leaving the Indian in desperate danger of starvation and
turning the flowering prairies into a stinking bone-
yard. Fields of heavenly blue flax and flaming wild
geranium drew color across the landscape to relieve
the monotony of sagey gulches. The country provided startling beauty but scant provision of food.
Hunger was a constant companion. Without meat the
men grew morose and taciturn, but whenever Fremont ordered an ox to be slaughtered, good humor
miraculously returned. "There seemed little else to
enjoy." Several mules and horses had dropped along
the way from sheer exhaustion. American horses were
of no serviceable value, Fremont observed, until they
have become accustomed to an all-grass diet.

As it was now mid-August, Carson advised Fremont to bypass Bridger's Fort, midway between Fort
Laramie and Fort Hall. The Snake squaw left the
company to travel on alone with her children to join
her tribe. Eager to get into the region of the Great
Salt Lake, Fremont pushed on to Soda Springs. With
their flour and bacon near the bottom of the barrel,
Kit left the company camped there and, with one
companion, rode on to Fort Hall for a supply of food.
The company lived on stewed skunk, some roots and
serviceberries for two weeks before Kit returned with
only a meager handout. He found, on arriving at
Fort Hall, that the unexpected number of emigrant
parties had left few provisions at the fort.

The company now set out to find the lake. Feeling
their way along willow-fringed streams, they skirted
the Wasatch Range and came into Weber Valley. On

September 6, from a height on Little Mountain, the green lake came into sight. "The sudden view of the expanse of silent waters to travellers long shut up among mountain ranges, had in it, something sublime," Fremont was moved to write, emotionally.

Camp was set up in a grove on the Weber about nine miles from the lake and it was plain to see that there was not food enough for so large a party. Seven men volunteered to go on to Fort Hall to wait for Fitzpatrick's party while the others explored the great inland sea. Two decades had passed since Jim Bridger had accidentally come upon the lake while settling a wager as to the course of the Bear River. Dipping in his tin cup to slack his thirst, Old Gabe thought he had reached the Pacific Ocean. Existing maps still showed two outlets to the Pacific and many emigrants believed it was possible to reach California by water from the Great Salt Lake. Fremont wished to verify or refute the many tales of whirlpools and other mysterious dangers.

Only a few white men, Carson one of them, had ever before looked into its transparent waters. Jim Clyman had floated around the "sheet of brine" in his bullboat. Zenas Leonard had written of the lake surrounded by mountains and barren plains, with a peak near the center of it.[4] No one had ever attempted to cross to that mountain island. This was an ideal challenge for Fremont who once again brought out a large collapsible boat—this one of linen coated with India rubber.

Kit, a superb horseman who preferred to remain on dry land, consented to join Fremont, Preuss, and two of the company's most expert oarsmen, Bernier and Lajeunesse, for an exploratory trip to the large island fifteen miles from shore. "So long as we could touch bottom with our paddles, we were very gay; but gradually as the water deepened, we became more still in our frail batteau of gun cloth distended with air and with pasted seams," wrote Fremont later. Midway across, one of the cylinders began to deflate. Only constant working of the bellows kept the craft afloat. A landing was made about noon along the low white salt-covered cliffs which from a distance Kit had mistaken for a flock of pelicans.

The island was found to be a bleak rock, completely barren of trees and the high peaks already dusted with snow. Luckily, they had brought along a day's supply of fresh water for there were no fresh-water springs. Fremont named the dismal spot Disappointment Island. (It was later named Castle Island by the Mormons and renamed Fremont Island.) While the scientific observations were recorded, Kit carved a cross "under the shelving rock." Fremont lost the cap to his telescope and it intrigued his imagination to think who might find it on the wild island where no white man, and possibly no red man either, had ever before set foot. A shelter of driftwood was put up and that night the men "lay down for the first time in a long journey in perfect security."

As the little boat started next morning for the mainland, menacing clouds began to bank above. Fremont, thoroughly alarmed, urged the men to pull for their lives. By almost superhuman effort at the bellows and oars, the shaky little boat was brought to land just before the storm struck, sending up mountainous waves. Men and boat were so completely covered with a white salty crust from the spray that they resembled a returning phantom ship and crew.

Carson and Bernier hurried to carry the valuable instruments to safe ground while Preuss and Lajeunesse began the long walk to the camp for horses to move the baggage. The storm, increasing in fury, almost swept the men off their feet as the winds churned the waters of the lake. With a salute from the howitzer the jubilant company greeted the returning "sailors" they had never expected to see alive. Next day, as they packed to move on, Fremont evaporated five gallons of water he had brought from the lake during the storm and got fourteen pints of "very fine grained and very white salt." It had seemed strange to be so near the Salt Lake and have none. (Fremont's report of this region was to have great influence on Brigham Young's decision to bring his followers to the area. When he announced "This is the place," he referred to the place Fremont had written about.) [5]

Carson brought down some seagulls to add to their "mournful diet" of distasteful roots and Fremont regretfully allowed one of the horses to be killed for food though neither he nor Preuss would touch it, "feeling as much saddened as if a crime had been committed." Great was the relief in the hungry camp when a rider galloped in with the news that Fitzpatrick's party had arrived at Fort Hall and Broken Hand himself was on the way with provisions for them.

Moving on along the Big Snake toward Fort Hall, the view of distant mountains was "like looking edgewise along the teeth of a saw." The big clay fortress had opened the same year as Fort Laramie, "saluted . . . with damaged powder and wet it in vilanous alcohol. . . ." According to Nathaniel Wyeth, its builder, the fort stood as "a terror to the sculking Indian and a beacon of saf[e]ty to the fugitive hunter."[6] After two years of hard luck, Wyeth returned East and the fort became the property of the Hudson's

Bay Company, which usually came out the winner in the game to "out-trap, out-trade and outwit" all competition.[7] Best of everything awaiting the exploring party was a plentiful supply of good butter.

Fremont's orders had been to map the Overland Trail to connect with the surveys of the Pacific Coast region, made two years before by Lieutenant Commander Charles Wilkes. As no mention was made of how the expedition was to return, the ambitious Fremont saw an opportunity to make a worth-while contribution to the information about the country and at the same time be assured of some good headlines. It was late in September when he announced to his company his intention of exploring the Great Basin to find, if possible, a new route to California. Eleven of his men refused to go on what seemed to them to be a foolhardy winter gamble. Oliver Wiggins was heartsick that Kit stood firm with Fremont who was furious at this action. Carson, the master conciliator, persuaded him not to call it mutiny.

With fifty fat cattle added to the herd, Kit led the party on in dust "half a leg deep." About this same time one of the emigrants sent a letter from Fort Hall to Iowa with the startling news that "Ft. Hall on the Oregon Trail had been delivered up to Lt. Fremont and Ft. Vancouver was believed to be next."[8] Beyond the lonely outpost, Fort Boise, the serpentine trail wound through a country "strange looking, one of fracture, violence and fire with rocks black and sombre-colored," yet the men felt a security they had not known on the open plains. There were no trees, only endless miles of pungent sage until, at last, the rich green country watered by the Columbia.

The Whitman mission, Waiilatpu, stood near the fork of the Walah Walah River and there the explorers were welcomed warmly by Mrs. Whitman, who remembered Kit from their meeting at the rendezvous on the Green, and Fitzpatrick who had piloted the caravan that had brought her across the mountains. Dr. Whitman was away on a trip to Vancouver. This was very disappointing to Fremont for the doctor had visited his camp in Kansas that summer while returning from a spectacular ride across the country to alert Washington to the uneasy situation in Oregon.

Waiilatpu, "the place of rye grass," was crudely built of adobe and cottonwood logs whitewashed with burnt clamshells and roofed over with large slabs of sod cut by a plow. The doctor himself had made the furnishings—rough tables, chairs with woven deerskin seats, and board beds nailed to the side of the house. The Whitman's only child, two-year-old Alice Clarissa, the first white child born in the Northwest, had fallen into the river and drowned several years before. An emigrant family of seven children whose parents had perished on the Oregon Trail was living with the Whitmans, along with several Indian children attending the mission school.[9]

The mission had started off very well in spite of extreme hardships but the influx of settlers had aroused the Indians of the region. Shortly before Fremont's expedition arrived, the Cayuse had burned the mission's mill. As a result, potatoes had to be substituted for the corn meal Fremont had expected to purchase there. Warned of difficulties ahead, Carson persuaded Fremont to leave the carriage and wagons at the mission and proceed over the mountains by pack mule.

To complete the assigned expedition, Fremont left Kit and Broken Hand in charge of the camp at The Dalles while he and Preuss set out by canoe for Vancouver where he hoped to pick up supplies and political information for Senator Benton.[10] Kit supervised the repairing of equipment and the making of packsaddles until Fremont returned with a three-months' supply of dried peas, flour, and tallow.

Frustrated in his attempt to find a new passage through the Rockies, Lieutenant Fremont was determined to approach California from a different direction. He hoped also to establish proof whether or not there was a Buenaventura River which the few existing maps—those of the fur companies—had shown rising in the mountains and flowing into San Francisco Bay. The Gallatin map had omitted it altogether. Senator Benton was convinced that the fate of Oregon depended upon whether or not there was a river parallel to the Columbia. If not, it was essential for the United States to possess Oregon for the sake of trade with the Orient. If there were such a stream, Fremont hoped to follow it to the Pacific.

Thirty-five seasoned men, a hundred mules, and a large herd of cattle "to be driven on the hoof," set out to follow Carson along the Cascade Range and into the Great Basin. Before them was some of the roughest terrain in all the West, a vast hitherto un-penetrated area of rock, forest, and desert. Before them, also, the unconquered High Sierras—thought to be part of the Rockies—and before them, most of all, the dreaded winter.

At first their direction was almost straight south from The Dalles through glacier-scratched rock so rugged that in order to bring along the gun carriage —the only thing on wheels—it was necessary to chop down trees and at times even dismember and carry the bothersome cannon. The only human beings seen were a few starving, half-naked Indians living in huts of sagebrush, the desolate earth providing scarce food and almost nothing to clothe against the cruel cold. These frightened people had never before seen white men and shut their disbelieving eyes to avoid looking at them. They cautiously accepted gifts of food and blankets but stoically refused to be friendly.

The animals fared badly. At least fifteen were lost or abandoned with broken hoofs and legs injured by the jagged rocks. Every available piece of iron was converted into horseshoe nails. Only Kit's and Broken Hand's experience in mountaineering brought the company safely through, after what seemed an interminable time, to the Upper Klamath Lake, picturesquely set in a bed of somber lava, thrown up in some primordial upheaval. Here a young Chinook Indian asked to join the white man's company and was taken on. Hostiles seemed to be lurking everywhere but only a few ventured near enough to be seen. One night, when Fremont's camp was almost surrounded by campfires and trouble seemed certain, Zindel was ordered to fire the howitzer. As the sound crashed the night silence, the fires hastily disappeared. A Klamath chief and his terror-stricken wife came out of the darkness into the camp to give themselves as sacrifices to save the lives of their people. Carson made signs to assure them of their friendliness and they accepted gifts to take back to the tribe.

Fremont's party was approaching the northern boundary of California but instead of going on in that direction, turned southeast into the Great Basin. Preuss noted in his record book that they were "off at a fast clip toward the East." Coming out of the high wooded area, Kit began to recognize the country he had explored with Bridger and they found themselves on the edge of the desert. Low-hanging clouds and a blinding glare of sun on the ice com-

pletely screened the mountains from view. Several
small lakes were found and one "handsome sheet of
water," named Lake Abert in honor of Fremont's
chief, was ironically discovered to be fetid salt water.
Another, deeper blue with a scalloped treeless shore
line, had "a very remarkable rock, a pretty exact outline of the Great Pyramid of Cheops," rising six hundred feet out of the water. Fremont named it Pyramid Lake.

In vain they searched for the Buenaventura. Kit
and Fitzpatrick looked for beaver cuttings which would
be found only along waters with an outlet to the
ocean. Christmas came without cheer though the cannon was fired to celebrate and Fremont brought out
a bottle of brandy, husbanded for the occasion. Kit
discovered a strange river that was given his name.
It ran broad and deep between steep banks with tops
of trees rising out of the water, the trunks completely
submerged. The flow of water sank rapidly and disappeared into a swampy area named Carson Sink, then
emerged in Carson Lake, twenty miles long. At times
the river mysteriously reversed its direction because
the basin also received the overflow from Mary's
River. Named for the Indian wife of Peter Skene
Ogden, the Mary's was sometimes called the Ogden.
Fremont changed the name to the Humboldt in honor
of the great German naturalist, Baron Alexander von
Humboldt, who never saw his river.

By the middle of January, convinced at last that
there was no Buenaventura, Fremont abandoned further search and decided to try for a direct crossing
of the Sierras into California. The expedition had
reached a point twenty-five miles east of the site of
Reno and snow reached halfway down the mountains.
Though warned by the Indians that the snow was

dangerously deep, Fremont considered this only more of a challenge.

An ancient Indian was finally bribed to guide the party. He had never been on a horse and would not consent to ride though his moccasins wore through on the sharp-edged rocks. Not trusted too far, the old man was shut in at night in one of the lodges with Kit lying across the entrance. Eventually he escaped, taking with him two of Fremont's best blankets. A number of Indians were seen circling wide on snowshoes and a few came to barter rock salt and piñon nuts, the savory and nourishing seeds of the miniature pine.

The higher they climbed, the deeper the drifts, some piling as high as twenty feet. Only painfully slow progress could be made by packing down the snow when it was moist at midday and hoping it would freeze enough during the night to bear the weight of the animals. The men plunged into the drifts on horseback, each going as far as possible before turning back, others followed pounding with mallets and covering the path with branches. Nearly exhausted by this desperate driving effort, they slept huddled close together against the cold. Up before the sun could soften the snow crust, they doggedly pushed and dug their way, stopping only to warm their near-frozen feet by fires built in the hollows of old cedar stumps. At times the blizzard filled in as rapidly as the clearing could be made. To add to the misery, the Chinook, believing he would never see his people again, began a pitiful lament.

Fitzpatrick, in charge of the mules and the few scraggly cattle that were left, was so far in the rear he forwarded meat by sled to the others. Through it all, Fremont remained undismayed, confident and not un-

mindful of the beauty around them—"glorious sunrise . . . crimson peaks rising into an air of greenish-
orange . . . a moon rainbow." His record of January
25 showed the temperature had warmed enough during the day for their moccasins to get soaked from
the melting snow but suddenly turned so cold they
froze stiff. That night, he brought out a little brandy
and the mercury fell to 2° below zero before morning.

One particularly disheartening day when the meat
train did not arrive, Fremont reluctantly gave Alex
Godey permission to kill and cook the little dog
Klamath that had followed them faithfully. He prepared it Indian fashion, scorching off the hair and
washing the skin with soap and snow water, then laid
the pieces on the fire. A supply of mule meat arrived
by sled and the nearly famished men were treated to
"an extraordinary dinner—pea soup, mule and dog."
At Kit's suggestion that the mule's head was the most
tasty part, they boiled one all night and even Preuss
called it delicious.

When the last of the cattle was killed, the desperate men were wagering whether their fate was to
starve or freeze to death. Some of the mules, too weak
to bring themselves up the path, floundered, scattering their loads down the mountainside. The cannon
was finally abandoned January 29, to lie at the bottom of the canyon.[11]

At last a level spot was reached where the snow
could be cleared for a grazing ground and camp was
set up. While the poor mules were given a chance
to revive, the men made snowshoes and sledges for
a new assault. With his customary optimism, "Field
Marshall Carson"—as Preuss called Kit—led a few of
the stronger men single file through the snow-choked
pines to scout ahead. Looking westward from a small

ridge, Kit recognized the low coastal range he had seen on his first trip to California. "There is a little mountain—it is fifteen years since I saw it—but I am as sure as if I had seen it yesterday," Kit told Fremont.[12] The words sounded incredible to the disheartened company but gave life to their waning hope of surviving.

Many bleak and blizzardy miles were still to be conquered before the summit would be reached. With hope revived, there was strength enough to start on. Fitzpatrick waited for a gun signal before moving ahead and after driving the herd eight miles was forced to lead them back to the old camp site where he knew grass could be found. He put the mules into two classes—"them as is beat out and them as is balky."[13] The animals were in an almost hopeless condition, their legs torn by the sharp ice crust, and they were so hungry they ate their packsaddles and even each other's tails. Those that could go no farther were killed for food and Broken Hand did not believe the rest could be taken over the pass even if they reached it. Kit reminded his old friend of the many tight spots they had pulled through triumphant. He went out in a desperate search for food for the mules and, returning to camp, "sung out from a hill: 'Life yet —I have found a hillside sprinkled with grass enough for the night.' "[14]

"All went to work with a will to tempt the pass," and reached it February 20—a thousand torturing miles from The Dalles. Carson carved his name and the date on a tree and Fremont named the Sierra opening Carson Pass. It was inconceivable that the road they had pioneered with such hardship would, in a very few years' time, be a well-traveled emigrant route to gold fields just beyond.[15]

The descent took three days and proved to be the most treacherous part of the ordeal, the path literally having to be cut out by ax and maul. So near the end of the journey, all mourned the loss of a mule that slipped on the dry pine needles and plunged over a precipice, carrying with it a pack of rare plant specimens. Fremont himself fell into a stream when the smooth sole of his moccasin slipped as he attempted to follow Kit, who had jumped easily across. Kit leaped into the icy water to pull him out but in the fall Fremont lost his gun. It was found after a search under the ice at the edge of the stream. Several of the men — de Rosier one of them — undernourished, snow-blinded and numb with cold, became deranged and wandered off. Preuss was lost several days, keeping alive on a few acorns and ants. He found a frog in a puddle, pulled off the legs and ate them greedily. But not a man was missing when they came down at last into the sun-warmed valley of the Sacramento where "the banks were absolutely golden with California poppy."

One of John Sutter's *vaqueros* was the first person they met. Fremont and Carson followed him to Sutter's Fort with six of the men, leaving Fitzpatrick to look after those too weak and emaciated to cover the remaining miles to comfort. Returning with food for them, Fremont was greatly moved to see the pitiable condition of "his gallant men." Of the sixty-seven horses and mules that had started from The Dalles, only thirty-three worn-out pack mules survived. The entire company remained two weeks at the fort as guests of Sutter. "It requires all your forebearance here at Sutter's," wrote the lieutenant in a letter to Jessie, "to prevent plenty from being more hurtful than scarcity was before."

Sutter had prospered since he had seen Kit Carson at the Wind River rendezvous five years before. He had taken Kit's advice and gone to Vancouver, then shipped off to winter in the Sandwich Islands (Hawaii) and in the spring captained a sailing schooner by way of Sitka to arrive at San Francisco Bay in July. Declaring his intention to become a Mexican citizen, Sutter was allowed by Governor Juan Bautista Alvarado to go up the Sacramento in search of a suitable place to build an outpost. The governor was interested in such an establishment as a convenient spot from which to observe the activities of his principal rival, Don Mariano Vallejo, a prominent ranchero of Sonoma, across San Francisco Bay. Eventually Sutter received a grant seventy miles square and proceeded to build an empire in the wilderness.

Built of unburnt adobe, the fort stood where the Sacramento was wide and deep enough to carry trading schooners to his pier. Twelve cannon, said to be those surrendered by Napoleon at Moscow, pointed in all directions and a garrison of forty Indians and twenty white men was on constant guard. Sutter was especially friendly with the American settlers who were rapidly filling up the valley—so much so that the Mexican government was becoming suspicious of this principal landowner, though Sutter maintained an appearance of fidelity.

Captain Sutter was greatly impressed by the gracious Lieutenant Fremont and granted him passports on his authority as a Mexican magistrate. During his stay at the fort, Fremont realized how feeble the control of the Mexican government actually was. The American emigrants had enjoyed almost complete independence from the central government until Santa Anna had sent a convict army to enforce the antiquated laws and demand tyrannical taxes. Native *Californios* joined with the Americans to protest and came out victorious. Governor Alvarado was demoted to a mere customs officer and Sutter was lucky to come out of the scrape without losing his life or the fort.

Thanks to Sutter's generosity, Fremont's party was now well equipped and in high spirits. When the expedition began its homeward journey, the genial Swiss rode part way with them and Fremont was mounted on a beautiful white stallion named Sacramento, a gift from Sutter. It was Fremont's intention to leave California quietly by a central route and continue exploring the Great Basin. The company—minus several men who were not sufficiently recovered to continue—was a conglomeration of nationalities: American, French, Spanish, German, a Chinook, two California Tulare Indians, and Fremont's devoted free colored servant Dodson. The herd numbered about a hundred horses and mules, some well shod to prevent "the foot-evil disease" but most of them half-wild mustangs. They started out across fields of flowering blue lupine and poppies, then turned toward the mountains and "the land of the yucca."

While camped on Pass Creek, April 13, a party of Indians happened along, led by a well-dressed *vaquero* from the San Fernando Mission. In fluent Spanish he explained to Carson, the interpreter, that the Indians had been trading and were returning to "a great river in the eastern desert." He told of an easier trail over Tehachapi Pass whereby the explorers could avoid an arid and barren desert that had repulsed all attempts to penetrate it. Kit advised Fremont to change his route. He was agreeable and the company was spared the dangerous waterless waste later to be called Death Valley.[16]

On the Old Spanish Trail, a party of six Mexicans, driving a herd of thirty horses, was moving some miles in advance of Fremont's expedition. They had started ahead of the great caravan to be assured of grass but after several uneasy days, had decided to make camp and wait for the caravan to overtake them. One of the men was on horse guard with an eleven-year-old boy when the camp was suddenly overrun by Indians. Only the herders escaped by riding through a barrage of arrows and unexpectedly came upon Fremont's camp on the Mojave. In a matter of minutes, Carson and Alex Godey, the daredevil Frenchman who was hunter for Fitzpatrick's party, were saddled and off in pursuit of the culprits. They returned thirty hours later shrieking out a victory war whoop and driving the herd of horses before them. As a token of victory, two bloody scalps dangled from Godey's gunstick.

The two men had followed the trail by moonlight, slept a few hours in a hidden defile and discovered the herd in the morning. Crawling cautiously to the top of a ridge, they looked down on a number of Indian lodges below. When a stir among the animals alerted the Indians, Carson and Godey charged down into the village with no idea of the number they would find there. Both fired. Godey missed his mark, reloaded and fired again. With only three shots, the Indians had fled to the hills. Alex narrowly escaped injury when a fallen brave suddenly rose up and shot an arrow through his collar, then fell over dead. Several of the horses had been killed and prepared for a feast and in one of the lodges they found the only Indian left in the village, a small boy stoically picking the meat from a boiled horse's head. After rounding up the remainder of the herd, Kit and Alex located the Mexicans' camp only to come upon the gruesome

sight of the horribly mutilated bodies of two men.
The two women had evidently been taken captive.

Fremont called this adventure "among the boldest
and most disinterested in the annals of the West, considering the time, place, object and numbers involved
. . . two men in a savage desert, pursue day and night,
an unknown body of Indians into the defiles of an unknown mountain—attack them at sight, without count-
ing numbers—and defeat them in an instant—and for
what? To punish the robbers of the desert and to
avenge the wrongs of the Mexicans whom they did
not know." When Fremont's party passed the scene
of the massacre, the Mexican boy found his mother's
little dog that was "frantic with joy to see Pablo again."
Pablo and the other Mexican, Fuentes, continued on
with Fremont's company.

The desert, though ornamented with "cacti in rich,
fresh bloom," was no kinder than before. There were
stretches of fifty miles and more without a trace of
water, no dew or rain, only the juicy pulp of the
bisada to moisten cracked and blistered lips. Every
day some of the horses fell with feet too sore from the
cracking alkali to go farther. When a horse died, the
feet were cut off to save the horseshoes. Indians followed like beasts of prey, scattering over the hills
and ravines. Some demanded tribute to pass unharmed
across their lands but none thought it wise to attack
so large a party. On one occasion, only a ridge separated them from a fierce intertribal conflict.

By early May Kit had guided his followers back to
the shores of Utah Lake which they had left the September before, having covered 3,500 rugged miles.
(Fremont mistakenly thought this to be the southern
arm of the Great Salt Lake.) Having pushed on at
a strenuous pace, the lieutenant decided, May 9, to

give himself and his men one full day of rest. It was near dusk when Carson aroused Fremont from a nap to tell him that Jean Tabeau, who had gone out earlier to look for a stray mule, was long overdue. As the search for the missing man began, Kit was appalled to see a fire signal rising above a cottonwood grove for he knew that as a sign to tell the tribe that another white man had been struck down. It soon grew too dark to search farther and dawn revealed signs of a death struggle, with grasses beaten down and caked with blood near the Virgin River where Tabeau's body evidently had been dragged and thrown in. That evening Tabeau's mule returned to camp and eventually recovered from an arrow wound. All the men, who had lived so closely together and endured so many hardships, were grieved to lose one of their number —"a brave and noble-souled fellow"—so near the end of their journey. Another would die accidentally from gunshot.

Better luck was to be with them. The last leg of the trek was easy, across Kit's old trapping grounds. Near Robidoux's post on the Uinta, Kit visited the little outpost he had built with Stephen Lee ten years before. A few days after Fremont's party had left Robidoux's, the fort was attacked and burned by the long-suffering Utes. All the men were killed and the women carried off. Antoine escaped only by being absent.

Kit fought off any hint of fatigue as he pushed on, leading the weary company across the Balla Salado, his favorite haunt in the Rockies, now abloom with columbine, shooting star, and fringed gentians, and the air sweet with the pungent aroma of summer sun on pine needles. His thoughts were all of Josefa. Perhaps some news had gotten through to her and she would be waiting at Bent's. The worn but jubilant explorers arrived at Bent's in time for a sumptuous Fourth-of-July dinner and Josefa was there, more beautiful than Kit had remembered.

Fremont went on to Washington, taking Pablo and the other Indians with him. Ten thousand copies of his report to Congress were published and through them, Kit Carson became the great hero of the West. President Tyler commissioned Fremont a captain of the Corps of Topographical Engineers. Colonel Abert invited the Fremonts to dine at his home where the mutinous Jessie was treated with "courtly consideration."

Fremont had paid well for one of the greatest scouting services on record and Kit looked forward to a more settled life with his lovely Josefa. Before returning to Taos, Kit decided to go up to Fort Bridger on a short trading trip for William Bent. He was eager to see Old Gabe again and Josefa could ride with him to see for the first time the country he knew so well and the scene of some of his greatest adventures.

An Oregon-bound emigrant, John Minto, who had stopped at Fort Bridger, told of meeting Carson there. "I went to my wagon where my trunk was . . . and found Capt. Morrison getting his plow irons out. He had traded one of the cows and the plow irons for flour brought from Taos. The man he was dealing with was very different from those here apparently on show. He was receiving the different parts of the plow . . . and telling about its now being late in the season for us to get to Oregon and said he had been in the country about Salt Lake the preceding fall and thought it would be a good country to settle in, thus talking and tying up the plow irons, a party passing stopped and asked what he was going to do with them.

He replied, 'I'm going to try farming for a while down at Taos. . . .' He was a man five nine or ten at most, strong framed in breast and shoulders; light brown hair, flaxy at the ends; eyes steel blue or gray. I watched him ride away. . . . I saw him throw the plow irons down at a camp close by the trail and continue up to the stockade, whither I followed him. . . . Jim Bridger was doing his own trading . . . a powerful built man about the height of Carson—but coarser made and coarser minded, as I thought. I passed the camp and a very comely woman was saddling and packing two of the finest mules I ever saw."[17]

Kit and his good friend Dick Owens for some time had "concluded they had rambled enough" and wanted to settle down. They had talked of getting a land stake on the Little Cimarron about fifty miles from Taos and building a ranch which might one day grow into a settlement. During the winter they made their plans and started building in the spring. After four months of hard work they had put up a house, several small huts for the Mexican workers, and fenced in a large corral. A crop, sown in the rich bottom land, showed prospects for a good harvest of grain. Everything was progressing well when the unexpected happened. An express arrived from Captain Fremont reminding Kit of his promise to join any future expedition he might make. Fremont was then at Bent's Fort preparing for a third expedition to the West, this one to last perhaps two years, with significant political as well as scientific purpose.

It was not easy for Kit to put aside his dream of a home and a life of comparative tranquility for another long absence from Josefa but his word once given was honor-bound. Owens was eager to go along. They sold their holdings for less than half the value, sacrificing four months' labor as well as the funds used to purchase stock and equipment. Within four days after Fremont's message was received, the two pioneer farmers had made an about face and were spurring their horses toward Raton Pass. Josefa was left in the care of Charles and Ignacia and before Kit would see his young wife again, stark tragedy would come near her.

A new star had been added to the flag whipping over the gate at Bent's Fort, for Texas had been annexed in March of that year 1845. Senator Benton opposed the "re-annexation" of former Mexican province, fearing the already strained relations with Mexico might break. Daniel Webster was more interested in the possibility of acquiring California, which he considered "twenty times as valuable as all of Texas." The new President, James Knox Polk, expressed the hope that some arrangement might be made to buy the land around the harbors from Mexico. Soon after Polk's inauguration, Benton had taken Captain Fremont to call on the President, who was not overly enthusiastic about spending much money on mapping service. This, however, could not dim Fremont's enthusiasm for the new venture and he thought himself as much an emissary for the State Department as a surveyor for the army. Benton and other "exuberant expansionists" termed their policy of peaceful extension to the Pacific "Manifest Destiny."

NOTES ON CHAPTER SEVEN

1. The quotations are Fremont's unless otherwise noted.
2. Benton, *Thirty Years' View*.

3. Bennett, James, *Overland Journey to California* (New Harmony, Indiana, 1906).

4. Leonard, *Narrative*.

5. Stone, *Men to Match My Mountains*.

6. Morgan, *The Great Salt Lake*.

7. Chittenden, *The American Fur Trade of the Far West*.

8. Brown, *Fort Hall on the Oregon Trail*.

9. Richardson, *The Whitman Mission*.

10. William Gilpin, later governor of Colorado, also accompanied Fremont and left the expedition at Vancouver.

11. The howitzer was raised and brought to Virginia City, Nevada, in 1861. Dellenbaugh suggests that it would have been wiser to have brought the same weight in beans.

12. In his *Autobiography*, Carson is very modest about his discovery: ". . . we could see the green valley of the Sacramento, and in the distance the Coast Range. I had been there seventeen years before and knew the place well."

13. Phillips, *Jessie Benton Fremont, a Woman who Made History*.

14. *History of New Mexico* (Los Angeles, 1907).

15. Fremont boiled water to determine the altitude of Carson Pass and recorded the miscalculation of 9,338 feet instead of the correct 8,634 feet. A bronze inscription on a boulder marks the spot. The section of tree with Carson's name and the date can be seen at Sutter's Fort Museum, Sacramento.

16. Johnson, Henry Warren, "Where Did Fremont Cross the Tehachapi Mountains in 1844?" (Historical Society of Southern California, Vol. XIII, Part 4).

17. Minto, *Reminiscences* (Oregon Historical Society *Quarterly*, 1901).

With Fremont in California (1845-1846)

He wrote his biography and left it
where the edition will never grow dim.
The alphabet he used was made of rivers,
the plains, the forests, and the eternal heights.

SALT LAKE TRIBUNE

FREMONT'S COMPANY of sixty qualified sharpshooters included a special bodyguard of twelve Delawares. The Chinook was with the party, returning to his tribe, but the California Indians had remained on Benton's horse farm in Kentucky. Pablo was in school in the East.[1] It was especially gratifying for Fremont to have Carson join him again at so great a sacrifice. "This was like Carson, prompt, self-sacrificing and true," he wrote later. Fremont did not know Dick Owens but accepted him on Kit's word. The three stalwarts were: Carson—"quick to see advantage as well as chances for defeat"; Godey—"insensible to danger, resolute and with perfect coolness"; and Owens—"equal in courage and far-sighted, with the calculating mind of a chess player." "They might have become marshals under Napoleon."

The expedition started from Bent's in the middle of August, following Pike's old trail along the Arkansas and through the Royal Gorge to its headwaters, crossed over to Piney River, proceeded along the Grand, the White, the Green and the Uinta to Provost Fork and on to Little Utah Lake, then by its outlet into the valley of the Great Salt Lake, the whole route entirely in Mexican territory. Two famous mountain men were picked up along the way. Old Bill Williams, roaming the hills alone, was hired for a dollar a day to guide. In the valley of the White River, they met

Captain Joe Walker who had crossed the Sierras a decade before to discover the incredible beauty of the Yosemite. With Carson, Williams, and Walker, Fremont had the services of the most experienced and capable trackers and trailers in the West.

The Salt Lake held a deep fascination for Fremont. After their camp was set up at a spot below their former encampment, Fremont, Kit, and several of the company visited another of its islands, riding their horses across the white floor of the lake, which looked like ice through the clear shallow water. They were surprised to find a large herd of antelope roaming the island and shot several to bring back for mess. That evening, as the men sat around the campfire watching the fat drip from the savory cuts roasting on forked sticks stuck in the ground, an old Indian appeared to inform them that all the antelope belonged to his tribe. Amused, but respecting the red man's demands, Fremont ordered a mule unpacked to give the Indian a piece of red cloth, a knife, a blanket and some tobacco to pay for their supper.

Leaving the "Dead Sea of the Great Desert Basin," the company passed through Skull Valley, which divides the fertile land from the desert—the eastern slope verdant while the land on the western slant lay sterile and lifeless except for patches of scrawny sage. They rested four days at the springs to enjoy the last of "the sweet, cool water." With two expert guides in Carson and Walker, Fremont again decided to divide the company to gain the benefit of double information. The main body, under the command of Theodore Talbot, with Walker guiding, was to take the heavy equipment over the emigrant road while Fremont, Carson, and eighteen others attempted a direct crossing of the salt flats. According to Indian legend, this had never been done for no grass or water could be found there. Old Bill Williams, wanting nothing to do with such a crazy idea, turned his mule and rode off to Fort Bridger. The two parties were to meet at a large lake which Walker had discovered the previous year at the edge of the desert near the Sierras. Fremont promptly named it Walker Lake to honor this veteran explorer.

Though fully warned of the great risk involved, "Fremont was determined to cross. Nothing was impossible for him to perform if required in his explorations," Kit mentioned in his *Autobiography*. Far in the distance could be seen by the telescope what appeared to be a green mountain peak. Carson agreed to ride ahead with Maxwell, Archambeau, and the faithful Lajeunesse and return a smoke signal if he found grass and water. They started after the sun went down, taking a pack mule with a load of water and a supply of food. They crunched across sixty monotonous miles of salt crust in the eerie moonlight, seeing no moving form or shadow, nothing but gray salt desert. Their hopes were sustained for when they reached the mountain, they found a perfect camp site. Fremont's party, moving toward them, saw the signal smoke many miles away and Archambeau was sent out to meet them. The inviting mountain was named Pilot Peak.[2]

Mindful of the miles ahead, Kit hurried the company on across a country seemingly devoid of everything, including human beings. After following a dry river bed on a particularly trying day, they were jubilant to find a good grassy plot with a spring which appeared to have been recently cleaned out. Except for a few naked footprints near the water, there were no signs that Indians might be somewhere about. That evening as the men were resting around the fire, smoking and telling yarns as usual, Kit suddenly bolted upright exclaiming: "Good God! What can that be?" An old Indian squaw was coming slowly toward them from out the shadows. She was nearly naked and her long grizzled hair blew about her shoulders in the chill breeze. Seeing the white men, she screamed and started to run away but was brought back and offered a blanket and warm food. The woman had evidently mistaken the camp for that of her tribesmen who had abandoned her. In times of famine, abandonment and suicide were considered commendable acts to provide food for those more likely to survive. When the company moved on, the pitiful old woman was left with a supply of meat.

For hundreds of miles the country offered only empty plateaus, salt marshes, and sage desert; the soft colors of far vistas belying the forbidding surface of the earth. Thirsty at times beyond endurance, the men ran to the sparse water holes before the animals could foul the water. The few Indians of the region were as mysterious as the land they lived in. One day a file of a dozen or more following some religious ritual walked with downcast heads close to the explorers and disappeared over a ridge without any sign whatsoever of recognition.

As Kit led the shabby, bearded outfit through a broken stretch, he noticed a thin spiral of smoke rising out of a small ravine. Motioning the others to approach cautiously with leveled rifles, Kit discovered a solitary Indian brave, "naked as a new-born babe," boiling ground squirrels in an open earth pot. Too frightened to move, the handsome young Indian stood as though transfixed. When assured of their friendliness, he offered to share his meal. Fremont gave him presents and all admired his handsome hunting arrows tipped with polished stone, beautiful specimens of skill and artistry. When, after going on a short distance, Fremont discovered that his Delawares had stolen some of the arrows, they were ordered to return them immediately. This special bodyguard was treated in every way equal with the white men of the company and they agreed to anything Fremont asked of them.

The two segments of the expedition were reunited at Walker Lake as planned. After a few days together, Walker and Talbot started on, planning to cross Walker Pass into the San Joaquin Valley where they were to wait for Fremont, whose party was to take the Truckee route directly to Sutter's Fort.

Once again Kit and Fremont explored the region of Carson River and the strange lake that resembled "a vast vat of lye with pieces of pumice floating on the surface."[3] Around the marshy sink a heavy growth of tule rushes covered with a honey-dew, attracted swarms of tiny insects which the Indians pressed into balls for a confection. Kit did not feel too honored that the fetid lake and malodorous sink had been given his name. Other members of the company were recognized with similar honors as Fremont mapped the region, giving their names to rivers, springs, mountains, lakes, and valleys.

Fearful of Sierra snows but grateful for benign weather, Carson pushed on across Truckee Pass without difficulty and brought his party to Sutter's on December 9, 1845.

The Mexican authorities had shown considerable alarm over Fremont's previous visit. A delegation, sent to investigate the fort, had been won over by Sutter's hospitality and had offered him $100,000 or the lands of the Mission San Jose for his holdings.

Sutter refused, though it was a high price for the poorly constructed and ill-equipped outpost.

Fremont was greatly disappointed to find Captain Sutter absent from the fort. John Bidwell, in charge of the ranch, could furnish him only wild mustangs instead of the mules he had hoped to buy. Fremont feared he might run into other unexpected obstacles. When Sutter returned after a few days, dapperly dressed in the best the West could offer, topped by the broad-brimmed white hat he always wore, he soon reassured the much perturbed Captain Fremont. Preparations were made for Fremont and a company of eight to leave at once to call on Governor Pio Pico at Monterey, using Sutter's copper-bottomed launch for the trip. Carson was to lead the rest of the company overland by the same route he had taken years before with Ewing Young.

As Fremont's boat came into San Francisco Bay, the sunset filled the hollows of the hills and shimmered in the quiet waters of the bay. With poetic praise, he called the entrance to the beautiful harbor Chrysopulae —the Golden Gate, little dreaming the real significance of the name. At Yerba Buena, the tiny village of less than a hundred huts that would one day be San Francisco, the unhappy captain wrote his wife a disconsolate letter telling of the many hardships and anxieties that were turning his hair grey before its time. Continuing down the coast, Fremont's party reached Monterey Bay late in January. The reliable, indestructible Carson was waiting for him.

The picturesque harbor teemed with trading schooners from world-wide ports come to buy hides and tallow. "Yanqui" traders from Boston brought complete stocks of goods to be sold directly from the boat to the customer. The floating stores moved from bay to bay offering everything from pins and iron pots to shoes made from California hides carried around the Horn to Boston and back.[4]

An intense rivalry existed between Governor Pico and his Chief of Army, General José Maria Castro. Pico, a ranchero of aristocratic family, owned a large estate near Ciudad de Los Angeles, where he wished to have the capital moved. Castro favored Monterey as his interests lay in that area. Consequently, most of the government business was left to Castro who had less than a hundred men under arms. The general was a swarthy, heavy-set fellow with formidable mustachios who wore his sleek blue-black hair carefully brushed into a cluster of curls at the nape of his neck. He was more likely to be seen dressed in the gold-embroidered riding suit of a ranchero than in military uniform.[5]

The customs collected at Monterey were the sole source of government income and most of it was absorbed by Castro. Native *Californios* were properly outraged at the corruption and feared their land titles might be forfeited. As Mexico's hold on this remote province grew more strained, Great Britain, France, and the United States all eagerly watched the fast-developing confusion. In the words of Thomas O. Larkin, the American consul, "The pear is ripe for falling."[6]

Captain Fremont took Kit with him when he went with Mr. Larkin to call on Governor Pico. Finding the governor absent, as he often was, General Castro granted permission for Fremont to carry on his explorations. The travel-worn outfit, driving before it a disreputable herd of footsore cattle and pack mules,

moved on toward San Jose where Fremont had hoped
to purchase fresh mounts before setting out to look
for Talbot's party. Indians threatened all the way and
succeeded in capturing all the cattle that had not fallen by the roadside. A few wild horses were lassoed
and killed to provide meat enough for the company
to reach San Jose. Carson and Owens left the company there to go in search of Talbot's party which
was supposed to be camped somewhere on the San
Joaquin. This company, mistaking the Kings River
for the San Joaquin, had bogged down in the tule
marshes of that area and was turning toward San
Jose when Carson and Owens met them in a jubilant
exchange of shots.

Already far into February, the exploring company,
with all its members together again, turned back toward Monterey where Fremont planned to secure a
new outfit before starting on to Oregon, hoping to
be home by September. They stopped at the vacant
Laguna Rancho where the news soon circulated that
Fremont had cash to pay for stock. The camp became a popular mart and meeting place of the farmers. Seemingly in no great hurry, Fremont went on
to the Hartnell Rancho within twenty-five miles of
Monterey. (He probably was killing time, waiting
for the news that war had been declared by Mexico
over the annexation of Texas.)

When General Castro, suspicious of Fremont from
the start, heard that the American company had set
up camp so near Monterey, he took a company of
soldiers to the old San Juan Bautista Mission, an ad-
vantageous height from which to watch the camp. On
March 3 Castro sent his aide, Lieutenant Chavez, with
two letters demanding that Fremont move on at once.
This peremptory demand by Castro seemed a breach

of faith to the volatile Captain Fremont and perhaps portended future difficulties. Instead of complying, Fremont ordered his men to build a substantial log fort on Hawk's Peak in the Gavilan Mountains, a short distance above their camp.

Castro watched this defiant action and when the Americans moved into the fort and audaciously raised the Stars and Stripes above it, he sent a party to inspect the deserted camp. When his men came back with some worn bridles and other discarded equipment, Castro immediately sent a dispatch to Governor Pico saying he had forced the enemy from his stronghold and captured his munitions. He called on all *Californios* to defend their glorious country, "polluted by a foreign and unholy invader."

From the summit above the little fort, the Americans could see by the glass Castro's men drilling and firing off their guns in an effort to frighten them into leaving. Fremont's sharpshooters were ready for the *Californios* to move and the Delawares eager to get Castro's "big scalp." They waited through the night for the attack that never came. Castro suddenly led his force away, probably never intending to send his men into so obvious a death trap. Among Castro's force were several American settlers who had joined with the *Californios* to resist the obnoxious Mexican army but refused to fight against their compatriots.

The Americans stayed four days on the mountain and when by accident the flag pole toppled over, Fremont decided it was the opportune time to move on toward Sutter's.

A friend of Kit's, the great mountain man, Jim Clyman, was in California at this time. He had piloted a wagon train the year before, bringing in several men who were to play important roles in California history: William Ide, a schoolmaster; Robert Semple, a printer; James Marshall, a cabinetmaker, and others. Clyman, a shrewd, observant man, kept an interesting journal in which he had noted on January 12, that the morning was frosty and he had heard that "Mr. Fremont had arrived at suitor's Fort. No information has yet arived of the politicks of the states. In fact information of all Kinds travels slow and is uncertain. When it has arived you know nothing certain unles you see it yourself." He went on to give his opinion of the government of California and on March 17 recorded: ". . a rumore that Fremont had raised the flag on Monteray and all citizens caled to apper at Sonoma armed and equipped for service under Gen. Byaho [Vallejo] to defend rights of Mexican citz." Four days later, Clyman corrected himself: "Mr. Fremont raised the American flag at camp near mission of St. John No report However can be relied on as few men in this country can write. You may form some idea of what reports are carried from 1-200 miles by ignorint supersticious people."[7]

When Fremont's expedition reached Sutter's, the jubilant settlers welcomed the men with a fiesta and barbecue. Clyman was there and offered to organize a party of vigilantes to join Fremont. The offer was refused because, Fremont insisted, he was only "pursuing science and shunning war."[8] Satisfied that a conflict was not imminent, Clyman left soon afterward to guide Lansford Hastings' party east over the salt trail Carson had pioneered the previous fall. A part of it became known as the Hastings Cutoff.

Fort Sutter had long been denounced as a den of sedition and Castro had gone so far as to bribe the Indians not to work for Sutter. As a result, Captain Sutter had been obliged to reduce his herds and wheat acreage and there was a rumor afloat that one of his more trusted men had been given a gun to kill him. Sutter admitted that he was "in a very hot stew."[9]

In the meantime General Castro had ordered signs raised in the billiard halls and other public places to inform the people that a band of highwaymen led by Fremont had been driven from the country. He even chartered a vessel for six hundred dollars to take the news to Mexico City. Consul Larkin, called upon to explain Fremont's action, agreed to take up the matter with Washington. He wrote letters to Fremont and the commanders of American ships lying at anchor off San Francisco Bay and Monterey, alerting them of the situation and suggesting that all unite in case of revolt. Fremont replied dramatically that he had "in no wise done wrong to any of the people and if we are hemmed in and assailed, we will die every man of us for the flag and his country."

Fremont did not linger long at the fort but started on toward Oregon as he said he would, Kit piloting the expedition through the densely wooded country of northern California. They stopped at various ranchos along the way and rested two weeks at Peter Lassen's post to pack supplies for the homeward trek. While they were there, a delegation of ranchers came to ask Fremont's help in driving back the hostile Indians that threatened their homes. He responded by sending some of his best men. The Indians were scattered and many killed. "A perfect butchery," Kit called it. He disapproved the wholesale slaughter of the red men but hoped it would discourage future attacks on the homesteaders.

In mild weather the men did not bother to put up shelters every night as they had at the start of the expedition. Tired from long hours in the saddle, they threw down their blankets where they stopped and were content to take whatever weather came. The Delawares believed guardian spirits in the form of eagles watched from the sky just out of sight. A dropped feather would render the finder invisible and invulnerable. Some of their white companions also carried charms but most of them were callous to danger.

By the sixth of May the exploring party had reached the lava beds near Upper Klamath Lake and had set up a camp within twenty miles of Fremont's camp-site of seventeen months before. The captain planned to spend some time in this region making maps of the almost unknown country. The Indians living near the lake showed surprise at seeing the Americans but appeared to be friendly. Fremont was eager to find the Klamath chieftain who had come to the camp with his squaw to ask mercy at the shot from the howitzer.

Near the close of the second day in the camp on the quiet lake, "a strange sight presented itself—almost an apparition."[10] Two horsemen came riding out of the timber, shouting excitedly so they would not be mistaken for Indians. They were Samuel Neal, a rancher from the Sacramento Valley, and William Sigler, a blacksmith who had been with Fremont's previous expedition, bringing the startling news that a Lieutenant Archibald Gillespie had arrived by sea from Washington with instructions to find Fremont wherever he might be. Gillespie had come ashore from the sloop *Cyane* at San Francisco harbor to receive a surprisingly warm welcome from Ex-governor Alvarado, in charge of customs. Suspecting the handsome young officer of coming to spy, Alvarado invited him to attend a ball where it was hoped, with the aid of their good wines, he might become talkative. Gillespie managed to slip away by midnight and started for Sutter's, where he hoped to locate Captain Fremont.

Four men volunteered to guide him over Fremont's trail. They had ridden three hundred miles through the rough country when the lieutenant's horse gave out. Neal and Sigler were sent ahead to locate Fremont's party which they could tell from signs was not far in advance. Hearing this amazing story, Fremont, Kit, and ten men saddled up quickly and raced out hoping to reach the men before any misfortune befell them. After about twenty miles, they were happily surprised to see Gillespie and his two companions riding toward them.

The lieutenant handed Fremont the first mail he had seen in eleven months. There were instructions from Secretary of State James Buchanan, political as well as family news from Senator Benton, a dispatch from Secretary of War Marcy informing Fremont that his status had been changed from Captain of the Topographical Corps to Colonel in the Army, and an affectionate letter from Jessie. The men sat up late around the campfires discussing the news from the world outside while Gillespie gave Fremont the information he had carried in his mind since destroying all papers before leaving his ship. Fremont was brought up to date on the state of affairs with Mexico. The government proposed to annex California by peaceful means if possible but by force if necessary. Fremont was warned to "keep a watchful eye on events in California, conciliate the good will of the inhabitants and be especially alert to the intentions of the British and other foreign schemes."

Tired and excited, the men threw their blankets under the low cedars near the fires and soon fell asleep. Fremont, too stirred by emotion to close his eyes, sat alone rereading the precious letters. Hearing a disturbance among the horses, he picked up his pistol to investigate. In the flooding moonlight he found nothing to alarm and the horses quieted. By this time Gillespie had awakened and the two officers talked a while longer. Finally, overcome with fatigue, they joined the others in sleep.

About one o'clock, Kit was aroused by what sounded like the murderous thud of an ax. Fremont heard him call out, "What's the matter over there?" At the alarm, all grabbed their weapons as the Klamath tribesmen, led by their chief in full war dress, came yelling and shrieking into the camp. One of the Delawares grabbed an unloaded gun which he tried to fire, then use as a club until felled by five arrows. Kit had accidentally broken the tube of his rifle while cleaning it the night before and was left with only his pistol. He fired at the chief, cutting the string that held his tomahawk. Maxwell's bullet found his leg and the crack of still another rifle brought the great man down mortally wounded. When the chief fell, his warriors fled without waiting to gather up their arrows, spread fanlike on the ground. In the dim light of the fire, they could see that Basil Lajeunesse, who had been with all the expeditions, had been the victim of the first death-dealing blow, and another of the Delawares was dying, struck by a poisoned arrow.

Kit could not hold back his admiration for the courage of the chief. "That was the bravest Indian I ever saw," he said, and the arrows, headed with lancet-like steel and poisoned to a depth of six inches, were the most beautiful and warlike he had ever come across in all his Indian fighting. The chief's war hatchet bore a Sheffield mark, leading the Americans to suspect the English had aroused the Klamath against them to further their cause in Oregon.

There was reason to regret for this was the only night they had failed to post a guard. If it had not been for the alert ear of Kit Carson, all might have been murdered and then the history of California would have been a different story. The blankets they had hung from the trees for some protection were shot full of arrows. Kit remarked that he did not know how fine a weapon the bow and arrow was until he had had them fired at him at night, more sure than firearms because they were "fired by feel."

The Indians had probably spared Fremont when he had gone out alone earlier, keeping to the shadows until the moon sank into the trees so that they could wipe out the whole number. Especially shaken was Gillespie, who realized the attack had probably been planned for him. He recognized the slain chief as the Indian who had rowed in from the lake the day before to bring him a salmon and in return he had unpacked his roll to give him a present. The Delawares claimed the chief's scalp.

Stunned by the horror of the brutal attack, the grieving men were determined to avenge their dead companions. They carried the bodies with great difficulty through ten miles of dense underbrush until impossible to go farther, then buried them "secure from wolf and Indian." Carson took fifteen men experienced in Indian warfare and easily picked up the fresh trail of the Klamath. Smoke rising above the trees revealed their village of about fifty lodges on the far side of a small river. In spite of extreme caution, the Indians caught sight of them as they came over the ridge above the village, and they fled in their canoes. Twenty or more were killed as the horsemen

followed along the bank safe from enemy arrows that
needed elevation to shoot across the water. Here Kit
made one of his rare miscalculations, motioning the
men to ford at a spot where they plunged into water
over the horses' heads. That meant wet powder and
useless rifles. Luckily for them, Fremont rode up with
the rest of the company.

All charged down into the now deserted village and
set fire to the lodges. Not without regret, at least
from Kit, for they were skillfully constructed of inter-
woven reeds and grasses in intricate artistic pattern.
Kit was a compassionate man though he did not hesitate to attack a hostile if it meant saving a life or
righting a wrong. The Indians' nets, boats, and scaf-
folds for drying fish were all destroyed. "We gave them
something to remember; the children we did not interfere with," Carson wrote later. A dead brave was
discovered sitting upright as if defiant in a boat that
drifted to shore with the current. His hands were still
on the paddles and on his feet were Basil's shoes.[11]

Riding back to the camp on Lake Klamath, Fremont had an opportunity to thank Kit for saving his
life by returning the favor. He jumped his horse
Sacramento on a warrior "bending his bow to the
pull" as Kit's rifle misfired. The Delaware Saguda,
following close to Fremont as he always did, killed
the Klamath with his war club and lifted the scalp.
Lucien Maxwell also barely escaped a poisoned arrow
that passed over his saddle just after he had jumped
to the ground. Not to be outdone, Kit happened
to spy a young brave ambushed behind a rock, dismounted, and crawled up behind him and disposed
of him with a bullet. Gillespie, who was amazed to
witness such strange and daring feats, was given the

Klamath's beautiful bow and quiver of steel-pointed arrows.

With the situation changed in California, Colonel Fremont turned his company southward, retracing the inland trail Carson had broken through to Oregon. Soon the settlers who were uneasy in California would move over that route toward what they hoped would be a less troubled spot in the Northwest. Wagons would not be taken through for some years to come.

Sutter was finding it extremely difficult to sit comfortably on the fence. With a pretense of loyalty, he had informed Castro of Gillespie's arrival but not until the young lieutenant was far on the way to meet Fremont. Several settlers were waiting for Fremont when he reached Lassen's post. They brought word from Sutter suggesting the expedition make camp at the Marysville Buttes, a natural fortress about sixty miles from Sutter's Fort. Fremont found it an ideal camp site and sat down to await further orders from Washington. Lieutenant Gillespie was sent by Sutter's launch to ask for supplies from the commander of the United States war sloop *Portsmouth* lying at anchor in the harbor of San Francisco Bay.

The political situation in California was deplorable. Few believed Mexico could long keep her hold on this remote province. There was even a rumor that Castro, eager to make the best deal for himself, had approached American officials to inquire if he could expect the rank of brigadier general if he should turn his influence toward the United States. Don Mariano Vallejo, while concerned over "the unbroken line of wagons from the United States," was not unfriendly toward the Americans. He was not in agreement with

Castro or Pico, who favored cessation to England, and denounced these leaders who would barter their country's future for gold. Therefore he was not in good standing with either of them. Not knowing which way the pear might fall, this loyal *Californio*, anxious to remain neutral, released the soldiers under his command at Sonoma, leaving his extensive holdings virtually unprotected.

With his force now enlarged to six hundred men by the addition of Vallejo's soldiers, Castro decided to move. He sent a large herd of horses, taken from Sonoma, into the Sacramento Valley to be used against the Americans in case of an attack. The settlers, greatly alarmed, sent a delegation to the Buttes to ask Fremont's help. He assured them of his firm support but explained that he had no political or military authority to use force. He made no objection, however, when Carson and thirty-three members of his company, itching for action, asked to join with the farmers. A few days later, June 10, hoping to create an incident that would provoke Castro to strike the first blow, thirteen of these reckless adventurers, led by Ezekiel Merritt, a gaunt trapper of Fremont's company, surprised Castro's lieutenant and captured the horse herd by running the animals through wild mustard that grew high as the horses' backs. Castro's men, indignant at being caught off guard, were somewhat mollified by the return of their own weapons and mounts.

Encouraged by the success of this bold move, the rebellious settlers moved toward the estate of General Vallejo at Sonoma, adding recruits as they went along. Carson remained with Fremont at the Buttes. At daybreak of June 14, 1846, the band of backwoodsmen and trappers secured the guard "a little way out of town" and surrounded Vallejo's residence. There was no violence. The aristocratic don got out of bed, dressed in his uniform, and offered wine to his captors. Assured that his household would not be disturbed, Vallejo signed capitulation papers and was taken, along with his brother Salvador, a relative, Jacob Leese, and his secretary, to Fremont's camp. Schoolmaster William Ide, chosen to command the captured garrison, issued a proclamation announcing the action which has been called "the first act of aggression by Anglo-Saxons on this continent." Indirectly, it won for the United States the rich prize of California.[12]

On June 20, the little band of captors raised the flag of the Republic of California, a rough piece of unbleached domestic with a strip of red petticoat flannel sewed across the bottom. A crude grizzly bear and an irregular five-point star had been painted on it with a mixture of Venetian red, linseed oil, and lampblack by William Todd, a nephew of Mrs. Abraham Lincoln. The bear — looking more like a pig — was chosen as a symbol for "its courageous qualities which never give the road to man—attacks any number, fights to the last with increasing ferocity, amazing strength and incredible tenacity." The star was a gesture to Texas.[13]

General Castro, still entrenched at San Juan Bautista, sent out a proclamation asking all *Californios* to unite in one supreme effort to "fall on and kill the Bears of Sonoma and then return and kill the whelps afterwards."

During this history-making event, Kit had remained at the Buttes with Fremont, the man who, perhaps involuntarily, had "stirred up the hornet's nest." Momentous developments had played into his hand far beyond his most fantastic dream. He did not yet know

that war with Mexico had been declared a month before, on May 17, and refused to take the responsibility for Vallejo and the other prisoners. Carson was
ordered to escort them to Fort Sutter. Though distasteful to Vallejo, he took his predicament with good
grace and was treated with consideration by his rival,
Sutter, also soon to be dethroned. Warned that Castro
was planning to recapture Sonoma, Fremont and Carson, with several hundred farmers armed with pitch-
forks or whatever they could find to use for weapons,
started toward the former Mexican outpost.

At four o'clock on the morning of June 29, one of
the twenty-four men on guard at Sonoma reported
hearing horses approaching—not only heard them but
saw them enter the darkened canyon and feared they
might be Castro's men. William Ide tells the story:
"They had advanced to within two hundred yards
of the place I stood. The impatience of the men at
the guns became intense, lest the enemy come too
near, so as to lose the effect of the spreading of the
shot. I made a motion to lay down my rifle. The
matches were swinging—'My God! They swing the
matches!' cried the well-known voice of Kit Carson.
'Hold on! Hold on!' we shouted—' 'T is Fremont!
'T is Fremont!' in a voice heard by every man of both
parties. . . . Captain Fremont dashed away to take
cover behind an adobe house and a moment after, he
made one of his most gallant charges on the fort; it
was a noble exploit. He came in at full gallop, right
in the face and teeth of our two long 18's!"

"Kit Carson," Ide wrote later, "probably saved us
from a pretty bad disaster which, had it happened,
would have resulted from Fremont's failure to give
reasonable notice of his coming." Confidently expecting to be acclaimed the leader of the conquest, Wil-

liam Ide believed it would be a simple matter to arouse all California to join the new republic. However, many of the settlers thought him too visionary and there were whisperings that he intended to turn the republic into a Mormon state. Fremont was asked to take over and Ide, stepping out of his brief moment in the spotlight, reluctantly turned his 234 followers over to Fremont's command.[14]

The first bloodshed came when two settlers, Thomas Cowey and George Fowler, who had volunteered to go to the Fitch ranch for a supply of powder, were captured and killed by Mexican guerillas. William Todd was caught carrying a letter from Fremont but escaped without injury. Three Mexican citizens—one found carrying information from Castro advising his aide at San Rafael of an expected attack on Sonoma —were captured and ordered to be shot by Fremont who said he could not take prisoners, an unfortunate impulsive act he would have cause to regret later.[15]

The Fourth of July was celebrated at Sonoma in fine style by opening Vallejo's choice wines and the Declaration of Independence was read with fervor. Kit had a reunion with his brothers, Moses and Lindsey, both employed at the Fitch ranch on the Russian River, north of Sonoma. (In contrast to his slightly built half brother, Moses Carson, foreman of the ranch, was about sixty years old, six feet tall, weighed over two hundred pounds, and had one eye and several fingers missing. Twenty-five-year-old Lindsey, an adventurer like Kit, had come to California the previous year.) To add to the excitement of the occasion, the news arrived that war between the United States and Mexico had been declared six weeks earlier. Gillespie, who had come in with supplies for Fremont's men,

was left in command of the fort while Fremont and
Carson turned south to look for Castro.

As soon as Commander John A. Montgomery of the
Portsmouth was informed of the Bear Flag raising, he
dispatched the news to Commodore John D. Sloat on
the flagship *Savannah,* commanding the Pacific squadron at Monterey. Sloat, assuming Fremont had acted
under official orders, unfurled the Stars and Stripes
and ordered the flag hoisted over Monterey at 10:00
A.M., July 7. As nothing had been heard from Castro,
it appeared that California had been annexed without
the semblance of a battle, "by four small ships and
the wildest wild party of backwoodsmen."[16]

Commodore Sloat was under orders to keep a close
watch on the Pacific coast and occupy Monterey at
the first sign of hostility. He was a cautious old man
of long service and though he knew war had been
declared, he did not arrive at Monterey harbor until
June 2. At that time his offer to salute was rejected
by the Mexicans on the excuse that they had no powder
to return it. It was rumored that they were waiting
to welcome the English fleet which Sloat had outwitted
by starting toward Honolulu, then turning back. The
veteran naval officer now found himself in the difficult position of having to direct a land force. He
called for good rifle shots among his tars to volunteer
for shore duty. These "Horse Marines," led by purser
Daingerfield Fauntleroy, took some of the ship's short
carronades and started forth to drive Castro from his
stronghold.

On July 9, Commander Montgomery, accompanied
by seventy men from the *Portsmouth,* went ashore to
the little adobe settlement of Yerba Buena and raised
a second United States flag. Lieutenant Joseph W.
Revere—a grandson of the famous Paul Revere—was

sent on the launch of the *Portsmouth* to Sonoma where he found all quiet except for some of the women violently objecting to the crude Bear Flag. Montgomery's young son, who had accompanied Revere, took down the historic piece of muslin to carry home for a souvenir and the American flag went up over the garrison. Going on to Sutter's, Revere saw the scalp of the Indian sent to kill Sutter hanging over the gate. At sunrise next morning, as the cannon saluted, Revere pulled the rope raising the colors of the United States to replace those of Mexico over Sutter's Fort. The long-hoped-for annexation had come but John Sutter's troubles were just beginning.[17]

Fremont's chief topographical engineer, Edward Kern, who had replaced the invalided Preuss, was placed in command of the fort. Kern was enthusiastic over the "bold and beautifully managed affair" at Sonoma and wrote home: "If Castro has valor, he is devilishly shy of using it."[18] Governor Pico demanded that the American consul explain the "downright robbery" of Sonoma and, to make matters even worse, Pico decided to march against Castro, who had pulled out of San Juan Bautista toward Santa Clara. Fauntleroy's Marines arrived at the old mission to find Fremont in possession only two hours. Now Fremont's party learned for the first time that the American flag was flying over Monterey. The usually reserved Kit Carson threw his arms into the air shouting: "The whole country will be at our feet. Californians don't know how to fight." Leaving a few men on guard, Fremont, with the Horse Marines added to his motley band, started for Monterey where a cheering populace was waiting for them when they arrived July 19.

This probably was California's most unique parade,

three hundred men marching in a square with the horses and cattle herded in the center. There were bearded trappers in deerskins and broad-brimmed beaver hats; Delaware Indians with decorated topknots and few clothes; weather-beaten backwoodsmen looking like Indians and enjoying being mistaken for them; shaggy mountaineers in flapping trousers and new blue middies of Navy issue; farmers in homespun with an assortment of weapons; and dandies from the gambling halls in "butterfly waistcoats and Railroad trowsers, frilled shirts and polished boots, their bowie knives encased in stained crimson velvet sheathes." Only the Horse Marines were in uniform. Leading this strange procession was Kit Carson, in comfortable trapping outfit, by the side of handsome Colonel Fremont who made a striking picture in blue cloth trousers and naval shirt left open at the neck, fringed deerskin hunting jacket across his shoulder, moccasins on his feet and a cotton handkerchief jauntily tied on his head. They sang and yelled as they marched through the streets of the capital city, confident they were the conquerors of California.

The day after Fremont and his company arrived at Monterey, Her Majesty's flagship *Collingswood*, carrying eighty guns, rode into the harbor leading the largest fleet ever before seen in the Pacific. The British sailors, seeing "a patch of color, small but of great meaning,"[19] realized they had come too late. Britain, who had lost out in Oregon the same day the Bear Flag was raised, now saw her hope of annexing California wrecked. Admiral George Seymour, of the *Collingswood*, unperturbed, told the British consul to consider the American occupation as only temporary.

The exploits of the frontiersmen were well known

in Europe through the writings of men like Sir William Drummond Stewart. So great was the curiosity of the British seamen that several were permitted to visit Fremont's camp on the plain above the city. Asking for a show of rifle skill, Mexican dollars were put up for targets to be shot at 150 yards, the coins to reward the men who hit them. Ready for any kind of contest, the sharpshooters responded eagerly but the supply of silver soon ran out.

Col. Fremont had with him one or two who enjoy a high reputation on the prairies. Kit Carson is as well known there as the Duke [of Wellington] is in Europe. . . . They are allowed no liquor, tea or coffee only: this no doubt has much to do with their good conduct and the discipline is very strict. They marched up in an open space of hills near the town under some firs and took up their quarters in messes of six or seven in the open air. The Indians lay beside their leader. (From the report of Lieutenant Hon. Fred Walpole of the Royal Navy.) [20]

Commodore Sloat, greatly disturbed to learn that Fremont had acted without written orders, instructed Commander Montgomery not to issue any more supplies to his company. He was extremely cool toward Fremont, evidently uncomfortable in his position as commander of a delicate and dangerous situation.

There was general relief with the arrival, July 23, of Commodore Robert Stockton on the frigate *Congress* to replace the unhappy Sloat who sailed at once for Washington to report the momentous events of the past weeks, believing the contest for control of California satisfactorily settled. Stockton, young, aggressive, and, like Fremont, "ambitious and far from home," in a vigorous speech in the square, denounced Castro for having "shamefully violated international law and hospitality by hunting and following with

wicked intent, Capt. Fremont of the U.S. Army and
his band of forty men who had entered California
for rest and refreshment." Vallejo was pardoned and
allowed to return to his ranch which he found stripped
of livestock but otherwise undamaged. The aristocratic don became an enthusiastic American. Far more
resolute than his predecessor, Stockton suggested that
Fremont resign from the army and become a naval
officer. His force, reduced to a hundred and fifty men,
was renamed "The Navy Battalion of Mounted Riflemen." They sailed on the *Cyane* for San Diego to
intercept Castro's retreat to Mexico. Stockton was to
join Fremont with a force for a combined march on
Los Angeles.

The sea was rough on the four-day voyage and Kit
made a poor sailor. It was the worst part of the war
for him and he vowed it was the last time he would
take his feet off solid ground if he could get a mule
to carry him.

Stockton landed at San Pedro with 360 men, "miser-
ably clad and wretchedly provided for,"[21] and entered
Los Angeles, August 13, without opposition. Fremont,
unable to find horses for his men, arrived a few days
later. Both Pico and Castro had fled across the border
into Sonora after tearful addresses to their indifferent
followers. Stockton appointed Fremont to act as military governor of California, with Captain Gillespie as
secretary, then left for Sacramento to enlist recruits
before sailing to join General Zachary Taylor at Mexico
City. To all appearances, the conquest of California
was complete.

NOTES ON CHAPTER EIGHT

1. Though given a good education by Fremont, Pablo returned to Mexico to become notorious as the bandit Joaquin Murrietta, according to Fremont's *Memoirs*, p. 409.   (Probably mistaken identity.)

2. Kelly, *Salt Desert Trails*.

3. Leonard, *Narrative*.

4. Lewis, *California in 1846*.

5. Revere, *A Tour of Duty in California*.

6. Lewis, *California in 1846*.

7. Clyman, *American Frontiersman*.

8. Benton, *Thirty Years' View*.

9. Revere, *A Tour of Duty in California*.

10. Benton, *Thirty Years' View*.

11. Fremont, Jessie B., *The Will and the Way Stories*.

12. Bancroft, *History of California;* DeVoto, *The Year of Decision: 1846;* Cleland, *History of California: The American Period;* Sabin, *Kit Carson Days*.

13. Benton, *Thirty Years' View;* Eyre, *The Famous Fremonts and their America*.

14. Ide, *Who Conquered California?*

15. Carson was reported to have been one of the firing squad. His part in the regrettable affair has been called "the only black mark on Carson's escutcheon." Probably, because of his great regard for Fremont, Carson does not mention the incident in his *Autobiography*.

16. Fremont, Jessie B., *The Will and the Way Stories*.

17. Revere, *A Tour of Duty in California*.

18. Lewis, *California in1846*.

19. Fremont, Jessie B., *The Will and the Way Stories*.

20. Bigelow, *Memoir of the Life and Public Services of John Charles Fremont*.

21. Bryant, *What I Saw in California*. Bryant, who had come west with Clyman, joined Fremont at Sutter's Fort.

With Kearny's Army of the West (1846)

Thank God! the land is rousing,
like a giant from its Sleep. . . .

GEORGE SHEPARD BURLEIGH,
*Signal Fires on the Trail of the
Pathfinder* (1856)

As a "REWARD for bravery and gallant service," Kit Carson was sent with a company of sixteen, including several Delawares, to Washington City as bearer of the all-important dispatches to the War and Navy departments. He left September 16, taking only twenty-five pounds of dried meat and a supply of parched corn and hoping to find sufficient game for the company. After a tedious month of routine desert hardship, they came to the familiar country of the Gila and followed it upstream to the Rio Grande. This was the land of the treacherous Apache but those of the tribe that came near their camp were surprisingly friendly and informed Kit that there was a new governor of New Mexico.

When war against Mexico was declared, May 17, 1846, Colonel Stephen Watts Kearny, a close friend of the Benton family and the man who had permitted Fremont to take the controversial cannon on his second expedition, was given command of the Army of the West with orders to move toward California by way of Santa Fe; the cannon to be sent around the Horn. He left Fort Leavenworth, "Missouri, June 30—ten days after the Bear Flag incident, marching with 1,700 men across the simmering hot plains to Bent's Fort.

By the time they reached there, they had been joined by several hundred trade wagons afraid to con-

tinue to Santa Fe now that a state of war existed with
Mexico. Camp was set up about nine miles from
Bent's Fort to wait for Colonel Sterling Price, who
was two weeks in the rear with an additional 1,800
men. William Bent, appointed colonel, agreed with
the help of Fitzpatrick to guide the army over the
hazardous Raton Pass. Many raw recruits, too ill to
continue, were left hospitalized at the fort.[1]

As the columns of cavalry and foot soldiers started
toward the mountains, the brass cannon in the tower
was fired in salute and burst. Traders, trappers, wagoners, Indians, their squaws and children, crowded the
roofs and walls of the fort to watch the incredible
spectacle of three thousand men and horses, a thousand mules and a long string of covered wagons disappear on the prairie. The Cheyennes did not believe there were so many in the whole white tribe.

Kit's Josefa may have been at Bent's Fort for she
had come with Ignacia and her children to stay at the
fort until conditions in New Mexico were more settled. Wherever she was, Josefa must have wondered
anxiously if her husband's expedition might be further
delayed by the war. Mrs. Fremont, sharing her worries,
had sent a letter by Mr. James Magoffin, traveling with
Kearny's army, to be left at the fort for her husband.

In temperatures soaring above 100°, Kearny's army
finally got over the craggy pass after several supply
wagons had overturned and rolled down the mountainside. To Fitzpatrick's great amusement, the first
Mexican prisoners brought in were five frightened
peons riding sleepy burros without reins and knowing
no English; they had no idea what was happening to
them. From a roof top in Las Vegas, Kearny made
a speech, interpreted by Antoine Robidoux, proclaiming New Mexico a part of the United States. On

August 18, 1846, five days after Stockton had occupied Los Angeles, the Army of the West entered Santa Fe without resistance.

So Kearny reported, but no mention was made that Captain Cooke and James Magoffin, a man of considerable wealth and great charm, had gone ahead with $30,000 appropriated by Congress to persuade Governor Armijo not to resist. They had found the governor amenable but with a show of strength he had led a force of four thousand to the impregnable Galisteo Pass, fifteen miles from Santa Fe, to await the American army. His second in command, Colonel Diego Archuleta, was determined to hold the pass at all costs but relented with Armijo's promise that he would be given command over the western half of New Mexico. The Mexican troops retired without firing a shot or knowing why. The alcade of Santa Fe shouted to the Americans that the pass was clear and Kearny's men poured over the mountain, sixteen hundred strong. Acting Governor Juan Vigil, Josefa's uncle, ordered a volley fired in salute as the Stars and Stripes were raised above the plaza. The exuberant American soldiers, much to the disgust of the sedate Kearny, put on a wild celebration ending in a near riot with fisticuffs and drawn sabres that brought court-martial proceedings to several offenders.

Kearny, now raised to the rank of brigadier general, found his troubles were only beginning. He drew up an elaborate document which he called "The Organic Law for Governing New Mexico," "seemingly unaware that such laws must be passed by Congress. It gave the governor broader powers than the President and it is difficult to believe that the whole affair was not a broad joke" (opinion of Congressman Lucian Chase).[2] The popular Charles Bent was appointed governor with Colonel Sterling Price in military command. The construction of a new fort, to be named Fort Marcy for the Secretary of War, was begun just outside the city.

Believing he had everything running smoothly in New Mexico, General Kearny prepared to move on toward California. He issued a general command to march from the city on September 25 with 300 dragoons, 100 artillery, 500 mounted volunteers, and seven days' rations. Accompanying the army was Thomas Fitzpatrick to guide and Antoine Robidoux as interpreter. They started forth to conquer California ten days after Kit Carson had left Los Angeles with the dispatches telling of the victory.

On October 6 the army pulled out from their camp site on the Rio Grande near Socorro, a hundred and fifty miles below Santa Fe, and had covered about three miles to the west when the advance scouts came riding back with a party of fifteen men "whooping like Indians," led by a stocky freckled-face horseman with long reddish hair blowing about his shoulders. It was, of course, Kit Carson's outfit bringing news that would blast General Kearny's hope of being proclaimed "The Conqueror of the Pacific Empire."

The meeting of Carson and Kearny in that empty desert country was a dramatic moment in the history of the West. Besides the element of surprise and the emotional impact, there was the significance of the news each carried and led to an unparalleled climax.

Carson, flushed with excitement, informed the general that "the flag was flying over every important position in the territory of California and the country forever free of Mexican control."[3] At least that was the situation when he had left there. At this startling news, the much perturbed General Kearny ordered Kit to give his letter pouch into the hands of his old friend Fitzpatrick for delivery to Washington City; Carson to return to California as guide for his army. Stunned by the peremptory order, Kit was at first almost defiant. He told Kearny that he had already worn out thirty-four mules on the sun-scorched desert trying to make record time and keep his promise to Stockton and Fremont to have the return dispatches in their hands in a hundred and twenty days. He could not betray their trust in him.

Kit had looked forward eagerly to visiting the Capital City and he carried letters of credit from both Fremont and Stockton addressed to important persons who might help their envoy along the way. It was bitterly disappointing to have the honor of the mission taken away from him so abruptly, and Fitzpatrick was no more enthusiastic about being the substitute. Most of all, Kit was heartsick to be within a few days of Josefa, whom he had not seen in fourteen months, and be compelled to retrace the difficult miles without seeing her. Kearny remained adamant. He believed he needed Carson's great experience to get his army successfully to the Pacific and refused to change the order. Kit was torn between what he considered his duty and what he was commanded to do. He seriously considered escaping at night but Maxwell persuaded him not to be rash. Not until convinced that Kearny had the power to order him, would Kit accept the decision.[4]

"It requires a brave man to give up his private feelings thus for the public good; but Carson is one such! Honor him for it," wrote Captain Archibald Johnston in his report to Washington.[5] Johnston, himself, would have the opportunity to show his own great courage before the Army of the West would reach the Pacific.

After hearing Carson tell of the hardships they could expect, the morale of Kearny's men was so deflated that twenty Mexican volunteers deserted. Only the presence of the famous scout to guide them served to bolster their sagging confidence. Kearny revamped his plans, sending all but a hundred men and two mounted howitzers back to Santa Fe under Major E. V. Sumner. He planned to resume march along the right bank of the Gila to the Colorado—the route he was to recommend as the boundary between Mexico and the United States. After the third day on the road, Carson advised Kearny that, considering the rate they were progressing and what lay ahead, it would take six months to reach the coast. He convinced the general that all baggage should be carried by pack mule and the wagons were immediately ordered back to Santa Fe to be turned over to Colonel Cooke, soon to leave with the Mormon Battalion to open a wagon road across the cactus waste south of the Gila.

Kit headed into Gila Canyon instead of taking Kearny's suggested cutoff across an almost impassable mountain area. The passage was overgrown with rank weeds and tangled grapevines and the sharp jutting crags forced several crossings of the river. Though they had covered only a fraction of the distance before them, the cattle were already sorefooted and the backs of the mules pitifully galled. The caissons carrying the cannon fared worst of all. At times they were so far in the rear they were feared lost and Lieutenant J. W. Davidson, commanding them, doubted they would ever come through. Bad as the trail was, Kit assured them it was "a turnpike road in comparison to the other route."

They passed through Apache villages without incident, some of the Indians even asking to be taken along for a chance to kill the despised Mexicans. "With a twinkle in his keen hazel eye," Kit warned that he would not trust one of them. Almost daily the camp was visited by some scraggly band with a few poor mules to swop for a couple of butcher knives.[6]

Grass was so sparse that orders were issued to caution against setting fires and endeavor to save the grass along the route as far as possible. Though disgruntled that the curtain had gone up on the California drama before he could arrive for the star performance, Kearny was aware of the historic role he was playing. A strict disciplinarian, sincere in his effort to win the support of the people of New Mexico, General Kearny would not let his men take any foodstuff without offering to pay for it.

Kit cut off the big bend of the Gila by pushing through a rugged, mountainous stretch and came at last to the flat plain. There, tensions eased considerably and even the weary pack animals seemed a little playful. The gun carriages that Davidson had managed to bring through after replacing most of the parts, began to roll with little effort. But Kit was serious. He knew they had "bid adieu to the grass and must henceforth subsist on willow, cottonwood and the long ephedra." The only food they could find was fish and a few wild ducks. With a dubious shake of his head, Kit told Dr. John S. Griffin, the army surgeon, "I never knew a party to leave the Gila without starving."[7]

Dr. Griffin had pulled the short straw at Socorro for the privilege of going with Kearny. In his diary he faithfully recorded the weariness and disgust along with his own impression of the forbidding country of thorns, tarantulas, and cracking river beds. Carson told the doctor he should be there in summer to observe the beautiful supply of rattlesnakes. Of all dis-

comfort suffered, by far the worst was from the alkaline dust mixed with autumn pollen.

The poor mules dropped from sheer exhaustion to
be devoured on the spot by white wolves waiting on
their haunches to fight over the carcasses. One heavily
loaded animal, rushing toward a stream with a last
surge of energy, fell into the water and drowned. At
times, the dragoons were forced to carry water in
buckets to their panting mules only to have the contrary creatures refuse to drink until they buried the
buckets in the sand and covered them with grass.
Nights grew so cold that water froze to an inch thick-
ness and the thirsty mules objected to drinking the
cold water brought up so laboriously through the ice
crust.

By November 22, Kearny's army had traveled no
farther than the junction of the Gila and Colorado,
near the border of Mexico. Anticipating trouble from
Castro in Sonora, Carson was sent with Lieutenant
William Emory to investigate several campfires seen
burning on the opposite bank. Approaching cautiously, they found a party of Mexicans camped near a
herd of some five hundred horses which, they told the
Americans, were being taken to market. Kit, noticing
some women's footprints, told Emory that he thought
it hardly likely that the fair creatures would have been
brought along if danger had been anticipated. Four
of the Mexicans voluntarily returned with Carson and
Emory to explain to General Kearny that they were
merely horse traders. They were, in fact, taking the
herd to Castro who was organizing a cavalry troop to
return to California.

The following day, a horseman was detained at the
river crossing and found to be carrying letters addressed to Castro from a General José Maria Flores

in Los Angeles. Kearny was stunned to learn through the intercepted dispatches that Los Angeles had been recaptured by a guerilla force under Flores two days before his army had left Santa Fe! Kit recognized one of the men accompanying the courier as a fellow he had talked with in Monterey but he could get no information from him beyond the advice that it would be foolhardy for the Americans to attempt to enter California without strong reinforcements.

This latest intelligence caused the already frayed spirits of Kearny's men to sag even lower. Dr. Griffin noted that they probably could expect "a small chunk of Hell." The volunteers were nearly barefoot and ragged beyond belief. Only those too ill to walk were permitted to ride. The good doctor treated them as comfortingly as he could for assorted aches and pains —rheumatism, gout, epilepsy, hernia, varicose veins, and dysentery to name a few—but he was confident, if given the opportunity, his boys would still be able to "deliver a good thrashing."

Before crossing the Colorado, Kit suggested that each dragoon tie a bundle of grass behind his saddle so that the mules would not only get safely across but be assured of at least one day's food, for beyond lay the dreaded Journado del Muerto—Journey of Death. Both men and mules suffered indescribably through the last of the thousand and fifty arid miles that brought them by December 2, with scarcely a ration left, to the Warner rancho, Agua Caliente, the frontier settlement about forty miles from San Diego.

Jonathan (Long John) Warner, who had come to California in 1827 as clerk for Jedidiah Smith's outfit and stayed to become a Mexican citizen, was at this time being held in San Diego on the suspicion of aiding the *Californios*. Kearny stopped for a day at

the ranch while Carson, Davidson, and twenty-five men
rounded up fresh mounts, then moved on to the Stokes
ranch. Stokes agreed to take a message to Stockton
at San Diego giving Kearny's location and asking escort. No mention was made of the fact that Kit Carson was returning with Kearny's army.

Three days later, Kit gave out a wild shout of joy
to see his old partner, Lieutenant Alex Godey, come
riding in with Captain Gillespie and a company of
thirty-five men. Among them was Midshipman Edward Fitzgerald Beale whom Kit had met in Monterey.
Beale, described by Fremont as "happy, spilling over
with good spirits," had come to California with Stockton on the *Congress*. Preparations were made to start
at once for San Diego despite the fact that Kearny
had been warned by Kit that a guerilla party of *Californios* was somewhere in the vicinity. After moving
on about ten miles, a reconnaisance rode in to report
a large enemy command encamped at the nearby village of San Pascual pretending to be horse traders.
Hearing this, Kearny ordered Lieutenant Godey back
to San Diego for more reinforcements. Kit assured
the general that he could not have chosen a better man.

There followed several days of anxious waiting with
no way of knowing whether or not Godey had been
successful in getting through to Stockton. Finally,
against the advice of Carson and his officers, the impatient Kearny decided to attack the village. Neither
Kit nor Gillespie expected much resistance but they
did not reckon with the infuriated young *Californios*
sworn to drive the "Yanquis" out of their country.
Tired as they were, Kearny's men seemed eager for
a fight.

At two o'clock on the cold and drizzly morning
of December 6, they woke to the call of "Boots and

Saddles!" and prepared to go out and capture "those gentlemen." Kit rode with Captain Johnston in the advance charge sent to capture the horses. Kearny was to follow with eighty men. When within a few yards of the village, perhaps luckily for Kit, his horse stumbled, throwing him to the ground. Crawling to one side, he avoided being trampled as the whole force passed over him. When he managed to get to his feet, he found the stock of his rifle had broken from the barrel. Running on ahead, he took up the carbine and cartridges of a fallen dragoon in time to join his company just as the main body of troops under Captain Benjamin Moore forced the *Californios* to withdraw. Moore took forty men in pursuit, only to be cut off from the rest of the command when the enemy suddenly turned to make a vicious attack.

The *Californios,* armed with gleaming lances, wheeled their handsome mounts to attack the helpless Americans on worn-out mules and half-broken mustangs. They turned to strike again and again, knocking the dragoons from their unmanageable mounts and stabbing heartlessly with their cruel blades. Kearny's horse was shot from under him. He mounted a mule in a desperate effort to lead his men out of the disaster, their weapons useless with damp powder.

By the time Lieutenant Davidson succeeded in rolling up the howitzers, he had all but carried across mountains, rivers and desert, the battle was over. For a final frustration, the mules pulling one of the caissons ran away to suffer the indignity of being lassoed by the Mexicans. Neither cannon was fired for both gunners were dead and the captured howitzer useless without American powder and shell.

The gory battle lasted only ten minutes and was over before dawn. Thirty-six of the forty men of

Moore's command were either killed or wounded—
the worst slaughter of white men Kit said he had ever
seen. It was a victory without the use of gunpowder
for only two Americans were injured by firearms.
Both Moore and Johnston were killed, Kearny, Gillespie and Robidoux were among the injured, Robidoux being blinded by a lance wound in the spine.
It was feared old Antoine would not live through the
day but he revived when one of the dragoons brought
out a treasured bit of coffee.

Though badly wounded, Kearny refused to accept
special care. He gave his command over to Captain
Turner but, undaunted by the fate that had dogged
him all the way, refused to call the engagement a defeat. In an eloquent report to the War Department
on December 13, 1846, he wrote: "The victory thus
gained over more than double our force may assist
in forming the wreathe of our national glory." Though
critical of Kearny's leadership, Kit felt great compas-
sion for the unfortunate general in his darkest hour.
He could not refrain from comparing Kearny and
Fremont, whom he not only respected but affectionately admired, and wondered what the outcome would
be when these two dynamic leaders met in California.

Not daring to move forward, the battered and despondent survivors stayed on the battlefield and in
the heavy night buried their dead comrades in a common grave under a lone willow "with no other ac-
companiment than the howling of the myriads of
wolves."[8] They started on next morning with Carson
and a detachment well in advance. The wounded,
delirious and dying, were carried by litter and travois
with exhaustive discomfort over nine miles of rough
ground to reach the Bernardo Ranch. Just ahead on
every hill they could see the *Californios*, now rein-

forced to a hundred and fifty men. When within a short distance of the stream where Carson had expected to make camp, the enemy charged on both sides forcing the bedraggled Americans to take refuge on a barren hill with no source of water.

To add to the unhappy situation, Lieutenant Godey was captured within sight of the camp as he was returning from San Diego with two companions. General Andrés Pico, brother of the former governor, now in command of the *Californios,* refused to exchange Godey for Kearny's one Mexican prisoner but released instead one of the other men who knew nothing of Stockton's reply. He could only report that Godey had managed to hide the dispatches under a tree before his capture.

As soon as the horses were loosened, most of them ran toward the water to be captured by the enemy. The dragoons dug frantically for a mere trickle of water to wash down the "mule-beef" that was their only food. Though their position was desperate, Kearny was still determined to go ahead regardless of the outcome. In the end he listened to his officers who were convinced that their nearly exhausted men could not face another battle without reinforcements. Their only hope was to get another message through to Stockton.

Kit volunteered with the naval officer, Edward Beale, and his young Delaware servant to attempt passing through the sentinel lines that stood three deep around the hill awaiting Kearny's surrender. Armed with a rifle, revolver and knife apiece, but refusing to take the last scraps of food, the three volunteers crawled out after dark through the brush and over stones and cactus, sometimes with only inches to spare between them and the lancers. General Pico, who kept his men moving, was heard to say: "Be alert, Carson is

there—*se secapare el lobo*—the wolf will escape if you
are not careful!"[9]

Kit suggested that they pull off their shoes and tie
them to their belts and throw away their empty can-
teens that rattled against the rocks. Lying flat against
the ground, they watched a Mexican sentry ride up
and stop so close they scarcely dared to breathe. When
Beale, believing their plight was hopeless, wanted to
rise up and fight, Carson whispered that he had been
in worse fixes and Providence had always saved him.
Once again it did; the sentry lit a shuck, smoked a
while, then mounted and rode off. After worming
their way past the last guard, the volunteers crawled
into the shelter of a gentle grove, having covered two
miles without daring to stand upright. Both Kit and
Beale had lost their shoes—the Delaware was more fortunate with his moccasins—and there were still thirty
miles between them and San Diego.

It was dusk again before they reached the outskirts
of the town. Their feet were swollen and bleeding
and young Beale, untrained to the wilderness, was
exhausted and irrational. Kit prodded him on, en-
couraging him not to give up so near their destination.
He advised each to try passing alone through the
Mexican picket line around the city and, miraculously, all got through safely. The gruelling experience nearly cost Ned Beale his life and Carson was
hospitalized for several days.

They found Commodore Stockton attending a baile
that was a nightly affair at the home of Juan Bandini,
with the musicians from the *Congress* supplying the
music. Stockton was dumbfounded to hear that Kit
Carson was back in California after having been trusted
with so important a mission. Without waiting to learn
the details, he ordered a hundred and seventy men

along with every horse he could find sent to Kearny's relief. They arrived to find that the dragoons had burned all the baggage preparatory to cutting their way through or die in the attempt. The *Californios* dispersed without a fight. When the once proud Army of the West finally reached the Pacific, Emory described it as "the most tattered and ill-fed detachment of men that ever the United States mustered under her colors."[10]

When Stockton's report of the great heroism of the three volunteers reached the capital, Senator Benton held the floor of the Senate for four days to tell of the superb feat and the startling events that had taken place in California. Kit Carson's fame was now assured. Not only was he the peerless mountaineer and daring Indian fighter, but a courageous soldier in the finest American tradition.

After an all too brief rest, the combined forces of Stockton and Kearny started north to recapture Los Angeles. There were about six hundred men in the force, two thirds of whom were sailors and marines. Kearny's men, still shaken from the horror of San Pascual, seemed fated to endure almost incredible experiences. When the feeble mules gave out, the men, poorly clothed with only canvas wrapped around their feet for shoes, were forced to pull the ammunition wagons over hills and through quicksand.

On January 12, 1847, when within sight of the whitened walls of the pueblo of Los Angeles, a procession of two thousand or more *Californios* rode out to meet the "web-footed Yanquis." Most of them were young rancheros, handsomely mounted and clad in velvet, with fluttering serapes and betasselled sombreros, carrying an assortment of weapons—beribboned lances, carbines, pistols, rifles, and sabres, and each division led by a musician. There were trumpets, guitars, bugles and even a fiddle or two playing as though it were some festive occasion.

Stockton, though of lower rank than Kearny, was in command. He ordered the men to form a square with the cannon set at the angles and wait for an attack. When a trigger-anxious tar fired prematurely, the Mexican cavalry under General Flores attacked but without success. Two minor charges followed and after each attack, the horsemen rode off toward the mountains to lasso fresh mounts—a side-show watched with great interest and admiration by the Americans. The battle for "the Angelic Capital" lasted only three and a half hours with one American private killed and thirteen wounded. General Flores turned his command over to Andrés Pico and left for Sonora.[11]

Pico led his men into the San Fernando Valley where Colonel Fremont had established headquarters at the old Cahuenga Rancho and surrendered to him. Lack of horses for his four hundred Mounted Riflemen had prevented Fremont from meeting Stockton and Kearny at Los Angeles. It is significant that the guerillas chose to attack Stockton and Kearny but preferred to surrender to the popular Fremont.

Carson and Fremont were reunited two days later when Fremont's battalion marched into Los Angeles. Now the celebrated dispute over who was to govern the new province arose between Kearny, the man who had been sent across the country to conquer California, and Fremont, who by his mere presence on the scene had done more than anyone else to accomplish it, had accepted the governorship and held the surrender papers.

From his headquarters on the plaza, General Kearny declared himself governor and ordered Stockton to cease all civil government. The indignant Stockton replied that he not only refused but would ask President Polk for Kearny's recall. Kearny also demanded recognition from Fremont, who sent Kit with a polite note of refusal.[12] Kearny's reply advised Fremont for the sake of his long friendship with the Benton family to reconsider and offered him half command. Fremont discussed the situation freely with Carson, whose counsel he valued deeply. Kit thought it almost cowardly that Kearny should attempt to sway Fremont by sentiment. The tone of Kearny's letter disturbed Fremont, a first intimation that serious trouble might develop.

When Kearny realized he could accomplish nothing with Stockton or Fremont, he capitulated and withdrew to San Diego where he was joined by Colonel Cooke and the Mormon Battalion that had successfully brought the first wagons over the southwestern trail below the Gila.[13]

Kearny sent Captain Emory by way of Panama with dispatches to inform the War Department at Washington of his unhappy situation. Stockton again ordered Kit Carson overland with all haste to the same destination with the other side of the story. It was Army *vs.* Navy; overland *vs.* seaway; the Navy order by land; the Army order by sea!

NOTES ON CHAPTER NINE

1. Among the sick was Lieutenant J. W. Abert whose Journal can be found in Ex. Doc. No. 41, 30th Cong., 1st Sess. See Emory, *Notes of a Military Reconnaissance.*

2. Chase, *History of the Polk Administration.*

3. Emory, *Notes of a Military Reconnaissance.*

4. Fremont in his *Memoirs*, p. 568, writes: "He had been so part of my life for eighteen months that my letters were chiefly indications of

points which he could tell them at home in fulness." It has been pointed out that since Kit was a courier for Commodore Stockton, he was under no obligation to return with Kearny as the Army has no jurisdiction over the Navy.

5. Diary of Captain Henry S. Turner, October 8, 1846 (House Ex. Doc. No. 41, 30th Cong., 1st Sess.).

6. See Emory *Notes*, also Corle, *The Gila*.

7. Griffin, *A Doctor Comes to California*.

8. Woodward, *Lances at San Pascual*.

9. Bonsal, *Edward Fitzgerald Beale*; Benton, *Thirty Years' View*.

10. In San Diego, on the plaza opposite Old Bandini House, a granite boulder with a bronze tablet marks the end of the Kearny Trail, December 12, 1846.

11. Revere, *Keel and Saddle*.

12. Phillips, *Jessie Benton Fremont*. Mrs. Phillips states that Fremont gave the letter to Carson for him to copy, further proof that Kit was able to write. (Theodore Talbot testified at the court-martial that he, Talbot, had copied the letter.)

13. For Cooke report see Ex. Doc. No. 41, 30th Cong., 1st Sess.; Bieber, ed., *Southern Trails to California* ("Southwest Historical Series," Vol. V).

Twice Across the Continent (1847-1848)

Kit Carson was a man among men. . . .
His nature was literally sweet—
sweet by its wholesomeness—
sweet as a clear-cut winter morning is sweet.

JESSIE BENTON FREMONT

FOR HIS SECOND attempt to get through to Washington, Kit had with him ten of Fremont's crack riflemen, including Theodore Talbot and Kit's old trapping crony, Rube Herring. The invalided Lieutenant Beale became so ill during the journey that Kit was obliged to lift him on and off his horse. However, because it was the spring of the year when the desert is more amenable and fragrant with delicate bloom, there was far less hardship though the water holes were as far apart. They traveled four hundred miles undisturbed by any threat of Indians, all the while Kit relentlessly scanning every ridge and ravine for any evidence of them.

One late afternoon he noticed a slight haze above the horizon, so barely discernible it would have gone unseen by a less trained eye. Believing it might indicate an encampment just beyond the great red mesa, Kit decided to employ a cautious trick of the mountaineer. Saying nothing to cause alarm, he ordered camp made at the usual hour and after supper, the men threw down their blankets to sleep. When all was quiet, Kit roused them, telling them to get up at once and move a mile farther down the road as quietly as possible. The animals were picketed close by on short tethers and each man was told to hold his packsaddle before him for a shield. They waited several hours hardly daring to move or speak and desperately weary for sleep. As expected, there was an attack during the night but the arrows fell wildly over the spot where they had first stopped. They started moving on at dawn, aware of spying eyes following their every move, and for a thousand miles they were scarcely ever out of sight of one tribe or another.

It took forty days to complete the tedious journey to Santa Fe and all the way Kit cared for Ned Beale with an almost pathetic tenderness which probably saved his life. "Dear old Kit," wrote Beale in later years. "O wise of counsel, strong of frame, brave of heart and gentle of nature!"

Great events had taken place in New Mexico in the twenty-one months since Kit and Owens had given up their farming to join Fremont. Sad and terrible news awaited Kit's return.

New Mexico, under the flag of the United States, had few men qualified to control the civil government. After General Kearny had pulled out for California, the newly appointed governor, Charles Bent, found himself in the midst of a seething unrest among the Mexicans and Indians of the territory. Several of their leaders were arrested and because of the touchy situation, Ignacia Bent and her children had not come to live in the Governor's Palace at Santa Fe.

Padre Martinez continued to attack with more inflammatory articles now that those he had branded as interlopers were conquerors of his country. His home became a gathering place for the malcontents, one of his principal allies being Colonel Archuleta, who felt he had been tricked by Armijo into nonresistance with a false promise of power. While these men were suspected of stirring up resentment, they were careful to keep their activities under cover.[1]

Governor Bent, returning to Taos for a few days' visit with his family, suggested that Narcisse Beaubien, Maxwell's young brother-in-law just back from school in the East, go with him to visit Ignacia's nineteen-year-old brother Pablo who lived at the Bent home. Josefa Carson was a member of the household and Ignacia's daughter Rumalda was also staying there while her husband Tom Boggs was away carrying dispatches to Fort Leavenworth. Though warned of danger by threats, Charles refused to become alarmed even though the brooding discontent might at any moment flare into insurrection.

The sounding of the Angelus on the morning of January 19, 1847, was the signal to begin a day of terror without equal in New Mexico's history. The Bent household was awakened by a shouting mob of Mexicans and Pueblos pounding on the door and calling for the governor to come out. As the violence in the street mounted, Charles tried in vain to reassure his panic-stricken family and at the same time attempt to reason with the rioters about to break down the door. Josefa and Rumalda managed to break a hole in the thick adobe wall, digging with an iron spit and ladle, and crawled through into the home of a neighbor where they disguised themselves as peons grinding corn.

Believing he could quiet the crowd if he but showed himself to the people he had always befriended, Charles Bent stepped unarmed before the savage mob only to be seized by an Indian and scalped alive with a bowstring. Covering his bleeding head with his hands, Charles stepped back into the house but before he could escape through the hole in the wall, a shower of bullets and arrows poured through the windows, door, and roof, killing him before the eyes of his terrified family.

The boys, Pablo and Narcisse, were found hiding under the straw in the stable and brutally slain. Eighteen Americans lost their lives that grim day, among them Sheriff Stephen Lee, the trader with whom Kit had spent one winter at Robidoux's post, and Juan Vigil, Josefa's uncle. The bodies of the victims were thrown into a pile on the plaza to be devoured by dogs while the insurgents, fired with *aguardiente,* paraded through the streets displaying the graying scalp of the governor nailed to a board. Ignacia and the three Bent children were left unharmed but were forced to remain in the room with the beheaded body of the governor for a day and a half without food or water until some friendly Mexicans took it away for safe and secret burial.

Vowing to kill all who had accepted office in the new government, the insurrectionists went on to Arroyo Hondo and other settlements along the Rio Grande where several more were killed. A former Carson man, the half-Indian Markhead, was seized with his trapping companion, William Harwood, and both shot in the back as they were being taken to Taos. Among others slain was Simeon Turley, a lifelong friend of the Carson family in Missouri.

A runner carried the grievous news of the massacre across the icy Raton Pass to Bent's Fort. Overcome by grief to learn the fate of his beloved brother, William doubled the guard at the fort, fearing it might also be attacked. The Cheyennes who loved Charles Bent signaled their nation that White Hat had been murdered and only William's restraining influence kept them from taking the warpath in revenge.

Ceran St. Vrain, stunned by the tragedy, enlisted a

company of volunteers to go into the mountains after the insurgents. Sheriff Lee's brother carried the news to Colonel Sterling Price at Santa Fe who immediately ordered a company of 350 men into the field. After bringing his men over an unfinished snow-locked road through the Canyon de Taos, so narrow in places that the cannon carriages scraped the canyon walls, Price was joined by St. Vrain's volunteers. Colonel Price gave the rank of captain to Ceran and together they drove five times their number from the narrow pass known as El Embudo—The Funnel.

The Mexicans, led by Pablo Montejo, a peon who had dubbed himself "The Santa Anna of the North," fled in disorder. Many took refuge in the ancient mission church of the Pueblos at Taos, believing the church would sustain those who had followed the exhortations of the priest, Padre Martinez. Price's men, reinforced by a company of dragoons under Captain J. H. K. Burgwin, reached Taos, February 3. Though his men were suffering from fatigue and frostbite, Price prepared for an immediate attack on the well-fortified insurgents. Rolling up the cannon, they bombarded the massive walls of dried mud for hours without making a dent. The attack was renewed early the next day but still the huge gray bastion held. The battle took on the appearance of a medieval assault with battering rams and hand-to-hand combat. At length a few breaches were made in the walls, six feet thick at the base, and shells were thrown in by hand. A near calamity was averted when a lieutenant picked up a shell that had fallen outside among the soldiers and threw it into the church only seconds before it exploded. The roof was set afire by soldiers climbing crude ladders under fire from the jeering mob inside. An eyewitness reported: "The mingled noise of the bursting shells and firearms, the yells of Americans and the shrieks of the wounded men was most appalling."[2]

All day long the siege continued. Finally the insurgents fled to the safety of the pueblos, turning in their flight to shoot down the flag Captain James Quinn had planted on the roof of the church. Some tried to escape into the mountains where they found St. Vrain's men waiting to round them up. Ceran himself was saved in a hand-to-hand struggle by Dick Wootton and the popular Captain Burgwin was killed.

The morning of the third day, the women came out of the pueblos waving white flags of surrender and fell on their knees to beg for peace. After more than two weeks of slaughter and terror, the bloody rebellion was ended with the complete destruction of the Mission of San Geronimo. A hundred and fifty of the more than six hundred barricaded in the church were killed and hundreds injured. Colonel Price lost but seven men with forty-five wounded.

There was the semblance of a trial for the leaders of the revolt with Dick Wootton acting as marshal; Captain St. Vrain, the interpreter; George Bent, foreman of the jury; and the grief-embittered Charles Beaubien as judge. When the widowed Ignacia Bent appeared at the trial with Josefa Carson, the young writer, Lewis Garrard, who had come from Bent's Fort, was struck by the unusual beauty of the sisters. "Senora Bent was quite handsome . . . [with] luxuriant raven hair; exceptional teeth, and brilliant, dark eyes," he wrote in his book *Wah-to-yah*. But it was Josefa who took his eye: "Her style of beauty was of the haughty, heart-breaking kind—such as would lead a man with the glance of the eye, to risk his life for one smile."

The Indian, pointed out by Ignacia as the murderer of her husband, sat unmoved with no show of emotion, though he knew her recognition had doomed him. Montejo, found wearing Governor Bent's coat when captured, was hanged in the plaza with five others. Nine more were to swing from the bough before the ghastly revolt was settled.

Kit's brief reunion with his beloved wife was filled with gratitude for her escape as well as grief for the loss of so many friends and relatives. He was now more embittered than ever that Kearny had ordered his return to California for he believed his great influence with the traditionally peaceful Pueblos might have calmed the revolt and prevented the tragedy.

After a few days at Taos, Carson and Beale took the Santa Fe Trail to continue their mission to Washington. Fremont's riflemen, who had accompanied them, were left to recruit their worn-out horses, returning east with a wagon train. They were joined by a young English writer, George Ruxton, whose articles entitled "Life in the Far West" were popular reading in England. The copious notes he kept have been some of the best sources of information about the early West. Ruxton wrote thus of Carson:

. . . the last in height but first in every quality which constitutes excellence in a mountaineer, whether indomitable courage, or perfect indifference to death or danger; with an iron frame capable of withstanding hunger, thirst, heat, cold, fatigue and hardship of every kind: of wonderful presence of mind, and endless resource in time of great peril; with the instinct of an animal and the moral courage of a *man*— who was taller for his inches than Kit Carson, a paragon of Mountaineers?

Small of stature and slenderly limbed but with muscles of wire with a fair complexion and quiet intelligent features, to look at Kit none would suppose that the mild-looking being had raised more hair from the head of Redskins than any two men in the western country; yet thirty autumns had scarcely planted a line or furrow on his clean shaven face . . . a credit to the diggings that gave him birth.[3]

Arriving in good time at St. Louis, Carson and Beale went at once to call on Senator Benton, who was avid for a firsthand report of what had happened in California. Kit, surprisingly at ease in the presence of this important legislator, told how he had met Kearny along the road and informed him that he was too late. Kearny had mentioned his friendship with Fremont and the Benton family and told Kit of his intention of making Fremont governor of California. The Senator was greatly impressed by Kit's forthright manner and invited him to be a guest in his Washington home where Mrs. Fremont was living with her mother during Fremont's absence.

In Washington, a hero's welcome awaited the weather-beaten envoys from the West who had accomplished the spectacular feat of covering three thousand miles in three months! Ned Beale, whose family was highly regarded in Washington society, insisted that Kit stay at his home. He was a little reluctant at first to go into the fine residence explaining that he usually met folks out on the road. The hero from the West stayed in the middle of the street shaking hands with the persons who crowded around him. The modest Carson was almost baffled by this first public acclaim but his openhearted friendliness won for him even more admirers.

When Kit, unaccustomed to sleeping indoors, did not rest well the first night, Mrs. Beale considerately fixed a bed for her famous guest out on the veranda. She noticed, one day, that something seemed to be disturbing Mr. Carson and asked her son to seek out the cause. After some urging, Kit confided to young Beale that he was bothered by the thought that it might not be right for him to conceal from the women of the household that he had once had an Indian wife, for if they knew it, they might not wish to associate with him. Then he loyally defended his Arapaho wife saying, "She was a good wife to me. I never came in from hunting that she did not have warm water for my feet."[4] To a straightforward man like Kit Carson, concealment was less than honest. Though there was no reason to speak out, he could not keep silent. It is touching to know that while considering the fine ladies of that well-appointed home, Kit had a tender thought of Singing Grass who had also sought to give him comfort.

Kit had looked forward to meeting Mrs. Fremont, but how could he tell her, without alarming her, what had happened to her husband during the long months since they had been together? When Kit was announced at the Benton mansion, Jessie ran to meet her husband's beloved Carson. She kissed his cheek and pulled a footstool up to his chair, begging to be told everything. Kit, at first uncomfortable in his new black broadcloth suit, white starched shirt, and neatly folded silk cravat, selected with Beale's help, was put completely at ease by the gracious Jessie Fremont. There in the elegant library of Missouri's senator, the unschooled but dignified Westerner unfolded the incredible story in his quaint and colorful language. Kit thought it best to keep nothing from her even though to hear it might be a blow to her pride.[5]

Some news of her husband's activities had indirectly come to Jessie. She had occupied some of her time during Fremont's absence by translating Spanish documents for the State Department and unofficially learned something of Fremont's part in the occupation of California. She was happily planning to sail with her little daughter Lily to California by way of Panama to join him. It was now Kit's painful duty to tell her of the clash between Kearny and Fremont, though Kit himself was unaware of the sinister turn of events that had taken place since he had left California.

Kit could not refrain from telling Jessie how much he admired the courageous way she had received the disturbing news. He liked her plucky and proud spirit—the perfect mate for a man of destiny like John Charles Fremont. On her insistent invitation, Kit came to stay at the Benton home for the remainder of his time in the capital. Senator Benton arrived shortly from St. Louis to take matters into his own capable hands and arranged for Carson to retell his story to a Senate committee.

"This statement I make at the request of Senator Benton," Kit told the legislators, "but had much rather be examined in a court of Justice, face to face with Gen. Kearny and there tell all at once all I know about Gen. Kearny's battle and conduct in California."

Jessie Fremont, years later, wrote at length of Carson's visit:

There were long delays at the State Department that tried his patience and he feared that the value of his long ride would be lost. "It is not fair to the Captain. He trusted me to come back as quick as I had come on. Now he is looking out for me and they won't give me the answer to carry back." He felt frustrated by the polite but vague answers to his anxious inquiries and it troubled him to find the almost reverential regard he had always felt for the leaders of the country weakening. "With their big houses and easy living, they think they are princes, but on the plains we are the princes—they could not live there without us."

Jessie continued:

My mother said to him one day, "You must have had a great many fights." "I never had a fight of my own but one. That was with a Frenchman. He said the Americans were cowards and darsn't fight. I told him I was an American and that I was his man and we fit." He turned back his collar unconsciously and simply showed the wound by the collar bone.

How he did appreciate Burns's verse.

> "The King may make a belted knight
> A Duke, an Earl, and all that
> But an honest man's above his might
> For a' that and a' that."

One of the troubled days he brought up to the library an illustrated Byron which had attracted him among the books in the Parlor below. The picture of Mazeppa bound to a horse, the frightened horse running madly over a solitary plain with only the stars for light, fascinated him. It made him too full of excitement to read it patiently. "Read it out to me—You will read it quicker than I can! It looks like Indian work—they're devils enough for just such work as that!" And then and often again I read it to him: there in my father's large library, among his father's and his own serious collections, I rendered Byron with all the dramatic effect I could manage.

Carson kindled to fury over the wild horse episode. His excitement culminated where Mazeppa says:

> "There never yet was human power
> That could evade—if unforgiven—
> The patient hate, the vigil long
> Of him who treasures up a wrong."

"That's so, that's so, He knows how a man feels! That's the way I felt. Until I paid them back, after the Blackfeet destroyed my caches and carried off my furs and skins. But I came back. I thanked them for their conduct. I had to wait for the right men to help punish the thieves. Then my time came and we left mourning in their tribe."[6]

Jessie Fremont immediately went into action, arranging a meeting with President James K. Polk, whose wife, by the way, was a cousin of Kit's former trapping partner, Joe Meek. Before leaving for the drive to the White House, Jessie picked up a beautiful crystal decanter and announced with a flourish that Mr. Carson and Mrs. Fremont would have a glass of sherry before going into battle!

The President—described as "lean, stiff, angular with sharp grey eyes, in a sad face, and long, grizzled hair brushed straight back behind his ears and devoid of humor"[7]—received this unusual couple cordially. He had just denied a request to permit the government buildings in Washington to be illuminated with new gas lights in honor of the triumphs in the Mexican War, fearing for the safety of the official records. He was evasive about the quarrel between Kearny and Fremont, hoping the whole affair would blow over before he would be obliged to side with either the Army or the Navy. The President was impressed by the straightforward, dignified manner of the famous frontiersman whom he described in his diary as "short, sturdy, weather-beaten and swarthy from the southwestern sun." Carson was requested to call again the next week and this further entry was made in Polk's daily record: "I saw Kit Carson again after night and had a full conversation with him concerning the state of affairs in California and especially in relation to the collision between our land and naval commanders in that distant region."[8]

President Polk wished to give some kind of reward

to Carson who had traveled so many perilous miles with extreme personal hardship to bring the dispatches from the far shores of the continent and was willing, without thought of reward, to carry back his replies. On June 9, 1847, Secretary of War Marcy received the following letter signed by the President:

Mr. Christopher Carsen of Missouri who has recently returned to the United States from California will accept the appointment of 2nd lieutenant in the Mounted Rifle Regiment. . . . A vacancy I understand exists in that corps produced by the death of Capt. Mason. I desire that Mr. Carsen shall be appointed a 2nd Lt. in that corps.[9]

Several conferences followed with many words spoken and written and after a final meeting with the Cabinet on the Fremont-Kearny matter, President Polk recorded in his diary:

All agreed as I did that both are gallant and meritorious officers and all regretted the occurrence. None of the Cabinet censured Gen. Kearny. The two former (Stockton and Fremont) have subjected themselves to arrest and trial but as all collision had been probably since that time avoided, I am disposed not to pursue so vigorous a course. . . . It has been decided to send Carson with despatches to both Kearny and Stockton to put an end to this most unfortunate controversy.

Though expressing himself as neutral, Polk appeared to favor the Army since it was more a land than sea operation. Furthermore, he was not too kindly disposed toward the imperious Senator Benton and had thought from the beginning that Fremont was too young and impulsive for his important assignment. Undaunted, Jessie asked for another White House interview. "Among those who called today was Mrs. Fremont. Lt. Carson was with her. Expressed desire

for her husband to remain in California. Left it to
the option of Lt. Col. Fremont to remain in the service or return and join his regiment now in Mexico."
So wrote the President, but Fremont would not be
allowed to make that choice.

Greatly honored that the President of the United
States had recognized his service to the country by
recommending his appointment to a lieutenancy, Kit
made ready to begin his return cross-country journey.
Entrusted to his care, along with official papers to the
military commands at Santa Fe and Monterey, was a
tender letter from Jessie Fremont to her husband, enclosed with an exquisite miniature of herself with the
words: "to wear over your heart until *le bon temps
viendra.*"

Lieutenant Beale had hoped to accompany Kit to
the West but became too ill to go beyond St. Louis.
After an almost tearful farewell with his devoted young
friend, Kit went on to New Franklin for a visit with
Adaline and his family before reporting to Fort Leavenworth. There he was given command of fifty volunteers being sent to Santa Fe as reinforcements for
Colonel Price. After the tension and limelight of
Washington, it was with relief that Kit turned to the
far-reaching quiet and freedom of his beloved prairies
and could once again sleep under the luminous night
sky. Somewhere along the way, Carson and Fremont
passed unknowingly.

After Kit had left California, Stockton had drawn
up a tentative plan of government which he turned
over to Fremont, then sailed off to resume his naval
career. Commodore Shubrick, who replaced him,
openly favored Kearny. Fremont, in the meantime,
had endeared himself to the Californians by sparing
the life of Don Jesus Pico, brother of the former gov-

ernor, who had been condemned to be shot for his
part in the insurrection. The firing squad was ready
when Dick Owens brought Pico's wife and child to
plead with Fremont, promising to devote their lives
to him if he would spare Pico's life. Fremont stayed
the execution and the families of the two men became lifelong friends.[10]

General Kearny, reinforced by Colonel Cooke's Mormon Battalion, arrived at Monterey in March to pro-
claim himself Governor of California and ordered Fremont to turn the archives over to him. Fremont was
now determined to have a showdown. Taking six
extra horses, Fremont, with his servant Dodson and
Don Jesus Pico, began a wild ride from Los Angeles
to Monterey. They covered four hundred and twenty
miles in less than four days' time, with fresh mounts
lassoed and saddled every twenty-five miles. Finding
no agreement possible with the implacable General
Kearny, who even refused Fremont's offer to resign,
the horsemen raced back to Los Angeles to set a record
of riding almost a thousand miles in seventy-six hours.
Kearny chose to ignore the order of General Winfield
Scott directing him not to detain Fremont but discharge him at once. Kearny was determined by this
time to discredit completely the man who had caused
him so much chagrin.

When Colonel Richard B. Mason arrived from
Washington on June 7, 1847, to take charge of
affairs, Kearny left for Mexico City. The new governor brusquely refused Fremont's request either to
join General Scott in Mexico or to be allowed to return east with his exploring party. Mason, going so
far as to threaten to put Fremont in chains, finally
disposed of the unhappy matter by ordering Fremont
to return east humiliatingly at the rear of the Mor-

mon Battalion. They crossed the mountains by the Truckee route and to them fell the gruesome task of burying the bodies of the tragic Donner party who had not survived the Sierra snows. At Fort Leavenworth Fremont was put under arrest to stand courtmartial.

Jessie Fremont, taking her maid with her, hurried to Kansas Landing to await the arrival of her husband whom she had not seen in over two years. A noisy ovation greeted the famous pair as they came down the gangplank of the river steamer *Martha* at St. Louis. General Kearny, who had recently arrived in the city from Mexico, tactfully remained in the background at Jefferson Barracks.

Meanwhile, Kit Carson was pushing down the Santa Fe Trail with his soldiers. They found encamped at Pawnee Rock a large Santa Fe-bound wagon train escorted by a company of volunteers for the Mexican War under Lieutenant Maloney. In the morning as a picketing party of Maloney's men led their animals to grass, a string of Comanche braves rode out of hiding and captured the horses after stampeding the cattle in the direction of Carson's camp. Kit's men succeeded in rounding up the beef herd but the United States lost twenty-eight good horses to the Indians, including the mounts of two of Carson's men who dropped the ropes that held them to fire at the Comanches. Three of Maloney's men were wounded and the sleepy guard responsible for the attack was required to wear the dress of a squaw for a day as punishment.

At Taos there was time for only a few days with Josefa. Kit was proud to tell her of his meeting with President Polk and of the appointment he had received. Then he continued on west with the all-important dispatches. Realizing that the route along the Gila had been swept clean of grass by three exhaustive crossings—Kearny's, Cooke's, and his own—Kit chose to take his company of sixteen over the Old Spanish Trail which was still hardly more than a mule path. The miles were covered without incident until late one day, as the men rode single file along the twisting trail by Muddy Creek that flows into the Rio Vergin, they suddenly found themselves at the edge of an Indian village that had been completely hidden from view. All at once they were practically surrounded by stony-faced red men whom Kit recognized as the hostile tribe that had ambushed and killed seven men the previous year.

If ever there was a time to be brash and brave, this was it. Any hint of hesitation would have been fatal. Carson ordered camp to be made on the spot and posted heavy guard. He refused to be deceived by friendly overtures, warning the Indians that he knew of their treachery and would kill any of them who did not leave the camp at once. Those who refused to move were fired upon with one killed and four wounded. There was no further trouble—an example of Carson's expert handling of a desperately critical situation with only a handful of men to stand off hundreds of savages with a minimum of bloodshed.

The lateness of the season tempered the desert sun and slackened the thirstiness. Rations gave out and mules were slaughtered for food but such privations were routine to Carson. "During all my life in the mountains," he told his men, "no more than twice a year did I have a full meal of bread, meat, sugar and coffee."[11]

The sensational Fremont court-martial was being

heard in Washington with Fremont conducting his own defense. Jessie Fremont attended every session, always dressed in her most becoming clothes, "for this was no mourning occasion." In the proceedings, Kearny denied, or failed to remember, that Carson had brought a letter to him from Fremont. The episode of the howitzer Fremont had taken on his second expedition was brought up to accuse Fremont of defying the orders of his superiors. Jessie, believing that matter closed, was shocked and outraged. After weeks of testimony, drawn out by Senator Benton's powerful oratory, Fremont was technically found "guilty on all counts: mutiny, disobedience and conduct prejudicial to order and discipline. Remission of penalty recommended and release from arrest to resume his sword and report for duty." Fremont chose to resign from the service. This did not, however, end the controversy which would still be argued after a century, with historians of equal importance violently partisan in the defense and condemnation of both Fremont and Kearny.[12]

It would be months before Kit Carson, then nearing California, would learn the news of Fremont's fate. Arriving at Monterey on November 22, he gave the letter pouch into the hands of Governor Mason. This was the first overland mail. Heretofore, letters had been accommodatingly carried by settlers or brought around the Horn and it would be years before California would have any regular mail service from anywhere in the United States.

A young lieutenant, destined for fame, was with Governor Mason that day in Monterey, his name, William Tecumseh Sherman. Recalling the event later, Sherman wrote:

I well remember the first overland mail. It was brought by Kit Carson in saddle-bags from Taos in New Mexico. We heard of his arrival in Los Angeles and waited patiently for his arrival at Headquarters. His fame was at its height from the publication of Fremont's books, and I was very anxious to see a man who had achieved such feats of daring among wild animals of the Rocky Mountains and still wilder Indians of the plains. At last his arrival was reported at the tavern at Monterey and I hurried to hunt him up. I cannot express my surprise at beholding a small stoop-shouldered man with reddish hair, freckled face and soft blue eyes, and nothing to indicate extraordinary courage or daring. He spoke but little and answered questions in monosyllables. I asked for his mail and he picked up his light saddle bags containing the great overland mail, and we walked together to Headquarters where he delivered the parcel into Gov. Mason's hands. He spent some days in Monterey during which time we extracted with difficulty some items of his personal history. He was then by commission a Lieutenant in the Regular Mounted Rifles serving in Mexico under Col. Sumner and as he could not reach his regiment from California, Col. Mason ordered that for a time he should be assigned to duty with the First Dragoons at Los Angeles.[13]

Sherman, ten years younger than Carson, was to be closely associated with him in government service years later after each had achieved outstanding military recognition.

After years of unstable government, California had settled down to enjoy an era of peace and quiet. The families who had moved into Sutter's Fort during the rebellion had returned to their own homes. A large number of Mormons from Cooke's battalion had chosen to remain in the vicinity of Sutter's to engage in agriculture. John Sutter had moved out of the fort to his large farm and was elated over the abundant harvest and prospects for the future.

Looking forward to an influx of new settlers, Sutter had contracted with James Marshall, the cabinetmaker who had come west with Clyman, to build a sawmill on the south bank of the American Fork about thirty miles from Fort Sutter. The project had not gone well for the flutter wheel had been placed too low for the water to flow. While digging a deeper channel for the millrace, on the "clear, cold morning" of January 24, 1848, Marshall noticed something shining through the water that ran a foot deep through the ditch. Picking up several small pebbles, he showed them to another worker and they decided it did not look like gold.

A few days later, after he had picked up about three ounces, Marshall changed his mind and hurried to show Sutter what he had found. Sutter pledged all who knew anything about the discovery to keep it secret for at least six weeks so that proper claim papers could be filed, then went out to see for himself how things were progressing. He expressed the hope that the discovery would not interfere with the work on the mill. Then picking up a nugget or two, which he rolled around in his huge palm, Sutter said he would see "a ring got made of it."[14] Marshall was sent with another man to take several specimens to show to Governor Mason. Lieutenant Sherman, who was with the governor when they arrived, took an ax and a hatchet and beat out a large piece which they decided "beyond a doubt was metal and pure metal."

Sutter's men pressed for claims but as yet there were no United States land laws in effect. As far as anyone knew, California was still officially a Mexican province. (The treaty of Guadalupe-Hidalgo, ending the war, was signed February 2, 1848, eleven days after the gold discovery, but news of it would not reach

Monterey until September.) Realizing this might be an important strike to be handled with extreme care, Mason and Sherman arranged to go at once to Sutter's to see for themselves. The governor placed a sample of ore in a tea caddy to send with his report of the strike to Washington. He decided to send it by sea, the route considered more certain of safe delivery than by overland mail.

It was impossible to keep the news of the strike secret for long. It first leaked out when one of Sutter's teamsters offered gold dust for a drink of whisky at the store run by the Mormon leader, Sam Brannan, who also published a little news sheet which he called *The California Star*. His competitor, Dr. Robert Semple, who had printed California's first newspaper, *The Californian*, on an old press he had found abandoned at San Juan Bautista, pulled a scoop on Brannan by printing the story of the gold discovery two weeks before *The California Star* carried the news on April 1.

At first there was no great rush, for the miners of the region were more interested in the high prices paid for quicksilver. In an effort to stir up some excitement over the story, Sam Brannan took a bottle of gold dust and climbed on a soapbox in the plaza at San Francisco to show the world that his story was no April Fool's joke. Soon every available pick, shovel and spade was digging in the soft sand rock of the American Fork. When the supply was exhausted, the gold seekers dug with spoons, butcher knives, and even their bare hands. So many deserted from the occupation forces that Governor Mason feared Los Angeles might be retaken by the Mexicans. Trading vessels, with not enough crew to man them, were tied up in the harbors with rusting anchors. The almost distraught governor had one consolation—all were so intent on getting rich, there was hardly time for mischief.

John Sutter had no conception of what might result from this invasion of his land. Things had been going well for him; he had contracted to sell all the wheat he could raise to the Russians in Alaska and trade was booming with the constant stream of new settlers passing the fort. Later, he remarked paradoxically, that if gold had not been found on his holdings, he would have been the wealthiest man in California. Instead, he was fated to spend his days in fruitless litigation trying to settle his land claims in Washington.[15]

During this time, Lieutenant Kit Carson was on duty with a detachment of twenty-five volunteers under Captain Andrew Jackson Smith guarding Tejon Pass to prevent Indians from taking horses through the mountains east of Los Angeles. He remained in that area until April when Governor Mason called him to Monterey to carry official dispatches once more across the continent.

Preferring to travel unencumbered by a large party, Carson started May 4 with a small escort, retracing the Old Spanish Trail which in a few months' time would be threaded with the wagons of the "gold-blinded Forty-Niners." He carried ordinary mail as well as official papers and the first news the East would have of the gold discovery rode in Kit Carson's saddlebag.

Accompanying Kit's party to Taos was a Lieutenant George D. Brewerton who kept an interesting journal of the difficult journey. "It is a country of eternal rock and sand like the crater of an immense volcano that had been afire and hadn't got quite cool yet," wrote Brewerton.[16] Desert travel was measured not by days but by *jornadas,* the distance between water holes. They found an occasional well that had been opened up by wolves whose keen sense of smell could detect water running beneath the sand. The holes were dug out and laced with willow branches to prevent the sand from caving in. The almost exhausted horses would sometimes drink as much as five four-gallon buckets of water apiece.

As sometimes happens in a parching desert, a river is found at flood stage. So it was with the Grand River. Two log rafts were hastily put together and half of the party crossed safely. The second raft capsized in midstream throwing Lieutenant Brewerton and the rest of the men with all their equipment into the swirling waters. All managed to swim back to shore but were forced to wait, wet and half-clad, in the chill desert night until an axe could be brought over next morning and a new raft made. It was a particular hardship to lose the sorely needed saddles, bridles and rifles.

In spite of this, luck seemed to be with the travelers as they covered hundreds of miles without any Indian trouble. When they were within fifty miles of Taos, Kit's face grew serious as he pointed out unmistakable Indian sign. "Look here," he said. "The Indians have passed our road since sun-up and they are a war-party—no sign of lodge poles and no colt tracks . . . a dropped feather . . . we'll have trouble yet if we don't keep a bright outlook."[17] The Indians appeared as expected—a band of a hundred and fifty Apaches and Utahs. Kit immediately ordered the animals held in the chaparral and the men to stand back to back for an attack. The Indians approached cautiously, demanding toll for passing through their territory. Kit shouted a warning for them to keep their distance and told them his men were in such destitute condition he had no presents to give them. A few came forward with gestures of peace and while these negotiations were taking place, an Apache brave rode up on a "speckled horse" lathered with sweat after a fast ride in the hot sun. The warriors listened with no sign of emotion to the news their scout had brought, then suddenly whirled their ponies and rode off into the desert haze.

Though it was growing late, Carson continued down the trail, following a rule of the frontier that in time of danger it is safer to be on the move than encamped. Brewerton was ordered to fall behind and if an attack were made, he was to shoot the mule carrying the mailbags. Pushing cautiously ahead for ten miles, they came face to face with a detachment of two hundred volunteers sent out from Taos in search of marauders. This seemed incredible good fortune but Kit understood at once why the Indians had left his party so abruptly. The Apache scout had seen the soldiers and rushed to warn his people not to start any trouble. The following day, Kit's bearded and bedraggled company arrived at Taos.

With only chance communication from the far West, Josefa Carson was prepared for the sudden appearance of her now famous husband and hoped each return might bring some assurance of a more permanent life together. She accepted her role as wife of the country's greatest adventurer with courage and optimism and the very uncertainty of the future made their rare hours together all the more precious. Kit, now a lieutenant in the Army on special assignment, explained that this mission was of extreme importance and he must proceed to Santa Fe and on to Washington City at once.

One of the greatest disappointments of his life awaited Kit Carson at Santa Fe. Colonel Edward W. B. Newby, in command of Fort Marcy, had the unhappy task of informing Kit that the United States Senate had refused to confirm his appointment to the lieutenancy. This meant that he could expect no reward for his great and responsible service as bearer of dispatches twice across the continent. Though deeply hurt at the rebuff, Carson refused to listen to friends who urged him to leave the mail with the officials at Santa Fe and be spared the long journey to Washington. Kit gave no thought to such advice for the dispatches had been entrusted to him by men who considered him the most competent person to deliver them safely in the shortest time. "It does not matter," he told them, "whether I am a lieutenant or a mountaineer when performing a service for my country."[18]

The Senate's denial probably had not been intended to be in any way derogatory to Carson. After several unfortunate experiences, they were hesitant to recommend the appointment of civilians, over those trained in the military. Some said it was a final slap at the Benton-Fremont clique. Senator Benton expressed the opinion that it was refused because Carson had not gone through the West Point Gate. A later historian, Milo Milton Quaife, called it "stupid pettiness . . . an act of vindictive meanness. . . . The idea that Kit Carson was undeserving of a lieutenancy in the American Army in 1848 is one to make the gods weep."[19]

Unwilling to trust anyone but himself to break the disturbing news to his adored Josefa, Kit rode back to Taos, resigned but not embittered at this unexpected blow to his pride. Never was the strength of

Christopher Carson's character more clearly shown than in his dignified acceptance of the decision against him.

Enlisting his ten best men, Kit chose a route north through the broken country at the edge of the mountains, hoping to outwit the warring Comanches. In this they succeeded but did not escape a brush with another hostile tribe—a band of Kiowas who appeared to be friendly, even inviting the white men to share their food and smoke with them. Before the calumet ceremony began, Kit overheard the chief tell his braves that when the pipe was passed the third time, they were to rise and kill every one of the white visitors. Maintaining complete composure, Kit told his men to stay with the horses as though nothing were wrong and he would lift his hand as a signal to shoot if necessary. He sat and smoked with the Kiowas, giving no hint that he understood what they were saying or knew of their malevolent scheme. As the pipe started on the third round, he leaped to his feet and leveled his rifle on the chief saying he was Kit Carson and understood what they were planning. It would be better, he told them, to use their arrows to hunt rabbits and rode off unharmed with his men.

The country was familiar ground to Kit as he led his men across the flat open stretch bordering the foothills of the Rockies, generally referred to as the "coasts of Nebraska." Beyond rolled the plains, dipping like a sea of grass and in the deep distance, the meeting of sky and earth barely discernible.[20] It was still the unexplored, unbroken, and unpeopled wilderness Washington Irving had called irreclaimable. Kit's company at length reached the Platte and followed a circuitous but pleasant route to Fort Leavenworth.

Kit went on alone by boat and railroad to Washington where he was surprised to meet, of all people, his old trapping crony, Joe Meek. Meek had come down from Oregon to bring the grievous news of the massacre of the Whitmans by the Cayuse Indians. Kit, who had heard many accounts of horror on the frontier, was too overcome at the news to speak. The Cayuse had ravaged Waiilatpu mission by tomahawk and firebrand, not for any personal grievance against the doctor or his lovely wife, who had befriended them, but as a warning to white settlers not to commit further atrocities against their people. Joe Meek's own little daughter, Helen Mar, and Jim Bridger's Mary Ann, were among the children killed.

With the crude and uncertain modes of travel, the lack of communication, the great distances involved and the hazards of traveling in 1848, it is incredible that Carson should just happen to meet so many different persons and be present for so many historical events. Joe Meek visited an important relative in Washington—none other than his cousin, Mrs. James K. Polk, the wife of the President. Meek generously aided Kit from his "contingent fund" and together the two ex-trappers were a great curiosity in the capital. One fine lady asked Joe if his wife was afraid of Indians. "Well, she shouldn't be," replied Joe, "for she is an Indian herself." He confided to Kit that the rustle of silks in the White House was far more frightening to him than the war whoops of a hundred Blackfeet.[21]

Another of Kit's adventurous friends, Alex Godey was also in Washington. Alex was very proud of his beautiful black wavy hair and despite all hardship, always gave it the best possible care. One evening while attending a concert in Washington, he overheard two ladies sitting behind him admire his smooth and shining locks. One, speaking in French, remarked that it probably was a peruke, at which Alex turned to inform them that he had lifted more than one scalp but the hair he wore was his very own.[22]

Kit was again entertained in the home of Senator Benton. Fremont, now thirty-five, had returned to private life, his spirit still unshaken by the ordeal of the past months. Whatever criticism is made of Fremont for being an arrogant opportunist, shielded by a powerful father-in-law, it must be said that he won the admiration and respect of the men who served under him. "I cannot forget his treatment of me while I was in his employ," Kit says in his *Autobiography*, "and how cheerfully he suffered with his men when undergoing the severest hardships. His perseverance and his willingness to participate in all that was undertaken, no matter whether the duty was rough or easy, are the main causes for his success; I say without fear of contradiction, that no one but he could have surmounted so many obstacles, and have succeeded in so many difficult services."

Great joy came into the lives of the despondent Fremonts that summer of 1848 with the birth of a son who was named Benton. Kit was proud to act as the baby's sponsor at the baptismal service, August 15, at the Episcopal Church of the Epiphany in Washington.

Four days later, the *New York Herald* came out with the first printed mention of the discovery of gold in California. The official report from Governor Mason would not leave Monterey until August 28 when Captain Loesser sailed on the schooner *Lambayecana*, bound for Valparaiso where he hoped to meet a British steamer at Payta and reach Washington with the sample of ore by December. The "sickly season" and the lack of manpower had delayed the start.

The *Herald's* story repeated almost word for word the account that appeared in Brannan's *California Star,* which without doubt was carried east in Kit Carson's mail pouch.[23] There was no other way for it to have arrived since Carson was the only courier, with the exception of Joe Meek, to cross the continent, west to east, that year. Major Beale arrived in September after a fast crossing of Mexico carrying official papers which were said to contain word of the gold strike. Captain Loesser came in late in December, shortly before President Polk delivered his annual message to Congress in which he mentioned "the existence of precious metal known for a considerable extent." These words signaled the start of the Gold Rush across the country—the climax to the drama of California.

NOTES ON CHAPTER TEN

1. See Twitchell, *The History of the Military Occupation of New Mexico, 1846 to 1851;* Keleher, *Turmoil in New Mexico.*

2. Beckwourth, *Life and Adventures.* Beckwourth, a versatile mulatto mountaineer, operated a store in the Sacramento Valley. When war with Mexico seemed inevitable, Beckwourth left for Santa Fe with a herd of several hundred horses which he offered for sale to General Kearny, who rejected them in favor of mules. Beckwourth joined St. Vrain's volunteers and wrote a vivid account of the battle.

3. Ruxton went home to England to publish his articles about the West. Returning two years later to join Fremont's Fourth Expedition, the brilliant young writer became ill and died in St. Louis. See Ruxton, *Ruxton of the Rockies.*

4. Fremont, *Memoirs of My Life.*

5. Phillips, *Jessie Benton Fremont, A Woman who Made History.*

6. Fremont, Jessie B., *The Will and the Way Stories.*

7. Smith, *The War With Mexico.*

8. Polk, *Diary.*

9. Old Army Letters Received 1847, The National Archives.

10. James, *Fremont in California.*

11. Carson, *Autobiography*.

12. See DeVoto, *The Year of Decision: 1846;* Kearny, Thomas, *The Mexican War and the Conquest of California;* Nevins, *Fremont, Pathmarker of the West.*

13. Sherman, *Memoirs.*

14. Sutter, *Diary.*

15. Sutter's mansion at Hock Farm was damaged during the disastrous flood in 1862. He left with his family in 1868 to settle among the Moravians at Lititz, Pennsylvania, where he died June 17, 1888.

16. Brewerton, *Overland With Kit Carson.*

17. Brewerton, *Overland With Kit Carson.*

18. Carson, *Autobiography.*

19. Carson, *Autobiography* (ed. by Quaife), editorial note p. 126.

20. See Dodge, *The Plains of the Great West;* Webb, *The Great Plains.*

21. Victor, *The River of the West.*

22. Fremont, *Memoirs of My Life.*

23. See California Historical Society *Quarterly,* X, 298-301 (1931).

Rancher (1848-1854)

Always a gentleman where gentlemanliness
was possible and courageous
in defense of the weak.

WILLIAM F. (BUFFALO BILL) CODY

FREE NOW OF ALL government commitments and also jobless, Kit began a lonesome journey home. Stopping briefly in St. Louis, he bought a mahogany rocking chair to take as a gift to his niece, Mrs. Leander Amick, who would accept no payment for the care of Adaline. Kit was proud to hear of the progress and popularity of his daughter at the Female Seminary in Fayette and promised to take her back to New Mexico on his next trip east.[1]

The stage trip from Westport was easy compared to Kit's first crossing by muleback but the great expanse of open land was still as unchanged as when he had first seen it. There was less violence on the trail since the well-armed stages could outrun many dangers. As always in the autumn of the year, the brilliance of the sun was screened by "the unmistakable haze of Indian summer," arising from grass fires set by the Indians to pen up game for their winter food.

Kit was back in Taos by early October, determined to treat himself at last to the luxury of home. In the six years of their marriage, Kit and Josefa had lived together less than six months. Lucien Maxwell had also returned and had come into possession of the vast estate of his father-in-law, Judge Carlos Beaubien. Several former Carson men had decided to settle near Taos.

Carson was not to be long out of service for the Apaches were warring and all New Mexico was threat-

ened with their depredations. Major Benjamin L.
Beall, in command of troops at Santa Fe, called on
Carson to guide an expedition "to pursue, overtake
and chastize the culprits." A force, sent out previously
under an inexperienced officer, had returned to report that because of the depth of the snow it was
impossible to cross the mountains. With Kit guiding
and Beall taking command personally, the company
of dragoons managed to get through the snow-blocked
Sangre de Christos but found no Indians. Forced to
turn back for lack of supplies, Kit happened to spot
the well-concealed Apache village. An attack was made
without casualties but two chieftains were captured.
Though skeptical of their promises of good behavior,
Kit advised Beall to release the Indians to return to
their people, explaining that an Indian considered
himself disgraced for life if arrested and preferred death
to confinement. Major Beall wisely accepted this sage
advice and an all-out war was probably prevented.

Some years before, Bent & St. Vrain had built an
adobe fort for Kiowa trade on the Canadian River
in the Texas Panhandle. Though well constructed
with nine-foot walls, the post was continually attacked
and finally abandoned during the Mexican War as
too remote and vulnerable to be practicable. Now
that there was peace, William asked Carson and Maxwell to go with a small party of traders to reopen the
post. Kit agreed though it meant leaving Josefa again.
The fort was repaired in a short time and opened for
business but the daring attacks continued. After one
of the herders was killed and the horse herd driven
off, it was decided to cache the furs and robes taken
in trade and try to get back to Bent's Fort.

Their only animals were two pack mules that had
been tied within the enclosure of the fort. These were

loaded with all the ammunition they had and a few supplies for the agonizing walk over rough stones and cactus spines that tore their moccasins to shreds. The Indians, not satisfied to have put the white man to flight, followed menacingly at a distance. Huddling close to their pack animals, the traders repulsed an early morning attack, killing three Kiowas and several horses. Realizing this was a severe loss for so small an amount of loot, the Indians rode away without further threats. Kit and Lucien were given horses to return to Taos after a few days' rest at Bent's Fort. (The next spring Dick Wootton returned with several men to retrieve the hidden goods. After barricading themselves in the fort, they carried on what trade they could by throwing goods through a slit cut in the wall. After that, William gave up and ordered the fort destroyed to prevent it from becoming an Indian stronghold. The ruins, known as the Adobe Walls, served as a windbreak for occasional hunters. Years later it was to be the scene of two great Indian battles, one of them, Kit Carson's finale.)

For years, Maxwell and Carson, with little hope of realization, had dreamed of one day establishing a ranch along the cottonwooded creek that cut through the picturesque valley the Mexicans had named the Rayado, about forty miles east of Taos. "One of the loveliest and most fertile valleys in the world," Colonel Henry H. Inman called it. Now Lucien owned the land—the largest privately owned estate in the United States, spreading over 1,700,000 acres of Ute and Comanche territory with the Santa Fe Trail running diagonally across forty-five miles of it. Plans were laid to start building early in the spring, hoping the houses would be ready for their families by summer.

Late in November, Kit's quiet life was disturbed

by the man who, of all his friends, was least expected.
Word was brought by courier that John Charles Fremont had arrived at Bent's Fort and wanted Kit to
join him there at once. After assuring Lucien that
nothing would disturb their plans, Kit started at once
to ride the two hundred miles of the Raton route to
Bent's.

After his bitter experience in Washington, Fremont
had set his heart on a Fourth Expedition at his own
expense, with some help from Senator Benton, to explore the Rockies in winter for the purpose of advising a railway company of conditions he would find.
Fremont had had his usual dramatic send-off, this time
touched with sorrow.

While in California, Fremont had given Thomas
Larkin three thousand dollars to purchase a homesite
he had especially admired overlooking the Pacific near
San Jose. It was Fremont's plan to cross the mountains with his expedition and meet Jessie and the children who would go by boat to San Francisco. After
promising Jessie's father that they would not try to
cross the mountains together, Fremont took his family with him as far as St. Louis. The day before Jessie
was to leave for Kansas Landing to be with her husband while the expedition assembled, their infant son
was found dead in his crib. Their grief was inconsolable but the plucky Jessie was determined to go with
her husband. She stayed six weeks near the camp,
living at the log-cabin home of Major Cummings, who
was in command of the government outpost. When
the expedition started on its way, Fremont was so
touched by the pathetic sight of Jessie bravely watching the wagons disappear into the unknown, that he
rode back ten miles to be with her for another hour.

Returning to St. Louis, Jessie Fremont was surprised

and distressed to learn that General Kearny was near death at Jefferson Barracks from a fever he had contracted in Mexico and had sent for her to beg forgiveness for the unhappiness he had brought to her and her family. Jessie refused to go to him for in her grief she felt she might have borne a healthier child if she had not been forced to endure the strain and anxiety of the long trial. She returned east and sailed soon afterwards for Panama with her small daughter Lily.

It was an added disappointment to Fremont that Kit could not be persuaded to guide his company as before. Kit explained that he was not free to accept because Josefa was expecting her first child and furthermore he felt too obligated to Maxwell to leave at this time. Besides, the snow already lay deep in the passes and he agreed with the other mountaineers that it would be foolhardy to try passing through them so late in the season. All signs pointed to a severe winter ahead. "No one should do it unless he's got a head as hard and pointed and empty as a buffalo horn," was Kit's opinion. Remembering their spectacular success in crossing the High Sierras, Fremont believed no mountain could stop him. He finally persuaded Bill Williams and Dick Wootton to guide him and the company of thirty-three men with a long train of pack mules started up the Arkansas in a foot of snow.

Wootton soon turned back, declaring it pure folly to go farther but the indomitable Fremont ordered his men ahead across the Greenhorn to Wet Mountain Valley, through Mosca Pass to the forbidding Sangre de Cristos and on to the Uncompahgre Mountains of the San Juan Range. There they were stopped by the sheer ice-coated walls of torn granite that would not allow a foothold and all trail marks were buried in ever-deepening drifts. Only the tops of the tallest

pines showed above the snow-filled chasms. The poor
mules, struggling belly-deep in snow, were so famished
they tried to eat their lariats and packsaddles. Many
froze to death and toppled down the mountainside
carrying with them the precious little food that was left.

Fremont and Old Bill disagreed violently on the
course and after unbelievable suffering the company
divided with the hope that some would get back to
level ground. Old Bill had grown reckless but he still
knew every trail and stream in the high country. What
is more important, he knew when to acknowledge the
supremacy of Mountain Winter. Desperately fighting
their way back through sun-blinding whiteness, the
men watched their companions fall and wondered
whether their own fate would be to die of cold or
hunger. There was no escape from the pursuing bliz-
zards and of the thirty-three that had started hopefully, only twenty-four returned alive.[2]

Fremont was taken to Carson's home in Taos where
he remained three weeks recuperating from a near-
frozen leg. Dick Owens and Alex Godey found and
guided the straggling remnants of the disaster to Taos.
The distraught Fremont bitterly blamed Williams for
the debacle, even accusing him of cannibalism. Hearing this, Kit replied drily: "In starving times, no one
who knew him ever walked in front of Williams."
All the valuable baggage was lost with the exception
of the small trunk Jessie had packed for her husband.

As the once-energetic John Charles Fremont lay day
after day in the warmth of Kit's comfortable but unpretentious adobe home, he reflected on the agonizing
events that in a few months' time had rocketed him
to sudden fame, then dropped him to dismal defeat.
Kit had no criticism or blame for his friend whose
spirit had ebbed to the farthest point of his lifetime.

He brought out the lovely miniature Jessie had entrusted to his care and from that time on, Fremont always kept it with him. He wrote Jessie of the luxury of a cup of hot chocolate Kit had brought to him in bed and and of other kindnesses that more than repaid the hospitality she had shown Kit in Washington. He made plans for the home they would have one day beside the blue Pacific and gave the letter to Ceran St. Vrain to carry with him when he left for the East. Arriving in Washington, Ceran found that Jessie had already set sail for California.[3]

For a time it was feared that an amputation of the injured leg would be necessary but the resilient Fremont recovered completely. Most of the men of his company who had survived the ordeal remained loyal and volunteered to go with him to California. The Army extended credit through Major Beall, and Carson, Maxwell, and Owens got an outfit together and escorted the party west with sixty horses, leaving them to join the other Forty-Niners on the Old Spanish Trail.

When Jessie reached San Francisco, Ned Beale was sent to tell her that from all reports it was feared that Fremont and all his company were lost. She refused to believe that any more heartache could come to her and valiantly remained confident that her husband would return to her. While she waited, Jessie lived in the home of Señora Castro, whose husband was still in exile in Mexico. Her faith was rewarded when Fremont arrived safely back in the territory that soon would honor him by choosing him to be its first United States Senator. He learned with much consternation that Larkin had bought for himself the lovely homesite Fremont had been dreaming about through the last trying months and had used Fre-

mont's money to purchase forty thousand acres of
mountain land hardly fit for grazing. Any disappointment over the deal soon vanished when a rich gold
strike was made at Mariposa and the Fremonts found
themselves immensely wealthy.

After the snows had melted enough to get through,
Bill Williams and Dr. Benjamin Kern returned to the
mountains hoping to recover Fremont's lost equipment which Old Bill had been accused of purposely
losing so that he could find it later. Both men were
ambushed and killed by the Utes, Old Bill ending
his days in the mountains he loved with a Ute arrow
stuck in his forehead. It probably had not been meant
for him for he was friendly with the Utes who had
made him a member of their tribe. Some of the lost
articles were later found by the dragoons in the home
of a Mexican farmer.

The ranch houses on the Rayado were ready for
the families to move in by April. They stood a short
distance apart, each with a surrounding adobe wall.
The Carson house was a two-story log building, the
lower floor consisting of four long low rooms built
around a patio with a long passageway leading to a
large wooden door on the outside wall. Within the
enclosure were also several small adobes built for
the Mexican workers and outside stood the stable,
slaughterhouse, and corral.

Maxwell put up the most pretentious house in New
Mexico—a block-long adobe with an enclosed garden
and encircling veranda. The Villa, as Lucien called
it, became the meeting place of notables. Stagecoach
travelers, delayed by floods, often stayed several days
as guests of the genial Maxwell. Women were not
invited into the dining room where Indian boys some-

times served as many as thirty guests at an enormous table set with a solid silver service. Mrs. Maxwell, the former Luz Beaubien, was a large handsome woman who, like her husband, was kind and considerate to all. They lived in a kind of medieval splendor employing over five hundred Mexican workers and ranchers. All transactions were verbal and few records were kept. Money, sometimes amounting to thousands of dollars, was kept in a bottom dresser drawer and an unlocked rawhide trunk in Maxwell's bedroom.

To forestall any Indian trouble, the Utes were welcome to roam and loaf anywhere they liked about the premises. Some of the rooms were furnished in the best Spanish-Mexican manner while others were bare except for a table and chairs for poker. If there were not rooms enough the guests slept on blankets on the floor with the Utes. Like Bent's Fort, the Villa had a billiard room, dance hall, and gambling room where Lucien and Kit would sit for hours at a time playing Seven Up. "Kit was usually the winner," according to Colonel Inman, a frequent guest, "for he was the greatest expert in that old and popular pastime."[4]

Kit, at the edge of forty, solidly built, healthy and clear-eyed, appeared much younger than his years. His happiness seemed complete; the ranch was prospering; he had established a home worthy of his aristocratic wife, and he had a son. The boy, born in May at Taos, was given the name Charles in memory of Charles Bent. A heartbreak similar to that suffered by the Fremonts came into the lives of Josefa and Kit Carson when their baby, a delicate child, did not survive his first year.

Kit's grief over the loss of this much-wanted son was borne with the stolid composure of an Indian. He worked long and hard on the ranch where ten

thousand cattle and forty thousand sheep grazed on
the grassy hills under constant guard. This ranching
enterprise of Maxwell and Carson was the first instance of cattle raising as a business in the United
States. (Carson's cattle brands: CC on the left hip
and a Cross-J are still to be seen in the Southwest.)
There was a race track at the corral which was a fore-
runner of the rodeo. Carson, an expert horseman,
helped break the wild mustangs brought in from the
far mesa and joined the roping and riding contests
that were reminiscent of the trappers' rendezvous.

Barracks were built at the Rayado for a company
of dragoons sent to guard the Santa Fe Trail. In
command was Major William N. Grier, described by
one of his men as "a fatherly old man designed as a
Methodist preacher whose patriotic spirit exceeded his
religious zeal." The dragoon, James S. Bennett, who
joined the force hoping eventually to get to the California gold fields, wrote of visiting the Carson home:
"It was the first good meal I had had in many months.
He is a small sized man with blue eyes and sandy
hair but has a heart of the first magnitude!" Kit's
warm cordiality and droll humor helped to relieve
many a case of homesickness.[5]

The rush for California—if plodding along by ox-
drawn wagon can be called rushing—brought thousands of emigrants down the Santa Fe Trail past Carson's home. Santa Fe was the halfway stop, a position
similar to Fort Laramie on the Oregon Trail. Parties
usually rested there for a week or so to lay in supplies and build up their animals for the rest of the
journey. Many stopped at the Rayado and all were
given a cordial welcome to camp as long as they
wished. Few had sufficient funds to see them through
and were grateful for the large cuts of beef Carson

and Maxwell brought to their camps. Kit enjoyed visiting around the campfires and after some urging would entertain them with stirring accounts of adventures he had had before settling down to the uneventful life of looking after his herds.

A Quaker named Pancoast, stopping at Carson's place for a few days, told Kit when he got to Santa Fe he hoped to visit his friend, James B. White, a prominent merchant there. He did not know that Mr. White and his family had gone to St. Louis on a buying trip. Carson warned those planning to follow Cooke's wagon road across the Mexican border that the feud between the Apaches and Mexicans had exploded into a brutal war. The Mexican government was offering bounties of fifty dollars for scalps of Apaches ten years or older.

At this time Kit, more or less resigned to routine ranch life, did not realize that his most exciting years were before him. One October day in 1849, a captain of the dragoons rushed up to Carson's house with the horrifying news that the merchant James White and his family had been attacked and murdered by Apaches while returning from the East. Believing they were well beyond dangerous Indian territory after they had passed the treacherous Point of Rocks, White, with his wife and small daughter, a Negro servant girl and two men, had left the wagon train piloted by Francis Aubry and started ahead in their dearborn carriage. They had gone only a few miles when a band of Apaches, hiding in the rocks, sprang out and demanded presents. When White refused, the Indians killed the three men and took Mrs. White and the girls captive. The Apaches fled to their hideout when a party of Mexican traders happened along just at that time, then returned to attack the Mexicans who had stopped to plunder the bodies. All escaped except a young boy, wounded by an arrow, who feigned death until Aubry's caravan came along and took him to Santa Fe.

When the news of the tragedy was relayed to Major Grier at the Rayado, he ordered a detachment of cavalry to ride to the rescue with Antoine Leroux and a veteran scout named Fisher—both rated in a class with Kit Carson—as guides and trackers. Kit offered his services at once but Leroux refused to take a subordinate position, probably because of jealousy. This caused an unfortunate situation which may have defeated their purpose. Riding across country at full gallop to the scene of the attack, they found the ground strewn with parts of broken boxes and luggage and the bodies of the victims mangled beyond recognition. After a quick burial, the Apache trail was soon picked up. It was difficult to follow, crossed and recrossed by buffalo paths and partly covered with new snow. The Indians had cunningly tried to confuse their trackers by dividing into small parties, then meeting and dividing again.

After twelve difficult days, the trail grew fresher. They had passed several camp sites where scraps of material were found, probably dropped by the captives with the dim hope that rescue might come to them. The dragoons were in the vicinity of Las Vegas when Kit told the men that they probably would find their prey just beyond the low ridge they were approaching. Riding on ahead, he discovered the Indian village and signaled to attack at once. Instead, Major Grier, to Kit's great dismay, called a halt on the advice of Leroux, who thought it advisable to ask the Apaches for a parley. The Indians, now aware of the presence of the white men, had the advantage of firing first. Grier narrowly escaped death when a bullet lodged in a pair of leather gloves folded in his breast pocket.

Hesitation was contrary to all rules of Indian warfare. Kit was proved correct for when the delayed charge was made, the dragoons found all but two Indians had escaped and the still-warm body of Mrs. White lay quiet with an arrow piercing her heart. She evidently knew that rescue was near for James Bennett saw her start to run away from a squaw who was trying to force her on a mule's back. The Indian woman then drew a bow and sent the fatal arrow. No trace was found of the little White girl or the servant.

Kit wept at the failure which might have been avoided by quicker action, though the poor ravished woman might not have survived in any case. He did not condemn the principal guide and the commanding officer for their inconsolable bungling of the affair. The dragoons followed the fleeing Indians until forced to turn back when their jaded horses refused to go farther. Back at the Indian village, Kit found a book with pictures showing him as a great hero slaying hostile Indians and making improbable rescues. It was probably one of many paperback novels that were popular reading at that time. Kit had never before seen one of these publications and was saddened to think that he could not have led a more successful rescue in answer to the prayers of the tortured woman.[6]

The utter frustration of the exhausting days of tracking down an enemy without any reward caused resentful bitterness among the dragoons. One of them, hearing a whimpering sound in the brush, discovered a papoose strapped to a headboard and before he could be restrained, threw the child into the river. The village was destroyed and 150 fine horses, left behind by the Apaches in their haste to escape, were captured. On the return to barracks, a violent blizzard drove the dragoons off the trail, forcing them to take refuge in a stand of cottonwoods until the fury of the storm died down. One of their number was frozen to death in the snowdrifts that blocked the way. The Apaches also suffered and lost several men in the cruel storm which Kit said was the worst he had ever seen.

The White girl was never found though Congress offered $1,500 ransom for her safe return. An Apache admitted later that the Negro girl had been killed when she was unable to keep up with the others. It was also reported that an Apache chieftain appeared in Santa Fe wearing Mr. White's false teeth on a necklace.[7]

The Apaches continued their devastating raids throughout the winter, keeping the dragoons busy recovering livestock. Two herders, injured one night in an attack, managed to give an alarm. As soon as it was possible to jump into the saddle, Carson was leading the cavalrymen and three of the ranchers on a chase to overtake the culprits. Five Indians were killed and Sergeant Leigh Holbrook brought in the scalps for vouchers. Asked to explain later to the Adjutant General in Washington, Holbrook said they had been taken by three Mexican herders who came up after the fight. All the cattle were recovered except four that had been killed for food.

Shortly after this scrape, one of the ranchers who had gone on the chase—Kit's old trapping partner Bill New—suddenly found himself surrounded by a dozen or more stone-faced Apaches while working on his farm. New, an experienced mountaineer who had brushed death many times in Blackfoot territory, was caught with an empty rifle. He held his assailants off for a time with the leveled gun until they suspected the truth and rushed in upon him. Using the useless rifle for a club, the helpless man fought desperately but soon fell bleeding to death from knife wounds. It was a particular sadness for Kit to lose another of his fast dwindling circle of old friends. Bill New and Carson had trailed together along the secret beaver creeks and had left their beloved mountain haunts together when trapping days were over. Bill's ranch in the Rayado Valley had been the realization of many years of campfire dreaming.

In May of that year 1850, Kit undertook a new business venture. Taking Tim Goodale, one of his ranchers, with him, he drove a herd of thirty mules to Fort Laramie to sell to the Oregon-bound emigrants who usually needed fresh stock by the time they had reached that point. The five-hundred-mile stretch—almost straight north from Taos—was the beginning of a cattle road one day to become famous in song and story as "The Long Trail." They found a good market at Fort Laramie and sold the mules for a substantial profit. The imposing fort, built at the height of the fur trade, had been a focal point in the drama of the West and now belonged to the government. Sublette, who had built it, had succumbed to tuberculosis and Lucien Fontenelle, the melancholic aristocrat among the fur traders, had committed suicide at the fort after a scourge of cholera had almost closed it. By this time, the buffalo had retreated so far that it was necessary to go as far as fifty miles for meat. Because of this, cattle raising had begun as a big business.

Kit remained at the historic post for a month, renewing old acquaintanceships but lost the services of

Goodale, who joined the expedition of W. M. F. Magraw, Superintendent of Wagon Roads, as guide and interpreter, hoping eventually to get to the California gold fields. Magraw agreed to share with Tim the profits from the six thousand pounds of liquor "in the hollow wood (kegs)," he was carrying at government expense. Tim got no farther than just beyond the divide where the partnership ended in a bloody fist fight.[8]

Warned that the Apaches were in the area and out for hair, Kit started for home with only a young Mexican boy for a companion, believing it would be safer without a company. All along the way, keeping close to the mountains, Kit noticed Indian sign. When they reached the Greenhorn that flows into the Arkansas, Kit and the boy came upon the camp of six men who were afraid to go farther after hearing the Apaches were waiting just ahead. Kit and his companion stayed in the camp six days to "recruit" the horses but could persuade only one of the men to join him.

Starting on after dark, they traveled through the night avoiding the well-known trail. Kit religiously practiced the rule of the West: "Travel by night if things ain't right." By daybreak, having covered almost forty miles of broken country, they stopped to rest at Trinchera River within sight of the "sky-propping" Spanish Peaks. Hiding the animals in the brush oak, Kit climbed the tallest cottonwood to scan the countryside, through the shimmering heat waves that rose from the plain, for any trace of Apache movement. Kit watched for hours, squinting in the brilliant sun, until he dozed and almost fell to the ground. Since life itself might depend on this sentinel duty, he could not trust his inexperienced companions to share the responsibility. About dusk, Kit's ten-hour-long vigil was rewarded by the sight of some minute moving specks. The long view, possible only in the rarefied atmosphere of the high altitude, showed the Indians moving slowly toward them about half a mile distant. With this definite information, Kit could now move on, knowing the exact location of his enemy. They kept to the brush and out of sight and arrived at the ranch by evening of the second day. It was not, however, the end of the Apache threat for he found that a band of that tribe had made a raid on the Rayado the night before and run off with most of his stock. Major Grier had hesitated to attack such a large number of hostiles but with Kit to lead them, the dragoons soon rounded up most of the valuable herd.

In spite of constant threat of attack, the early years at his hacienda in the lovely valley of the Rayado were the most serene of Carson's life. From the ranch house which stood "at the edge of the plain and the foot of the hills," he could watch the creek "lose it-self in the great dry plain below." The ranch was well on the way to being prosperous with over two hundred acres planted. Maxwell took a great delight in his vast estate and was especially sympathetic to the needs of his Mexican workers. Often he could be seen walking barefoot through the *acequias* that ran from the river to each ranch to take a personal inter-est in some farm problem.

Colonel Inman describes an evening at the Villa:

I have sat there in the lone winter evenings when the great room was lighted only by the crackling logs roaring up the huge throat of its two fireplaces . . . watching Maxwell, Kit Carson and a half a dozen chiefs silently interchange ideas in wonderful sign language until the glimmer of Aurora announced the advent of another day. But not a sound had been uttered during the protracted hours, save an occasional grunt of satisfaction on the part of the Indians or when the white men exchanged a sentence.[9]

A great favorite at the ranch was Josefa's vivacious niece Teresina Bent, who came to live at the ranch when she was ten years old. Teresina and Uncle Carson, as she called Kit, spent many hours riding together over the extensive ranch, Kit taking the place of the father Teresina had lost and the affectionate niece filling the spot left empty for Kit with the absence of Adaline. One day, a large party of Cheyennes, Arapahos, and Comanches eluded the guard and approached the Carson house. An attack seemed inevitable. Kit called Josefa and Teresina into a back room and told them that his gun held only two bullets but if the Indians should crash through the door, he would kill both of them rather than see them captured. To the intense relief of all, the outer gate held and the hostiles were driven off.

Some of the California-bound emigrants, stopping at the Rayado, decided to go no farther and settled on Maxwell's estate. True pioneers, intending to remain as permanent settlers, were welcome but Kit was concerned over the number of fugitives and drifters continually arriving in New Mexico. One of these, a shifty-eyed fellow by the name of Fox, was hired by two wealthy merchants of Taos, Samuel Weatherhead and Elias Brevoort, to assemble an escort for their wagon freight, soon to leave on a purchasing trip to St. Louis. Fox rounded up a gang of cutthroats with the idea of attacking the merchants and capturing the bags of gold they would be carrying. The diabolical scheme was uncovered when one of the men approached by Fox confided the details of the plot to Lieutenant Oliver Taylor of the dragoons.

The young officer rode out to enlist Carson's help, explaining that he wished to have Fox apprehended for nonpayment of debt. Kit refused. He was willing to go to any length to help anyone in danger but would not be imposed upon. When the officious dragoon revealed the truth, Kit was off at forced speed through the hills leading a party of cavalrymen and hoping not to arouse the Indians. They came upon the camp of Captain Richard Ewell with a number of recruits on the way to Santa Fe and twenty-five of the men were allowed the thrill of joining the chase with the famous Kit Carson. Hoping against hope that they would be successful in reaching the spot on the Cimarron chosen for the attack before it was too late, the riders spurred their mounts on as fast as horse-flesh could travel.

By the end of the second day, they sighted the wagons pulling toward the river. Kit rode on alone into the camp asking for Fox, who could do nothing in the face of Kit's pistols. In the meantime, the dragoons had surrounded the wagons and closed in on the scoundrels. When informed of their remarkable escape, the traders were overcome with gratitude. Brevoort, almost too choked with tears to speak, offered to reward Kit, who declined, saying he had only done his duty. "If there is a God in Heaven, He will reward me after." Kit believed his own life had been miraculously spared many times and this was one way of showing his everlasting gratitude. The merchant train was left with only a handful of men to take it across the hostile-infested plains. The renegades were taken back to Taos in the custody of Captain Ewell and to Kit fell the dubious honor of turning Fox over to the

authorities. He was placed in the adobe *calabozo* at
Taos where he stayed only long enough to dig himself out. No effort was made to find him as intent to
rob was not a crime.

When Brevoort and Weatherhead returned from the
East a few months later, they brought along a pair
of handsome silver-mounted pistols as a gift to Carson. Though Kit had always lived simply, he appreciated beauty and elegance. He used silver ornaments
on his bridles and favored carved leather saddles, the
high pomelled variety used by both *caballeros* and
Indians. His favorite hunting shirt was buckskin lav-
ishly trimmed with silken braid and sturdy handmade
boots had replaced the moccasins that had carried him
noiselessly through the forests.

With a steady increase of traffic on the Santa Fe
Trail, Kit marveled at the progress of transportation
and communication in the quarter century since he
had first traveled the historic road. Mile-long freights
were not uncommon with loads valued as high as
$200,000 and insured against everything but Indians
and acts of God. Some dared to travel without armed
escort, preferring to take the big gamble and save the
cost of guards that cut deeply into the profits. Most
of them got through without trouble. There was now
more danger from bandits than Indians and some reports of wagoners stealing the cargo.

Regular mail service between Independence and
Santa Fe by overland stage had been established in
1850 with the government paying $11,000 annually
for the mail contracts. A few small packages were
carried but regular express service would not be available for several years to come. Five dollars in gold
was required to send a package weighing half an

ounce. The contractors found at the end of the first year of carrying the mail that they had lost money by operating when they counted the cost of escort, tolls, and insurance. New contracts were drawn up paying $25,000 but the actual cost to the stage companies was nearer $30,000.

The coaches were quite elegant with brightly painted bodies built high enough to ride over the ridges and cross small streams without wetting the floor. They were well upholstered for comfortable sleeping, fitted with pockets for toilet articles and a sliding drawer under the driver's seat was the hiding place for valuables. Eight passengers could be accommodated and an equal number of guards, each armed with a Colt revolver, pistol, rifle, derringer and hunting knife—altogether capable of 136 shots without reloading. Horses were changed about every fifty miles at adobe rest stations. In hot weather, if there were no women passengers—and there seldom were any— the men stripped off most of their clothing to ride more comfortably. Each carried sufficient food for the entire trip and on one occasion, a large piece of cheese from one of the lunch-baskets was successfully substituted for axle grease when a hotbox developed in one of the wheels. The fare for the jolting ride through an unfriendly country was $125 in summer and $150 in winter, with forty pounds of personal luggage allowed from St. Louis to Santa Fe.[10]

After the war with Mexico, all the old trading posts—with the exception of Bent's Fort—had been taken over by the government for military stations. William Bent had refused an offer of $12,000 for his famous establishment, holding out for $16,000. He bitterly reminded the government agents, who seemed to treat him like an ordinary squatter, that General

Kearny had used the fort in 1846 as a storage station and hospital without payment and he himself had guided the Army of the West over the dangerous Raton Pass on the victorious march to Santa Fe. William had watched the prairie fortress grow into the biggest business in the West. He had outlived two Cheyenne wives and was the sole survivor of four brothers who had helped to build the empire. Besides Charles, cruelly murdered in the rebellion in New Mexico, Robert had also been a victim of violence, killed and mutilated by the Comanches. George Bent had died of tuberculosis at the fort.

Disheartened after several years of bickering over price, William moved all his belongings to a new site at Big Timbers, an oasis of the trail forty miles farther up the Arkansas. Returning to the great old fort that had been his pride for twenty years, he fired a powder keg and watched the tawny walls blow skyward and once again become part of the prairie earth —a climactic finale to a fabulous era in the saga of America. (The first published report of the destruction of Bent's Fort appeared in the *Missouri Republican* of Independence, September 27, 1849.)

Riding out from the barracks one day to meet the mail, Grier's dragoons were alarmed to see great oncoming clouds of dust and "soldiers never practised to pray, dropped to their knees."[11] Though it proved to be only a buffalo herd instead of the feared Apache, it omened the horror they were soon to see. At a treacherous spot on the trail, the horsemen came upon the appalling sight of eleven bodies partially devoured by wolves, mailbags ripped open and the contents scattered about, and several wrecked wagons with dead mules harnessed to the broken tongues. The ground was almost covered with arrows and blank government forms which had constituted the bulk of the load the eleven had given their lives to defend. The attacking Apaches had carried away only the big rolls which they mistook for money. In sorrowful ceremony, the victims of the massacre were buried in a common grave, thereafter to be known as Wagon Mound, a great landmark of the Southwest.

The spring of 1851 found Carson once again taking to the trail, this time in command of twelve wagons belonging to Maxwell which were headed toward Missouri to purchase supplies for the ranches. To Kit, who had made so many crossings of the trail, this one was too uneventful to record. The return trip would be a very different matter.

The army responsible for peace in the new West was pitifully ill-equipped and untrained for frontier warfare. With only a little more wisdom and restraint, peace might have been maintained. Many unfortunate incidences occurred owing to the lack of experience and understanding of the Indians. One such instance indirectly imperilled Carson and his wagon train returning from Missouri.

Colonel Edwin V. Sumner, newly appointed Governor of New Mexico, was en route with a company to Santa Fe when a young Cheyenne chief, visiting the camp, was struck across the face by an officer who accused the Indian of paying too much attention to his wife's jewelry. Because of this one regrettable incident, the whole Cheyenne nation put on war paint, vowing vengeance on all white men.

It was not long afterward that Carson's wagons pulled across Cheyenne country, returning to the Rayado by way of the Raton route to spare the animals the torture of the Cimarron waterscape and take advantage of the good grass along the Arkansas. Adaline was with the caravan, returning to New Mexico with her cousin Susan Carson, the bride of Jesse Nelson, one of the teamsters. Kit had expected no trouble whatever from the Cheyennes with whom he had been closely associated during his years as hunter for Bent's Fort. He had expressed great admiration for that tribe, calling them "the durndest fighters and the finest gentlemen of the Plains."

After camp had been set up late one afternoon about twenty miles from a Cheyenne village, several braves rode up and were invited to sit and smoke with Carson, who knew nothing of the outrage that had been committed against them. As the pipe made the circle, Kit became wary when he realized they were talking in the Sioux language. They had probably done some kind of mischief, Kit thought, which they wished the Sioux to be blamed for, but he gave no sign whatever that he understood everything they were saying. As they grew more excited, they began to talk in their own tongue of their plan to knife the wagon master while he smoked, boasting that they could kill the thirteen Mexicans with him as easily as if they were buffalo. Kit sat stoical as any of them, waiting for a chance to move, then quickly jumped to his feet and drew a bead on one of the chiefs. He ordered all to leave the camp and not come back unless they wanted to die. As the Cheyennes shuffled out to their waiting ponies, Kit ordered the wagons to roll at once, then turned to console the weeping girls. "Poor plunder to have along on a war party," grumbled Pete, a veteran French-Canadian teamster.

With one hand on a whip and the other on a rifle, the teamsters urged their tired mules forward while Kit, with his finger curled around the trigger, anxiously scanned the hills in all directions for an onslaught of Cheyennes. He kept the train moving till nightfall, then ordered camp set up near the river. That night, men, mules, cattle and the frightened girls huddled together within the circle of the wagons. The only food for the hungry animals was a few handsful of grass cut with sheath knives. After the camp was still, Kit secretly sent a Mexican rider streaking across country to the ranch with a message asking Major Grier to send some men to his aid.

The wagons were well on the way to Bent's new fort by dawn with no sign of Indians until the noon rest when five braves rode in with arms upraised in the truce sign. Carson informed the Indians that one of his men was at that moment riding to bring soldiers that would hunt the Cheyenne to the last man if any harm came to his caravan. At this the Indians turned back to look for tracks that would tell them whether or not Kit was telling the truth. That was the last sight of Indians for that trip.

When the Mexican courier overtook the company of Colonel Sumner, whose headstrong subordinate had started the trouble, Sumner refused to send any of his men to relieve the endangered wagon train. Carson's message finally reached Major Grier, who sent his aide, Lieutenant Johnston, racing with a squadron toward Bent's hoping to reach Kit's train before Cheyenne fury had annihilated it. The dragoons came upon Sumner's company on the road and thirty men under Major James Carleton were ordered to join Johnston. A few hours later, Kit's wagons were spied rolling peacefully along the trail towards Big Timbers. The famous Carson luck had held once more and the Mexicans, overjoyed to tears, gave the dragoons a reception long to be remembered. This was the first meeting of Carson and Carleton who were later to be closely associated during New Mexico's most crucial years.

Safely back at his hacienda, Kit looked forward to another peaceful interlude in his strenuous life. Adaline, returning after nine years, was affectionately received into the family. The attractive well-schooled young woman, with pale copper-tinted skin and dark eyes and hair like her Arapaho mother, was a fine horsewoman and extremely proud of her marksmanship. The following year, Adaline married George Stilts, whom she had met in Missouri, and went to live on a ranch near Mono Diggings in California.[12]

During the uneventful winter of 1851-52, Kit and Lucien, reflecting on their years spent in the mountains, decided to get some of the old-timers together for a sentimental last trap. They brought out the old horn beaver bottles, oiled the rusting traps, and got an outfit together. With Kit again the leader, eighteen veteran mountain men started out with the spring thaw along the well-loved trails, looking once again for the nibbled bark and delicate tracks that would lead them to the haunts of the silken beaver. They followed the Upper Platte and traced along familiar little streams and easy valleys to the Seedeskeedee. They ate their fill of "buffalo sausage," roasted to savory goodness on forked sticks over a greasewood fire and recalled the excitement of gone-by days. They found the beaver heavy-coated and plentiful after years of being unmolested and returned home without any sign of hostile Indians. These miles in company with his old comrades, Kit said, were the shortest he had ever traveled.[13]

After six years of a rather teetering peace full of Indian trouble and discontent, New Mexico began to feel the first rumblings of unrest between the North and the South. The farsighted Secretary of War, Mr. Jefferson Davis, was bending all efforts to promote a railroad from New Orleans to San Diego so the South would have a rail line to balance the road that was pushing westward from Chicago to San Francisco. At Davis' suggestion, President Franklin Pierce sent James Gadsden, a South Carolinian, to Mexico to acquire the narrow strip of Apache land south of the Gila, the section that had been crossed by thousands of California-bound emigrants following Cooke's wagon road. After much deliberation, Mexico agreed to sell 45,535 acres of this seemingly worthless land between the Rio Grande and the Rio Colorado for ten million dollars. Senator Benton opposed the deal quoting Carson's opinion that the land was so poor a wolf could not make a living on it. Critics called it conscience money to compensate Mexico for land acquired as the result of the unpopular Mexican War.

This was the beginning of the South's plan for the Southwest in event of a civil war. New Mexico was to be a focal point. Kit Carson watched this railroad game with intense interest and wondered, with other loyal New Mexicans, if in time they would become embroiled in the balance between North and South.

The Gadsden deal with Mexico was at first rejected by President Pierce but was eventually adopted by Congress though Northern legislators feared the position of the South would be strengthened. The purchase was so unpopular in Mexico that Gadsden, who had returned as United States ambassador, was forced to leave and Santa Anna was branded a traitor for accepting the terms.

The fine new fort Colonel Sumner had built for his headquarters at the junction of the Raton and Cimarron branches of the Santa Fe Trail, was named Fort Union, to show where his sentiments lay. Standing on the Mesa Grande, "an immense plateau that rose like a blank wall a thousand feet from the plain," the adobe fortress with its newly planted rows of cottonwoods gave an impressive show of strength.[14] Convenient for supplies were St. Vrain's store and gristmill at nearby Mora. Maxwell and Carson were given contracts to supply the post with beef and hay.

They happened to be present at the new fort one day when the mail arrived. Colonel Inman, opening a new periodical entitled *Day's Doings,* came upon a picture portraying Kit Carson as a brawny buckskin-clad frontiersman holding a rifle to defend a female in dire distress with six dead Indians lying at his feet. Inman handed the paper to Kit, who put on his spectacles to study it intently. After a few minutes, Kit remarked: "It might have been true but I can't recollect doing it." Kit was frankly disturbed over the exaggerated accounts of his prowess with the rifle, some even intimating that he purposely stirred up trouble so that he could pick up a few more laurels. When asked, as he often was, how many Indians he had run off, his modest reply was: "I sometimes ran after them but most of the time they were chasing me!"

Though more settled and secure than he had ever been before in his lifetime, Kit grew restless on the ranch and, like his fellow Missourian, Josiah Gregg, he longed to be on the wild roam again. Hearing reports of the fantastically exhorbitant prices paid for goods in California, Kit and Maxwell decided to take a drove of sheep to the west coast. They rounded up an immense herd—about 14,000 head—planning to be on the way early in February "before the grass is all eat off." They divided the herd and Kit started a week ahead of Lucien with Tom Boggs and Kit's cousin, George Jackson, from Glasgow, Missouri, several shepherds, and a pack of sheep dogs. They followed the Long Trail to Fort Laramie where their visit was recorded in July, 1853. The sheep nibbled their way along the Oregon Trail to Salt Lake, then by way of the Humboldt, through Carson Pass into the Sacramento Valley, arriving at San Francisco with small loss.

As the great herd cleaned a wide swath of grass across the country, Kit gave generous gifts of sheep to compensate the Indians of the region who feared the stripped grazing land might keep the buffalo away. By such fair dealing, the drovers and their herds were able to pass unmolested through areas considered hostile. Along the Humboldt, they saw countless graves, great numbers of dead stock and broken wagons, lost or left behind by the Forty-niners. Probably fifty thousand, who had started hopefully for the golden Sacramento Valley, never saw California.

"Humboldt, all things considered is the meanest river for its length on earth. . . . no sensible man would let his stock eat grass so coarse in structure and so alkaline by impregnation if there were any alternative. Here there is none. Cattle must eat it or die —many eat it and die— Here on the Humboldt, famine sits enthroned," Horace Greeley had written.[15] Kit called it "the burying ground of horses and oxen. . . . The river is nothing but horse broth but it's all we got so we have to swallow it."[16] The grass was dry and sere and the whole region, "tiresome as Hell." Kit meant this for a true comparison. He was not a profane man—at least his friend, the great mountaineer Tom Tobin, said Carson "never cussed more'n was necessary."[17]

Kit saw again the valley Fremont had named for him, a stretch twenty miles long and sixty wide—"certainly one of the most delightful spots on the face of the earth" in the opinion of one pioneer who got through.[18] But Carson Pass was the worst day of six months and a thousand miles. It was a personal triumph for Kit, who was greeted as a celebrity in San Francisco, which had grown into a city of 150,000 in the six years since he had left. The first thing Kit did was to go into a restaurant where he ordered six dinners and ate every bite. Maxwell came in on schedule and the sheep which they had bought for twenty-five cents a head were sold for five dollars and a half on a ready market.

After a reunion of the Carson brothers and other friends settled in the Valley, Kit and Lucien started home.[19] Kit was glad to escape from the attention he received everywhere he went. He said he would rather be fighting Indians than toasted as a hero. Maxwell could not persuade him to go to San Diego by steamer. The trip on the *Cyane* was still too vivid in his memory. Filling their saddlebags with gold dust, the partners took the Gila route and successfully completed one of the greatest gambles ever planned in the West. They arrived back at Taos on Christmas Eve, Kit's forty-fourth birthday, and found the plaza and rooftops of the village lighted by the traditional *luminarias* ("little bonfires") in observance of the last day of the *posada* which all Mexicans celebrate at Christmas time.

Awaiting Kit's return at Taos was a long-hoped-for son, born to Josefa October 23. This healthy boy, dark-eyed like his beautiful mother, was named William for Kit's great friend, William Bent. This happy ending to a ten-month journey marked for Kit the close of another phase of his life. Kit Carson, the unfettered mountain man, became a dedicated family man and his pride in his handsome son Billy knew no bounds. However, a quiet life with his family was not in the offing for Kit Carson.[20]

NOTES ON CHAPTER ELEVEN

1. See Sabin, *Kit Carson Days.*

2. See Brandon, *The Men and the Mountain.*

3. Senator Benton introduced a bill to the Thirtieth Congress, Feb. 7, 1849, calling for the building of a transcontinental road which he hoped would be "a plain old English road . . . a road which the farmer in his wagon and carriage, on horse or on foot, may travel without fear, and without tax—with none to run over him or make him jump out of the way."

4. Inman, *The Old Santa Fe Trail.*

5. Bennett, *Forts and Forays* [the diary of] *a Dragoon in New Mexico, 1850-1856.*

6. Henry Nash Smith, in *Virgin Land,* suggests that it may have been a twenty-five-cent paperback novel, *Kit Carson, Prince of the Gold Hunters,* by Charles S. Averill, published in Boston, in 1849. (Rare Books, The Library of Congress.)

7. See Duffus, *The Santa Fe Trail.*

8. See Jackson, *Wagon Roads West.*

9. Inman, *The Old Santa Fe Trail;* see also Keleher, *The Maxwell Land Grant.*

10. See Hafen, *The Overland Mail;* Root, *Overland Stage to California.*

11. Bennett, *Forts and Forays* [the diary of] *a Dragoon in New Mexico.*

12. Captain James Hobbs describes Adaline as "a noble looking woman, of mixed complexion, black eyes and long black hair, and could excel most men in the use of the rifle." Adaline separated from Stilts, "a reckless man," and went to live with a family by the name of Wilson at Mono Diggings where, it is said, Kit visited her in 1853. She died young and is buried on the shore of Mono Lake, the spot marked by a monument to "The Prairie Flower," unveiled August 3, 1930.

13. See Hough, *The Way to the West.*

14. Dodge, *The Plains of the Great West.*

15. Greeley, *An Overland Journey.*

16. Mack and Sawyer, *Our State: Nevada.*

17. Hewett, *Kit Carson, He Led the Way,* (Papers of the School of American Research, Archaeological Institute of America, printed by Car-

son Memorial Foundation, Taos, New Mexico, by permission of the Museum of New Mexico, Santa Fe.)

18. Bennett, *Overland Journey to California.*

19. *Missouri Historical Review*, Vol. 6, No. 2 (January 1912). William M. Boggs, eighty-six years old, recalls a visit of his brother Tom and Kit Carson to his home at Napa, California, in 1853.

20. Philmont National Scout Ranch is now located on Kit Carson's ranch.

Indian Agent (1854-1859)

They call me friend, and their friend I am,
Although I've fought them hard and long,
For the Injun's right in the Injun's way,
And the White is mostly wrong.
ARTHUR GUITERMAN, "Kit Carson"

IMPORTANT NEWS awaited Kit. He was informed by the Mormon delegate to Washington that he had been appointed Indian agent for the Utes, Pueblos, and Apaches soon after he had left for California. Gratified that at last some recognition had come to him from the government, Kit accepted the appointment though it meant a sacrifice to leave the ranch at this time. The years 1854-61, which found Carson serving as the understanding friend and counselor of the Indians, have been slighted by his biographers yet Carson himself said the last fourteen years of his life were far more exciting than the first forty-five. Few men who served as agent to the Indians were as qualified in honesty and strength of character to be given authority over these primitive people in the great period of transition.

Christopher Carson, looking ten years younger than his age, was a man in his prime. He had grown more stout; his hair, a shade darker, was still shoulder length; his eyes were "alight with rare good humor." His voice, high-pitched but gentle, commanded respect and attention. Though more talkative, "he was inclined to make someone other than himself the hero." He was admittedly the country's most traveled man or, as a mountain man would say, Kit was a "great leg."

As agent for the Indian, Carson was responsible for a great number of resentful nomads roaming over an extensive area without definite boundaries. His charges were the most aggressive tribes of the dispossessed and discontented people slowly being pushed to extinction into the arid lands no one else wanted. The choice of Carson pleased the Indians for they trusted and respected *Vih hiu-nis,* "Little Chief." He assured them their problems would be given thoughtful consideration as long as they remained peaceful but he promised to teach them the meaning of law and order even if it meant bloodshed. As agent, he could make recommendations and report crimes but had no power to punish.

The first attempt toward administration of Indian affairs in the Southwest came March 29, 1849, when the Council Bluffs Agency was moved to Santa Fe. When New Mexico became a territory the following year, James Calhoun was appointed to serve both as governor and Indian agent. Unfortunately, Calhoun died after serving but a few months. He was succeeded by William Carr Lane, a less vigorous administrator, who was soon replaced by David Meriweather, a capable but somewhat arrogant and visionary person who was in office when Kit reported for duty on January 9, 1854.

There were scarcely over 500 Americans in the whole territory, with 60,000 Mexicans and 45,000 Indians who were at times justifiably hostile and predatory. There were not more than 10,000 in the whole Army of the United States, with 2,000 of the number ineffective. Half of this meager force was scattered across the spreading frontier to maintain order where there had never been any recognized law. The relationship between the Indians and the military had worsened through the inhumane treatment the red men had received from some of the soldiers and officers.[1]

In a letter of March 21, 1854, to Acting Governor Messervy, Kit urged the government to try to arrange a treaty with his tribes.

Something ought to be done to protect the citizens and their property from depredations. Humanity as well as the plighted faith of our government demands it and the longer it is deferred, the more serious the consequences. . . . They should be made to *know* and *feel* the power of government. Then the policy of endeavoring to induce them to cultivate the soil for a living and settle in pueblos and villages might be attended with success.[2]

To be an Indian agent in New Mexico in 1854 did not mean sitting in an office listening to complaints and doling out supplies. Trouble began to stir shortly after Carson took office when a menacing band of Jacarilla (Little Basket) Apaches came within twenty miles of Taos. Kit rode out to hold council with the chiefs and was shocked to see how pitifully undernourished they were. They agreed to be quiet when Kit promised to go at once to Santa Fe to request a supply of corn and wheat for their use. Impatient after a few days' waiting, the Jacarillas continued their devastating raids. Not waiting for Carson's return, Lieutenant Davidson, who had commanded the howitzers at San Pascual, took sixty cavalrymen into the field determined to find and punish the Apaches.

Riding through "the darkest night ever," the dragoons lost their way and became scattered in the sleet and rain of a mountain storm. Low-hanging branches knocked off most of their hats and they rode on bareheaded and numbed with cold until they located the

Apaches' village of sixty or seventy lodges hidden on Embudo Mountain near the little town of Cieneguilla. Starting toward it for a sunrise attack, Lieutenant Davidson led his men straight into an ambuscade of several hundred warriors well entrenched on the height where they could not be reached on horseback. The dragoons dismounted and proceeded on foot to drive the Apaches from the mountain but found themselves completely surrounded by an enemy well hidden in the brush. After several charges, each with a terrible loss of life, retreat was sounded at noon. James Bennett, the dragoon who told this story, though shot through both thighs, managed to escape by seizing the stirrups of two horses and dragging his body for half a mile. The remnants of Davidson's battered company reached Ranchos de Taos by midnight with thirty-two badly wounded men and no doctor to care for them. Young Bennett survived after he was given up to die for refusing to have an amputation. Twenty-four men were left dead on the battlefield and only four of the entire command escaped injury.[3]

Carson learned of the battle the following day as he was returning to Taos with Teresina Bent, who attended the Academy of the Sisters of Loretta at Santa Fe. Riding over the same mountain road Colonel Price had taken in pursuit of the insurgents who had murdered Teresina's father, Kit and his niece came upon the ghastly battle scene. Sickened at the sight and realizing the Apaches had broken their promise to him, Kit hurried over the twenty miles to Taos and returned with help to bury the dead.

After the fight, the Jacarillas had scattered in all directions on the horses taken from the dragoons, making their escape through breaks and sunken canyons choked with heavy snow. A force of forty Pueblos and Mexican volunteers was hurriedly organized to hunt down and punish the offenders. When they took to the field, Carson accompanied them both as guide and Indian counselor. It was important for the agent to be present, for one friendly Indian taken captive by mistake could lead to a devastating war with his whole tribe.

Trailing was a fascinating but sometimes grim game of wits. The Apaches were very cunning with their tricks of purposely making crooked trails, walking backwards, crossing and recrossing their path to discourage their pursuers. The soldiers finally caught up with them and a skirmish without victory followed at Nutria on the Rio Ojo Caliente where the Indians threw their dead into the river and even drowned some of the children who had hampered their escape. They fled into the distant fastnesses of the winter-bound Sangre de Cristos, vanishing so completely that Carson advised returning to Taos to prepare a full-scale campaign against them in the spring.

A figure long familiar to Kit Carson, Lieutenant Colonel Philip St. George Cooke, was now military commander of New Mexico. Though Cooke had defended Kearny against Fremont, Kit expressed great admiration and respect for this testy frontier veteran who in Kit's estimation, was as efficient as any Indian fighter he had ever accompanied. Cooke called for volunteers and took personal command of the company that marched from Taos on April 3, 1854, through the difficult Arroyo Hondo. In crossing the flooded Del Norte, the horses were at times knee-deep in snow water and some stepped in holes over their heads. After the dragoons were across, the horses were sent back for the infantry. Carson crossed and recrossed the river about twenty times and with each crossing was thoroughly drenched in bone-chilling water.

Kit soon picked up the Apache trail and Cooke's company followed "through a chaos of deep slopes, rock, snow and bogs." The horses fell through the ice that bridged the streams and the mules were so drenched they had to be repacked before going ahead. All thought of fatigue seemed to vanish when the Apaches at last were sighted. The dragoons led off at a gallop, followed by the volunteers, but once again the Indians disappeared "like deer into the forest." Kit trailed them to a high tableland from which there could be no further pursuit. With extreme regret, Cooke ordered the second expedition to return to head-quarters. Such intense hardship without result was accepted as part of frontier soldiering. A third expedition was immediately organized under Major James Carleton to start in May to find the elusive Apache.

As before, Agent Carson accompanied the expedition. For some time he found no sign of a trail. He believed the Indians were either concealed on the western slope or had gone through Mosca Pass into the valley of the Huerfano.[4] Leading the company through the difficult Sangre de Cristo Pass, Kit discovered what he believed was the path of the Jaca-rillas, though the trail was so cold that weeds had grown in the hoofprints of their horses. They traced these dim markings over Maxwell Pass where they found the remains of an Indian camp.

The Indians from the pueblo at Taos with an instinct that was truly wonderful, then led off and after winding through deep woods, a tangled undergrowth, up and down moun-tains, through gorges, across deep streams and wide marshes and through prairies and open woodlands, the column was

encamped within a few hundred feet of the eternal snows
of the northernmost of the Spanish Peaks. Here again we
found another encampment perched like an eyrie high up
the mountainside in an almost inaccessible grove of quaking
aspens. . . . From the watch in the peaks, the trail led off
to the southeast and for some fifteen miles down a beautiful,
well-grassed valley, walled in by sandstone bluffs and mantled
by open pine glades . . . and crossed Purgatory River directly
into the Raton Mountains. (From the report of Colonel
Cooke.) [5]

Carson was now on what he considered a warm
trail. As the signs grew fresher, they passed three
encampments a day. On the morning of June 4,
Carson announced that they probably would overtake
the Apaches by two o'clock that afternoon. This
calm prediction so intrigued the imagination of Major
Carleton that he promised to buy Kit a new hat if
his calculations proved to be correct.

Climbing single file directly up the side of Fisher's
Peak, through a gorge covered with timber, Carson's
spies reached the crest of the mountain which they
found to be scooped out to form a deep amphitheater.
As Kit looked down into the great bowl of earth, he
could see a herd of horses and a number of Indian
lodges at the edge of the timber. Warning all to keep
the strictest silence, Carson and Carleton, on a reconnaissance, found an opening large enough for two
horses to be driven abreast across the mesa. As the
cavalry galloped over the ridge toward the camp, filling the air with shots and screams, the Apaches, taken
completely by surprise, fled in panic into the forest.
Finding it impossible to follow on horseback, the men
dismounted, some to search the woods and the others
to descend the precipice. To do this, it was necessary
to slide down a tree hoping to find a footing on the
ledge below, then descend farther by a rope made of

two lariats tied together. At the sound of "assembly," all returned to the abandoned Indian village where they found food still cooking in the ashes of the campfire. The Apaches had fled without taking anything with them, leaving their stores of furs, skins, and dried meat. Most important to the soldiers were thirty-eight good horses, recognized as those captured from Davidson's command.

Once again the Apaches had disappeared into thin air and the expedition against them was ordered to return to Taos. During the difficult campaign, Carson and Carleton became firm friends. A few months later, Kit received the fine beaver hat Carleton had ordered made especially for him in New York and on the headband were inscribed the words: "At 2 o'clock—Kit Carson from Maj. Carleton."

Later in the summer, Kit was called to testify at a court of inquiry on the conduct of Lieutenant Davidson at Cieneguilla. The dragoon, James Bennett, quite recovered from his injuries, rode with Kit to headquarters at Santa Fe and was invited to recite Plato's "Soliloquy on Immortality" before the session began. Davidson, who had shown unflinching courage at San Pascual, was found blameless for the debacle at Cieneguilla.

Kit used the large front room of his house in Taos for the agency office and commissary, reserving comfortable quarters off the patio for his family. The house stood just off the plaza, a low adobe with portico of hand-hewn timber shading the entire front of the building. The Indians under Carson's jurisdiction were welcome to come and go freely, Kit usually meeting them out in the open, laughing and talking with them. They felt his warm, almost paternal, concern for them and called him their "Father Kit."

When not actively campaigning against the unruly ones, Carson would ride great distances to smoke and hold council with the chiefs, hoping to achieve peace among the tribes as well as protection for the scattered white settlers.

In the agency office Kit soon found himself entangled in the inevitable government red tape. Conscious of his limited schooling, Kit had hired a young clerk, John Dunn, without official consent, to keep the records and take care of the correspondence which was considerable for so small an office. Dunn also acted as interpreter and looked after the agency while Kit was required to be away for weeks at a time tracking down the marauders.

There were repercussions and many irritations. The auditor insisted that Kit sign his name "C. Carson" instead of "Kit." A signed receipt was required for all travel expenses though most of the men employed could make only an "X." There was considerable correspondence between Carson and Meriweather over inaccuracies in the records. Kit, who had never before had his honesty questioned, naïvely believed his word should be sufficient for anyone. It appeared for one thing that he had omitted his own salary from the record—the salary: $2,294.81 for the period between January 1, 1854, to June 30, 1855.

To add to the difficulty of maintaining peace, there was constant friction between the soldiers and the Indians. Over-eager dragoons from the East did not seem to differentiate between hostile and peaceful Indians. Kit was infuriated to learn one day that a corporal had stolen a horse belonging to an Indian who had come peacefully to trade at Taos. A runner was sent to recover and return the animal to the grateful Indian. "Father Kit" gave presents to those in dire need of supplies without bothering to fill in the proper forms or wait for government funds when delay meant starvation and cold for those he was obliged to care for. He probably was never reimbursed for most of it.

The continuing raids on the ranch alarmed Kit, who was often away from his family. Several young chiefs boldly came to the ranch house one day demanding food while their braves were running off stock worth ten thousand dollars. Kit recognized them as hostiles but invited them to sit at the family table. During the meal one of the Indians made brash advances to the attractive Teresina Bent, demanding her for a wife. Kit managed to spirit the girl away and pacify the Indians with gifts until he could alert the soldiers at the barracks. The Indians rode away without further trouble with Kit close behind them to recover his cattle. After this alarming incident, Kit asked further protection for both the ranch and the vulnerable mail route.

The Apache, crippled but far from subdued, had taken refuge in the hidden canyons and gorges of the Canadian River. Under their colorful Chief Blanco, they planned further trouble for the white man. Blanco, a handsome fellow but most deceitful, could always be identified by the scarlet shirt he wore.

An epidemic of smallpox broke out among the Indians soon after they had received a shipment of government goods which they believed had been poisoned. A missionary was hired at four dollars a day as a special agent to vaccinate the Pueblos, and to Kit fell the task of assuring the skeptical Indians that it was done only to benefit them. The resentful Blanco led a band of survivors through some of the worst depredations recorded in Western history, culminat-

ing in an attack on Fort Massachusetts on Christmas
Day, 1854, when more than twenty dragoons were
massacred. The Indians plundered the vulnerable
mountain fort and gorged themselves on the stores
of food until many died of overeating. They carried
away what supplies they could but left the canned
goods on the shelves because they had never before
seen cans and did not know they contained food.

The Apaches were next heard from when word
reached Kit that Blanco's men, united with a band
of unruly Utes, had attacked a Mexican settlement
eighty miles above Bent's Fort. "The general impression is that it is in Kansas Territory," was the
indefinite information Carson forwarded to Meriweather, January 7, 1855. (Kansas, newly organized
as a Territory, extended from the Missouri River to
the Rockies.) "The Utes have evidently opened the
ball by commencing war. Nothing can be done unless they are well whipt. This is but the beginning
of what they will do in the spring. They are now in
the San Luis Valley surrounded by snowclad mountains and cannot escape if troops are sent against them.
They will plunder at will when the grass comes and
cannot be captured. Blanco, I have not seen. He only
comes if he intends mischief."

Carson's letter convinced Meriweather, who ordered
Kit to trail Blanco with six companies of mounted
volunteers which he rated better Indian fighters than
the cavalrymen from the East. Captain Ceran St.
Vrain was in command and after a rugged climb, they
found Blanco joining in a scalp dance with his braves.
They watched as the warriors moved in a ghostly
circle around the scalps stretched on willow wands
stuck in the ground, each singing with extravagant
gestures to show how he had captured the trophy.

As St. Vrain's small advance party approached, the
defiant Blanco taunted and jeered, ridiculously imitating their bugle calls to the great amusement of the
white men even in so precarious a situation. His
countenance changed expression when the main company of three hundred horsemen appeared over the
ridge and the Indians fled into the breaks in the
rocks. Carson trailed them for several days before the
volunteers closed in from all sides. After several attempts to escape with heavy loss to the tribe, Blanco
asked for peace. It was a complete defeat for the in-
tractable Apache and the last expedition led against
them.

A smoke was raised and runners sent in all directions to gather together as many as possible of the
principal men of the tribe for a council to be held
at Abiquii on the Chama River. "In a few days,"
Carson wrote Meriweather, "I shall depart for the
purpose of finding the Indians. They are very much
scattered. I presume I shall have to go to Grand
River. Not being able to employ any person, I shall
have to perform the journey alone but as I know the
country over which I shall travel, I fear but little
difficulty...."

In a later letter, Carson excused those who did not
remain friendly. "They had lost their families and
had nothing to live for except revenge for the deaths
caused by the white man. They have become desperate when they ask for peace, not respectfully submitted."

One Ute, killed for his blanket, and a horse stolen
by a Mexican started a bitter war with the Utes.
After many smokes and parleys, they finally agreed to
a treaty which, on Carson's recommendation, allowed
the Utes to keep the horses they had stolen, the gov-

ernment to pay damages to the citizens who had lost them. Carson persuaded his superiors that it was wiser to reimburse the settlers than allow unauthorized persons to take up arms against the Indians. The canny Carson could instinctively tell whether or not claims were justified. With an earnest effort to be fair to all, Carson would not blame the Indians for suspected mischief until he had seen them "to find out what report they had to make in the matter." The Mexicans stole from the Indians and the Indians stole from the Mexicans and Carson was kept busy recovering horses for both. "I do not wish to be misunderstood as accusing the citizens generally of dishonesty. I only allude to the class of persons that unfortunately reside among us who are, in the estimation of all intelligent persons, inferior to the Indians."

Great tolerance, sympathy and wisdom guided Kit Carson's decisions concerning the welfare of those committed to his care. He regarded them as citizens to be treated with the same consideration as anyone else and subject to the law. Before the treaty was approved by the Senate, the impoverished Utes came to the agency so often and in such numbers that Kit used his own money to buy supplies for them so they would not turn to stealing.

Besides trailing and pacifying hostile Indians, settling accounts with the government, advising the military, and looking after his charges, Carson had to put up with constant wrangling among the other Indian agents, many of whom were dishonest and disgracefully incapable of filling their jobs. (William Bent swore that he knew of one agent, receiving an annual salary of $1,500, who retired after four years with $40,000.) Some, resenting Carson's great popularity, fabricated rumors to embarrass him, and it troubled

Kit that any responsible person would believe them.

One agent who served with great credit to himself and the government was Kit's old friend, Thomas Fitzpatrick, the first Indian agent to be named. He received the appointment in 1847 when he had gone to Washington to deliver the dispatches that General Kearny had forced Carson to hand over to him at Socorro. Fitzpatrick was wise and fair and a man of action, sharing Carson's regard for the welfare of the Indians. He had once seized a load of whisky intended for Indian trade and poured it into the Platte. In 1850, Broken Hand, who had never married, surprised his friends by taking a teen-age bride, Margaret Poisal, the half-Arapaho daughter of a trader.

About the time Kit took office, Fitzpatrick was called to Washington for a conference on Indian affairs after a disastrous meeting of the Sioux and troops from Fort Laramie had resulted in increased attacks on emigrants. The Indians showed no respect for any government overtures and set their own terms of peace, which Fitzpatrick carried to Washington. The chiefs demanded that travel over the Platte route be stopped because the animals of the emigrants were destroying the grass, the timber was being wasted and the buffalo needlessly slaughtered. They asked four thousand dollars in money and the balance of their annuity in guns and ammunition. In addition, they demanded a thousand white wives![6] Soon after Fitzpatrick arrived in Washington, he contracted pneumonia and died there. Besides his young wife, he left two children, three-year-old Virginia and Andrew, age one. This great man of the West who had served his country nobly, lies buried in an unmarked grave in the Congressional Cemetery.

Carson and Meriweather did not always see the Indian problems in the same light. Kit did not approve the treaties, submitted by Meriweather, which would require the Indian to come sometimes as far as three hundred miles to receive his gifts and supplies. Kit thought the time spent in traveling might better be used for hunting or trapping so that the Indian could try to support himself and not depend on the inadequate government allowance with no incentive to work. Furthermore, the Indian was more likely to follow the bad habits of the white man than the good, and he should be left in his natural surroundings. "Every visit an Indian makes to town causes him more or less injury."

Kit divided his time between Taos and the ranch. Besides Billy—or Julian as he was called by his mother—there was now a daughter Teresina, who was born at Taos on June 23, 1855. Kit was a doting father, taking unto his care, besides his own growing family, several nieces and nephews and any waifs who were lucky enough to cross his path.

While on a routine visit to Ulora, a Mexican village in his territory, Carson heard that a white boy was being held captive by the Kiowas and immediately hired some Mexicans to meet the Indians and barter for the boy's release. The lad, so brown he looked like an Indian, was brought to the Carson home. He could understand no English, Spanish, or French, all of which Kit spoke fluently, but could talk in the Kiowa tongue. Aloys Scheurich, a young trader who had come to call on Teresina Bent, whom he later married, discovered that the boy could understand German. Kit sent out a general description which was recognized by the boy's father living in Texas. The state legislature of Texas appropriated

"$500 or as much as may be necessary for the reclamation of the boy." Kit, who had grown very fond of the boy in the five months he had lived with the Carsons, bought new clothes for him to return to his father but would accept no payment for keeping him through the winter.

There were other cases of recovered captives, one a Navajo woman stolen by the Apaches and brought to Taos to be sold to the Mexicans. Kit solved this difficult problem by buying the woman for "two horses and articles worth $300," then informed the superintendent of what he had done. "The squaw shall remain in my possession subject to your orders. I am ready to deliver her to the Navajos by their paying the sum I gave for her or they may have her without payment as you direct."

At another time, two Mexican women who had been captured by Comanches, heard that Carson was camped near the Indian village. They escaped to Carson's camp where they were protected until they could be returned to their people.

There were still no fences on the ranches and the usually good-natured Maxwell began to voice concern over the increasing number of squatters on his vast acreage. In the more remote areas, many suffered cruelly from Indian raids on their cattle and several pastors were killed. Their only protection was a few scattered fortified towers built of adobe that served as lookouts in the faraway places. Whenever Indians threatened, the women and children ran to the *torreón* while the men rounded up the cattle and sent up smoke signals for help. Rifles could be pushed through apertures in the walls and any hostile coming too close was doused with hot lard thrown from above.

The wife of one of the settlers, who was captured and given up for dead, came crawling back on her hands and knees after the horrifying experience of being thrown over a precipice and pelted with stones. Her child, taken at the same time, was treated with kindness, the Indians taking turns carrying her on their shoulders and sharing their scarce food with her. Troops sent out from the Rayado found the girl unharmed and returned her to her home.

Calls for help came to Kit from places far beyond his assigned territory. William Bent sought his assistance in securing a treaty between his Cheyennes and the Pueblos. He wrote Kit that he expected "considerable rowing" between the Kiowas and whites and was unable to say how he would come out. He asked Kit to be on the lookout for two horses stolen from the Arapahos, "one a cley-bank horse and the other a sorrel with flee-bitten neck and flanks." Kit was a busy man.

The daily mail brought news of memorable things that were happening to Carson's friends in the year 1856. John Charles Fremont, who had served as California's first senator, received the Republican nomination for President to oppose James Buchanan under the slogan: "Free Labor, Free Speech, Free Kansas and FREMONT!" Commodore Stockton, serving as senator from New Jersey, was also mentioned for the nomination. During the campaign, which was a bitter one, Fremont's opponents brought up the subject of the crosses he had carved on various mountainsides to charge Fremont with Catholicism. He was also reminded of the three Mexican citizens he had ordered shot at San Rafael as well as the court-martial. Senator Benton died that year, an unhappy man. He had been defeated for re-election two years before, after thirty years of service, because he could not accept slavery for his beloved Missouri. A lifelong Democrat, Benton supported Buchanan against Fremont, his son-in-law.

The first train had crossed the Mississippi River at Davenport, Iowa, pushing steadily westward to the distress of Mr. Jefferson Davis and bringing nearer plows to score the sod, and buffalo butchers to ravish the plains and push the already miserable Indians still farther into the barren lands. Davis ordered a railroad survey and came to the conclusion that camels might solve the problem of transportation "in the waterless wastes of the desert."

Edward Beale, then serving as Superintendent of Indian Affairs in California, had first discussed the idea of importing camels for desert transportation when he and Kit were crossing the desolate rift of desert later named Death Valley. The notion had come to Beale while reading aloud to Kit from Abbé Huc's *Travels in China and Tartary*, which he had carried in his saddle pack for campfire reading. Kit was very skeptical of the idea and recommended against it. As early as 1853, Beale took the matter up with Secretary Davis and convinced him that the camel was "the last instrument necessary before the Pacific Railroad to bend the uninhabitable frontiers of the country into contact and annihilate the wilderness."[7]

After two years of debate and delay, Congress appropriated thirty thousand dollars to purchase "camels and dromedaries for military posts and other purposes." In February, 1856, after the governments of

Arabia and Egypt were persuaded to waive their laws against the export of camels, thirty-three one-hump dromedaries were shipped from Smyrna tied to padded stalls in a kneeling position and after three months, arrived at Indianola, Texas. Forty-four more camels were landed the following February. In the meantime, John B. Floyd, who had succeeded Jefferson Davis as Secretary of War, ordered a survey by camel corps of the wagon road from Fort Defiance to the Colorado River under the command of Beale. Carson followed this costly experiment of the first —and last—United States Camel Corps with keen interest. The indifferent beasts were able to go without water for days but were much slower than mules and could not carry as heavy loads. They would eat only thorny bushes and the bean of the post oak and the attendants brought over to care for them were even more troublesome than the camels. Beale was the only one who seemed to be impressed by their efficiency and purchased several to use at his California ranch.

Through stage lines now extended to California with regular mail service twice a month from Tipton, Missouri, the western terminal of the railroad, to San Francisco. The stagecoach ride was a great gamble against the elements and often with hostile Indians in hot pursuit. Council Grove was still the frontier settlement and only an occasional buffalo could be seen moving through the sunflowers. The mail carried at risk of life often was thrown in a heap in the corner of the station with anyone privileged to hunt out his own letters. Overland express started a year later. The largest company, Alex Major's Merchant Express, maintained 4,000 wagons, 40,000 oxen, 5,000 mules, and employed 4,000 men who were required to sign a pledge not to drink or swear on the job.

Driving for the Overland Stage Company was a young man who had idolized Kit Carson since boyhood and at twenty had a reputation for steady nerve and a shooting eye comparable to his hero. It was said that Wild Bill Hickok could slit the throat of a chicken with a bullet at thirty paces without ruffling a feather. Patterning his life after Carson's, Wild Bill, in a few years' time, was to become the symbol of law and order in the West.

Padre Martinez had continued to publish a newspaper at Taos, though his press had been smashed and the type thrown into the Cimarron. The Pueblos turned against him after the insurrection that had destroyed their mission church but the priest had an active following among the Mexicans. Rumors reached Carson that Martinez planned to stage another uprising on the tenth anniversary of the day Governor Bent was murdered. When January 19, 1847, came around, there was tense watchfulness in Taos. Kit, who was known for his tolerance and respect for law, stated that he would like nothing better than to "put a bullet into that scoundrel." The peace was not disturbed and Martinez went on his iniquitous way until he was excommunicated five years later.

The town of Cimarron was organized in 1857 to fulfill the wish of Carson and Maxwell that there would be a permanent settlement in the Rayado. In May of that year, Carson was appointed Indian agent for the entire territory of New Mexico. John Collins had become Superintendent of Indian Affairs on the death of Meriweather. Shortly before he died, Meriweather ordered Kit to discharge his clerk, John Martin. In his answer, Kit wrote: "I kept Martin in employ disregarding the order of the Superintendent sooner than neglect the duties which I have sworn truly to perform." He enclosed a report of the unpaid account for Martin's service: $535 for one year and twenty-six days at $500 a year. A few months later, Kit informed the new superintendent that Martin was sick. He died two weeks later. Kit had paid Martin's wages out of his own purse and never was repaid.

The name of Kit Carson was still news in the East. A correspondent for the *Washington Union*, after an interview with Kit, sent the following description to his paper:

He is a mild, pleasant man in the expression of his face, and no one would ever suspect him of having led the life of daring and adventure which distinguishes him. He is refined in manner and very polite—his conversation marked with great earnestness, his language appropriate and well chosen though not pronounced with correctness. He had a strong mind and everything he says is pointed and practical except when indulging in a vein of humor which is not infrequent. . . . He has a jovial, honest, open countenance and a kindness of heart that is almost feminine. He is universally loved here and a favorite of all classes, Indians included. He never alludes to his career as an adventurer unless questioned. He is heavy framed and weighs about 170 lbs.—48 years old but does not look over 35.

To Kit's great delight, Ned Beale came to visit him at Taos the winter of 1857-58. Beale, making his sixth continental trip since he had first crossed with Carson, was in command of a "mapping and measuring expedition to survey and build bridges for the Southern Route" (Route 66). The company of 130 remained in Santa Fe for a month's rest. When the expedition was ready to start on west, Beale was pleased to have his orders brought by camel in recognition of that interesting phase of his brilliant career.[8]

Early in 1858 the War Department, concerned about the relations between the Mormons and the Indians, ordered Carson to be furnished an escort to visit the Utes and other tribes in Utah territory "with the view of ascertaining how far they have been tampered with by the Mormons and of holding them firm in their allegiance to this government." Utah territory included all the land west of the Rockies to California and north of New Mexico to Canada.

A key figure in bringing about the investigation was Jim Bridger, whose fort had been burned by the Mormons in retaliation for allegedly selling arms and ammunition to the Indians. All his stores of furs, robes, supplies, and livestock were lost and Bridger faced financial ruin. He moved his Shoshone wife and three children to a farm near Westport, Missouri, which he had purchased a few years before after a prosperous trading trip. Following repeated appeals to Headquarters at Fort Laramie asking the government to take some action against "the Destroying Angels," Bridger had journeyed to Washington, the city of his youth, to appeal personally to President Buchanan, who promised his support.

Carson took sixteen men on the assignment to Utah and reported meeting the Muahuache Apache.

I could have visited them without an escort but wished for proper discharge of duty. . . . I have but little fear of their joining the Mormons. . . . I have not said that I give them more food to purchase their peace and friendship. I only give you, I say, so that it being winter and no game in your country, to keep you and your families from starving and if you commit depredations, you will be punished. Have given freely in a manner I consider most economical for the government. . . . I have ardent hopes of their friendship. . . . The Muahuaches have a stream in their country, so says those Indians, over which U.S. troops have to pass, which causes instant death by their drinking of it and for Indians it is healthy and the Good Spirit would protect them.

At this same time, Bridger was guiding the forces of General Albert Sidney Johnston toward Salt Lake City where an agreement was reached with the Mormon leader, Brigham Young, who received a full pardon from President Buchanan. Disgusted and still empty-handed, Old Gabe Bridger returned to his Westport farm to find that his Indian wife had died, leaving him with another son.

A son was also born to the Carsons the same summer, Christopher Charles, born at Taos, June 13, 1858. In his complete happiness, Kit's sympathy went out to his old friend Bridger who now had a new sorrow added to his other misfortunes.

Maxwell had come into full possession of the land grant by buying out the Miranda share for a mere $2,475. Deposits of copper and gold had been found on the estate and Lucien carried a chamois skin bag of nuggets in his pocket. However, he was so well off with the profitable ranch business that he was not interested in mining. Kit and other old-timers knew there was gold in the hills. Old Father de Smet had told of it and Marcellin St. Vrain's children had picked up handfuls of shining pebbles near Fort St. Vrain ten years before.

Just a decade after the gold fever had swept California, the glittering spotlight was suddenly turned on the Rocky Mountain region called Colorado, which was part of Kansas Territory. Kit's cousin, George Jackson, who had gone with him to California to

help with the sheep, was a key figure in the drama.
Jackson had stayed to pan for gold without much
luck, and on his way back to Missouri he had stopped
to see what he could find in the streams of the Rockies.
Enough color showed to convince him that the hoped-
for treasure might be found there. He went on to
Missouri to get a grubstake and returned the next
year on the pretext of hunting elk. Leaving his two
companions in their winter camp, Jackson slipped out
alone, January 7, 1859, and dug a large chunk of
frozen gravel out of Clear Creek with his hunting
knife. After he had thawed it over his campfire and
washed it in a pint tin cup, he came up with a sizable
nugget and half an ounce of gold dust.

The big lode was discovered in April and soon
every mountainside was peppered with rough shanties
and every stream in the region invaded by an army
of hopefuls. PIKE'S PEAK OR BUST! was the slogan carried on the billowing canvas of thousands of
covered wagons drawn from the East into the country
which the Utes considered to be their unquestioned
domain. Claims were staked and towns laid out without any thought whatsoever being given to the rights
of the Indians. The gold-blinded mob came from
every station of life, from clergymen to outlaws—a
very different breed of men from the early trapper
and later settler. Kit Carson, as agent for the Utes,
was greatly alarmed.

The Utes, who had become a peaceful and friendly
nation under Carson's wise guidance, were aroused
at the invasion and resentment soon flared into violence. A party of Tabawache Utes descended on the
mining settlement on the Conjos professing friendship
but returned with five fresh scalps. Blanco's brother,
a powerful chief of the Muahuaches, voluntarily came

to Carson's office offering to send some of his men with Kit if he would find and punish the offenders. The chief feared the miners, not knowing one tribe from another, might punish the innocent and start a war. Kit agreed that the murderers must be caught and punished without delay. Such co-operation was the direct result of the confidence Carson had inspired in his Indians. Hearing that a party was being organized on the Platte to attack his Utes, Carson wrote Superintendent Collins that such a foolhardy move could only be disastrous and asked that a company of troops be stationed at the mine to maintain some kind of order.

Kit's territory stretched over such a great area that he was in the saddle most of the time. Whenever he could get away, he spent his happiest hours romping with the children of the ranch, his own, the young Bents, Maxwell's five daughters, and a horde of small Mexicans. There were many prominent visitors to the ranch house where Josefa presided as a gracious hostess. She was slightly taller than her husband and a superb horsewoman. One day when Billy was riding with them, Kit caught a glimpse of Indians riding toward them across an open stretch. Instantly alert, he put the boy on his mother's horse and told Josefa to ride home with all possible speed while he attempted to decoy the Indians by riding in the opposite direction. It was an anxious time for Kit as he watched his loved ones gallop out of sight but perhaps not out of danger. It ended happily—just another almost commonplace incident in Kit's adventuresome life.

Sympathetic toward the plight of the Indians, Kit could not refuse when tribes beyond his jurisdiction

came to beg for food. Fearing he would fall short of
his estimates, he asked for instructions how to treat
these Indians whose families were dying of hunger.
When they continued to stream in, he sent this appeal-
ing letter to Superintendent Collins:

April 20, 1859

Col.—

I have this day drawn on you for funds. I have expended
every dollar of my private money always making it a practise
to pay down for all. I purchase whether government money
is in my hands or not.

I gave one hundred dollars in provisions to Indians today.
They have gone and say they will not return before July.
God grant it. They have nearly worried me to death.

I am Colonel,
Very Respt.
Your Obt. Svt.

Col. J. S. Collins   (signed) C. Carson

Later in the summer, Carson made another trip
to the mining district to check on the behavior of his
Utes and enjoyed a few days' visit with Dick Wootton
at the fast-growing town of Auraria. Only five years
before, Fitzpatrick had pointed out the site as a good
location for a city and the name had been recently
changed to Denver City in honor of Governor Denver
of Kansas. Carson reported finding a more friendly
feeling existing between the Utes and the miners but
cautioned all to be discreet and judicious in dealing
with the rightful owners of that territory.

By the dawn of 1860, New Mexicans were convinced
that war between North and South was inevitable.
Carson, with the government indebted to him, felt
he could not continue without a more stable arrangement for administering the agency. In January, Kit
sent this letter to Superintendent Collins: "Owing to

the present state of affairs in the East, I do not think myself safe in advancing any money to the government's purpose and if you have no money at present the Indians must wait but if you will let me know how much you will give me and I will send you receipt for same. Request John to look well to the accounts to see if there is no mistake."

Near tragedy came to Kit later in the year while guiding a party in the San Juan Mountains—the region where Fremont's winter expedition had ended in catastrophe. Kit's horse slipped on a loose stone and fell, dragging his rider by the lariat down the mountainside. In the accident, Kit received internal injuries from which he never fully recovered, though many years of active service were left to him.

NOTES ON CHAPTER TWELVE

1. Hoopes, *Indian Affairs and their Administration;* Moody, "Kit Carson, Agent to the Indians in New Mexico, 1853-1856."

2. Letters quoted may be found in the National Archives, Old Army Section, in the Department of the Interior and at the Bureau of Indian Affairs.

3. Bennett, *Forts and Forays* [the diary of] *a Dragoon in New Mexico, 1850-1856.*

4. A lone peak near Pueblo called The Orphan.

5. Cooke report to General Garland, March 24, 1854. "Mr. Carson showed his well-known activity and boldness." Colonel Cooke left Fort Union in September to report to Fort Leavenworth where he was assigned to look into Indian trouble in Sioux territory.

6. Report of Indian Agent John W. Whitfield (Ex. Doc. 30, 33rd Cong., 2nd Sess.).

7. See Bonsal, *Edward Fitzgerald Beale, A Pioneer in the Path of Empire;* Lesley, *Uncle Sam's Camels.*

8. Jackson, *Wagon Roads West.* (See Ex. Doc. 124, 25th Cong., 1st Sess., Report of Survey of a Wagon Road from Fort Defiance to the Colorado River.)

Army Colonel (1860-1863)

Men look to the East for the dawning things, for the
    light of the rising sun,
But they look to the West, the crimson West, for the
    things that are done, are done.

MULLOCH

WHILE THE leading citizens of New Mexico wagered which way their territory would go when the time came to make a decision between North and South, Kit Carson pointed out that the problem of controlling the Indians was still of most importance. He continued to stress the need for more protection and more forts if peace was to be maintained and deplored the action of hotheaded officers that had brought on much of the trouble. In his opinion, one little company of infantry and a few dragoons were no more protection than so many stumps.

The military posts, established throughout the spreading territory that had come into the possession of the United States with the Treaty of Guadalupe Hidalgo, were crude and remote enclaves scattered over a vast, almost unpeopled area. The scenery was sublime but could not altogether compensate for the monotony, danger, and lack of adequate supplies offered to the frontier soldier. The post commander ruled with a despotic power over men who were required to be woodsmen, farmers, blacksmiths and carpenters as well as riflemen.

Because of the irregular express service—delayed by Indians, lack of escort, or drunken expressmen—equipment was slow in arriving. Some posts received no funds for more than a year. The broken terrain of the Southwest was anything but ideal for maneuvers.

The horses sank to the fetlock in mealy sand and rocks and thorny shrubs cut their feet and legs. Pack-saddles broke down, requiring the soldier to carry the load, tying bread in his handkerchief and filling the sleeves of his coat with rations. Raw recruits were sent into arid areas with inaccurate maps showing streams where no water was to be found. Their spent horses had to be refreshed from chance water holes, using camp kettles and even the soldiers' hats for buckets. There were times when a pound of meat had to be divided among twenty-five hungry men. But in spite of these and other difficulties, there was less sickness in the desert country than at the river posts.

Most of the dragoons were young men out for ad-venture who made excellent soldiers. Many hoped eventually to get to the gold fields. Some were fugi-tives, or otherwise wholly unfit for service. A few, homesick and afraid, tried to desert—a feat not easily accomplished in that hostile country. If caught, the deserter's head and eyebrows were shaved; he received a lashing and was drummed out of the service to the "Rogue's March," played on the bugle. The govern-ment did not offer much inducement for better men to join the service. "The fact of a man's being a soldier seems to imply that he is not fit for other employment," commented dragoon James Hildreth, who took an unashamed joy in discovering beauty where only desert wastes had been expected. "My anticipation has carried me over the ground more rapidly than my horse will."[1] Few had any sympathy for the Indian's tragic position but looked on him as nothing more than a target for rifle practice. Some officers proudly reported the numbers killed by sabres and sent scalps home for souvenirs. Carson was horrified at some reports he had heard of the actions of troops sent out to protect the frontier and warned against the wanton destroying of the flocks and herds of peaceful Indians who would be forced to steal or starve.

Such was the condition of military posts in the Southwest with a civil war looming dark on the far horizon. In November, 1860, a Kentuckian not nearly as well known as Kit Carson, was elected President of the United States and before he took office, six Southern States withdrew from the Union, choosing Jefferson Davis to be President of the Confederate States of America. While Secretary of War, Davis had secured the appointment of men sympathetic to the South to fill important posts in New Mexico, believing, in the event of war, the territory would unite with the Southern Confederacy.

In spite of his Kentucky-Missouri background, Kit Carson remained a loyal Union man. A month after war was declared, May 24, 1861, he resigned as Indian agent to accept an appointment at lieutenant colonel of the First Regiment of New Mexico Volunteers under the command of Colonel Ceran St. Vrain. At Kit's suggestion the Indian Agency was moved to Maxwell's ranch to get away from the distilleries at Taos.[2]

New Mexico found herself gradually being cut off from the rest of the nation. Stagecoaches discontinued their runs and mail service was paralyzed. Finally, in desperation, Colonel William Russell of the freighting firm of Russell, Majors and Waddell, came up with a plan to carry the mail by horsemen. He had thought of it first while crossing the Hasting's Cutoff to California in 1846. By posting relays, a Santa Fe trader, Francis Xavier Aubry, had made a spectacular dash from Independence to Santa Fe in five days and thirteen hours to set a record, win a wager from Carson, and convince Russell that pony express was possible. There was quick response to his advertisement calling for "Young skinny wiry fellows not over 18. . . . Orphans preferred. Wages $25 per week."

On April 3, 1860, riders started simultaneously from St. Joseph, Missouri, and Sacramento, California, streaking across the formidable country alone and unarmed on their small ponies. Relay stations were posted every fifteen miles or so with fresh mounts waiting. Each rider could cover about seventy-five miles a day on half a dozen mounts, the mail carried two thousand miles in nine days. Five dollars postage was charged for half an ounce and a maximum load of twenty pounds was allowed. The mail, written on tissue and wrapped in oiled silk, was sealed in a leather pouch that was unbuckled and ready to be thrown to the man holding an impatient fresh mount at the relay station. To keep up with the exacting schedule, the rider should be on his way after two minutes. He rested at the end of his run until he received the mail from the other direction, then galloped back over his trail. Eighty riders were on the road at the same time, forty headed west and forty riding toward them. Though the plan was carried out with efficiency, it was to function only for a year and a half.

As the telegraph line was strung east from California to meet the wire from the East, the need for the Pony Express diminished, in the end, running only between the gap or carrying messages between wagons. The transcontinental telegraph was completed October 24, 1861, at Salt Lake City, the first message proclaiming the West loyal to the Union. This marked the end of the Pony Express, a costly experiment not paying a tenth of the cost of operation. Only one mail was lost and the record ride—320 miles in 21 hours on 20 horses—was held by a fourteen-year-old Kansan named William F. Cody, later to become famous as "Buffalo Bill." The record cross-country run carried Lincoln's Inaugural Address to Sacramento in seven days and seventeen hours, a giant step forward since Kit Carson had carried the first overland mail fourteen years before.

Lieutenant Colonel Carson was assigned to headquarters at Albuquerque to enlist and drill a company of raw recruits, most of whom were Mexican farmers hoping to earn a little money for their families. No better choice than Carson could have been found for he understood their problems and molded them into a loyal, effective unit. Josefa and the children came to live with Kit at the Officers' Quarters where another son, Charles Christopher, was born August 2, 1861. Kit continued in his favorite role of loving father, sometimes giving military matters second place. He was probably the most unsoldierly officer in the army and could be found romping on the floor with his children swarming over him, searching for candy in the pockets of his uniform. But no officer was more loved and respected by the men under his command. In September, Carson was elevated to the colonelcy when St. Vrain resigned his commission for reasons of health.

During the first months of the war, New Mexico seemed on the verge of disintegration. The posts were almost without funds, the nearest telegraph was a thousand miles away, and the morale of the soldiers was at low ebb. Several high-ranking officers resigned their commissions to go over to the Confederates, among them, Colonel H. H. Sibley, who left his command at Fort Defiance and took over the rebel force at Fort Thorne, above El Paso. Later Sibley confided to friends that he regretted his "sickly sentimentality" in not taking his entire command with him. Colonel W. W. Loring, who had been assigned Commander of Forces in New Mexico, went over to the Southerners three months later, to be replaced by Colonel Edward R. S. Canby who, incidentally, was Sibley's brother-in-law.

It was reported that many officers stationed at the isolated desert post, Fort Fillmore, "were avowedly with the South and holding on to their commands to embarrass the government and at the proper time turn everything over to the South." Expressmen were offered bribes to deliver their goods to El Paso instead of Santa Fe. No effort whatever was made to recapture horses stolen from a mounted company stationed there though the soldiers pleaded to be allowed to recover their mounts. The officers not only tampered with the loyalty of their men but even ran up "a disunion flag."

Early in 1861, the section of New Mexico called Arizona voted to join the rebel cause. A third of the newly organized territory of Colorado was openly sympathetic to the South and two hundred Confederate partisans began drilling secretly at Mace's Hole, a hideout near Pueblo. Taos was bitterly divided. As a native Kentuckian who had grown up in Missouri, the rebel group had expected Carson to side with them as his brothers had. But Kit stood firm. When a crowd of rebel Taosenos gathered from the stores and saloons to hoist the Confederate flag in the plaza, Kit, with fire in his eye, walked unarmed into the

milling crowd, shouting in a shrill determined voice:
"Don Fernandez de Taos has been Union since 1847
and will stay Union. I will not be here much longer
and I want you to see that the flag stays up there!"
Then he helped Captain Smith Simpson nail the Stars
and Stripes to a cottonwood pole and set it in the
dusty plaza where the whipping post had stood. (The
flag still flies there night and day—one of five places
in the United States where the flag is never lowered.)

During the first year of the war, all the fighting
in New Mexico was between red and white men with
the army alert for any movement of Confederates in
Texas. The transcontinental railroad pushed steadily
westward, following the telegraph route. Neither war
nor Indian peril slackened the great "moving mass
of humanity," spreading slowly across the continent
toward the treasure fields and free lands of the West.
Courageous nesters built solitary houses of sod and
dug into the virgin soil wherever they found a favored
spot, determined to challenge the red man's right of
possession.

When Carson's company was moved to Fort Union,
the most strategically placed fort in the Southwest,
Josefa and the children returned to their home in
Taos. Kit led his volunteers into the field for what
he called a "searching scrutiny" to examine the mountain passes. He reported to Colonel Canby that he
believed it would be impossible for a force to make
a surprise attack. "Should the Texans attempt to
march upon the place, I shall fight them for every
inch of ground that I can make tenable and the country is well adapted for this kind of fighting."
The mail service had stopped altogether with the

burning of several bridges in Missouri and the pay-
master was unable to get through with any funds for
the forces on the frontier. With no money to pay
the dollar a day promised to the volunteers on en-
listment, they became an unhappy, disgruntled lot.
If it had not been for their love and respect for Carson, the volunteer company might have disintegrated
altogether. Abraham Lincoln had commanded a similar company of volunteers during the Blackhawk War
and, like Carson, had more success than officers trained
in the military because of his understanding and sympathy for the common soldier.

Rumor was almost the only source of news. A
widely circulated report that Mexican troops were
massing to march against Texas gave some faint hope
to the Union commanders in New Mexico bracing
for an attack from the Lone Star State. By February,
1862, the Confederates had occupied the lower half
of New Mexico. Rebel General Baylor had moved
from Fort Bliss at El Paso to Fort Fillmore at Mesilla
and reported "the road for five miles lined with panting famished soldiers who threw down their arms
. . . and begged for water." Major Isaac Lynde, the
Union officer who surrendered the fort without contest, was condemned later as more incompetent than
disloyal and dropped from the Union rolls.

General Baylor, confident the South was on the way
to victory, declared Mesilla the capital of Arizona.
"So far, Mr. Lincoln is not making much headway in
suppressing the rebellion. He has got himself thrashed
at every fight from Manassas to Mesilla and today we
dare them to attack us at any point." Confederate
Chief Justice McWillie wrote President Davis suggesting "it might be profitable to spend ammunition
on the game in New Mexico."[3]

The all-out Confederate drive against New Mexico began with Sibley, now a Confederate general, marching from El Paso with 3,500 men, most of them under twenty-five years and "the best that ever threw a leg over a horse." Sibley believed all of New Mexico would fall easily, leaving the road open to California where Jefferson Davis had envisioned a separate western republic sympathetic to the South. Gold from both California and Colorado would greatly strengthen the Confederate chance of success.

With Fort Union and Fort Craig the only important posts left to the North in New Mexico, Canby dispatched a courier with all haste to Governor William Gilpin, of Colorado, to send his company of Pike's Peakers to the defense of Fort Union, the main supply center. Colonel Carson and his volunteers were ordered to Fort Craig, midway between Santa Fe and El Paso, to keep Canby informed of Sibley's movements. Canby, with 5,500 men under his command, concentrated his strength at Fort Craig, "the best and the prettiest fort in New Mexico set in a grove of cottonwoods on a tableland above the Rio Grande." Here he must make a stand to protect Fort Union or all would be lost.

The Confederates were expected to bypass Fort Craig and move directly to Santa Fe but instead, Sibley took a stand "sheltered in the innumerable ridges of volcanic rock," directly opposite the fort. Canby held fast, refusing to be drawn into a battle at this point but wondered anxiously if Sibley was aware that many of his impressive cannon were merely painted logs. A severe dust storm delayed any Confederate action and after five days of worrying the Union men, Sibley moved a few miles farther "to a plain . . . just north of the high table mountains," the site of the abandoned rancheria of Val Verde.

Expecting to nudge Sibley on toward Santa Fe, the Union forces marched from Fort Craig on February 21, 1862, led by Colonel Canby and with Governor Henry Connelly as a spectator. Instead, they found the Confederates firmly entrenched in the heavy timber of the canyon with their batteries hidden in the old river bed. A Union charge held the Confederates from crossing the river but as Canby's men followed, Sibley opened fire with everything he had, including double-barreled shotguns. His men rushed down to the very muskets of their opponents, their bravery said, by some, to have been as much an effort to get to the water to satisfy their thirst as to fight Union soldiers. Carson was ordered to hold one end of the battleground. The one mounted company under his command, led by Captain Rafael Chacón, pushed a detachment of Texan lancers across the river and took protection in a thick grove only to find themselves under fire from their own artillery that came so close that shattered branches fell about their feet. Chacón's command, the only Union men to get to the east bank, succeeded in lassoing an enemy gun that had kept a steady fire on them and in hauling it off "cowboy fashion."

In the general confusion, neither side knew who had the advantage. It was impossible for Canby to use his cavalry in the fierce hand-to-hand combat for fear of trampling his own men. Three horses were shot from under the harassed Union commander. As the battle progressed, most of Carson's green volunteers, inherently afraid of Texans, ran from their position, leaving Kit and a handful of officers to hold firm with a few scattered batteries. Finally, to end the massacre, retreat was sounded an hour before sunset. Canby ordered his men to get back to the fort any way they could but he refused to surrender it to Sibley. Carson's cavalrymen, stranded far into the enemy lines, managed to escape through fire from the Union guns which luckily fell too short to cause harm. The final score was 40 Confederates killed and 100 wounded; 68 Union men killed and 160 wounded. Carson lost one man. Valverde was "the bloodiest battle for numbers involved in the whole Civil War."[4]

This was the first and only time that Kit Carson, veteran of many Indian fights, would witness a genuine military action with trained army officers pitted against each other. He vigorously defended those of his company who had run away from the battle, pointing out the fact that they had not been ordered into the central position. He charitably suggested that they be promptly discharged and allowed to return home to prepare their lands for spring planting rather than hunted as deserters.

Valverde was a Confederate victory but Sibley's laurels soon wilted. In spite of the fact that handbills had been circulated through the mining towns offering high prices for lead, shot, and arms, the citizens of New Mexico did not defect as Sibley had anticipated. The rebel army arrived at Santa Fe, March 23, 1862, to find the government offices had been moved to Las Vegas. After raising the Confederate colors, they advanced toward the grand prize, Fort Union, which had bolstered its strength with the arrival of 1,400 Pike's Peakers.

The opposing forces met March 26 at Glorieta Pass, a deep and narrow gorge used mostly by the Apaches. After an initial firing, both sides drew back. Colonel John M. Chivington, a giant of a man and an or-

dained minister, took five hundred Colorado Firsts
on detour and cut off the Confederate supply train
of eighty wagons with a guard of two hundred. The
wagons and goods were burned, the animals stabbed
or herded over the steep mountainside and the Confederates bottled up. Chivington showed remarkable
military skill for an untrained man and this un-
planned maneuver was the decisive defeat for the
South in New Mexico.

Neither Canby nor Sibley was present at Glorieta.
Canby remained at Fort Craig and Sibley was absent
"due to illness and weakness that made it necessary
for him to retire early"; the "weakness," described
by his critics, as an overfondness for the bottle. The
Confederates were permitted to take their dead and
wounded from the field but under the white flag
picked up a load of weapons as well. A few minor
skirmishes followed and Sibley was allowed to return
to Texas after his men had taken the oath of allegiance to the United States. Many would have stayed
where there was food but Canby found it impossible to care for 1,500 prisoners of war. Mrs. Canby
—Sibley's sister—helped to care for the Confederate
wounded, "capturing more Confederate hearts than
the old General ever did Confederate bodies."[5]

The rebel force finally got back to El Paso, hungry and thoroughly disillusioned after the Indians had
made their retreat as uncomfortable as possible by
throwing dead sheep in the only wells and harassing
them however they could. In spite of overtures by
the Confederates, the Indians had remained loyal.
Their devotion to the Union was of tremendous importance in the final accounting and Kit Carson was
directly responsible for their unwavering loyalty. The
battles of Valverde and La Glorieta, the only clashes

between North and South in New Mexico during the war, were of great strategic importance for New Mexico stood firm as a bulwark against a Southern drive to the Pacific.

Colonel Carson was left in command of Fort Craig with seven companies of his own regiment, two of the Second and one of the Fourth New Mexico Volunteers. His orders read: "The fort is to be held to the last extremity and the manner of doing this is left to your judgment and discretion." Governor Connelley, in a letter sent April 13, 1862, to Secretary of State William H. Seward, commended Colonel Christopher Carson for his zeal and energy and Carson's role as a key figure in the Southwest campaign was brought to the attention of President Lincoln.

An officer, serving under Carson, who shared his regard for the lowly Indian and the common soldier, was Lieutenant Colonel E. V. Wynkoop, who became Kit's close friend and confidant. One day at Fort Craig, as they listened to a fellow officer read aloud from the exploits of William the Conqueror, Kit was struck by the hero's favorite exclamation: "By the splendor of God!" Afterwards, Carson and Wynkoop, on their daily visit to the wounded men at the post hospital, found a sergeant quarreling with a convalescent patient and saw him draw a knife to threaten him. Carson, bringing up his pistol, stepped between the men, shouting in his high-pitched voice: "Drop that knife, or by the splendor of God, I'll let daylight through you!" Colonel Wynkoop said later that was as near an oath as he had ever heard pass Kit Carson's lips.[6]

Colonel Wynkoop was with Kit when he led a detachment toward the town of Albuquerque, which then was only a collection of dilapidated mud huts

on crooked lanes. At the ford of the river, flooded
with melted snows, they came upon two boatloads of
gaily bedecked Mexican girls on their way to the
cathedral across the river. As they were about to push
off, a rough-looking Mexican youth leaped into one
of the boats and refused to leave. Fearing the added
weight might capsize the boat, the boatman ordered
the ruffian out. Carson, watching this little drama,
swung down from his horse and tried without success to reason quietly with the young man. When a
more vehement tone failed, Kit raised his sheathed
sword and struck the obstinate fellow such a blow
on the side of the head that he toppled into the
water. Instantly, Kit jumped in and pulled the of-
fender to safety. Dripping wet but still in command,
Colonel Carson remounted and the company swam
their horses across the swollen river to be acclaimed
by the boatman and the grateful *señoritas*.

John Charles Fremont, commissioned major general, was at this time in command of the Department
of the West, stationed at Fort Leavenworth, with Wild
Bill Hickok as his Brigade Wagon Master. Fremont
had been in England at the outbreak of the war. He
offered his services and was given unlimited power
to organize and equip a hundred thousand men. He
accomplished this in three months' time, having to buy
and manufacture most of the clothing and weapons
and using some of his private funds. Fremont, who
remained a controversial figure, was relieved of his
command. The fact is sometimes overlooked that it
was Fremont who was first to recognize the potenti-
ality of an unpopular lieutenant named Ulysses S.
Grant and gave him his first independent command
contrary to the advice of the War Department.[7]

Another of Carson's great friends, Brigadier General James Carleton, was moving toward New Mexico with the California Column of 2,350 men and a large supply train. Three separate dispatch parties had failed to get through to headquarters. After enduring the varied tortures of floods, drouth, and Indian attacks, the army arrived at Mesilla in no fighting condition. Carleton found the Confederate headquarters moved from Mesilla but received no welcome from the citizens. The *Mesilla Aza Times* printed an account of Carleton's arrival from the west with a great number of wagons loaded with everything they could not carry horseback, adding the information that the settlers were "anxious to be rid of those locusts." This issue also carried the report of "a big fight at Manassas—10,000 federals killed and wounded . . . federals flying perfectly panic-stricken." Carleton announced the formation of the territory of Arizona with this exhortation: "Every man who has the development and prosperity of Arizona at heart must put his shoulder not only to the wheel but to his rifle!" Carleton then moved on to replace Canby as Commander of Forces in New Mexico.[8]

During the years immediately following, Carson and Carleton worked closely together, both devoted to achieving a lasting peace with the Indians and providing for their welfare. With only a handful of men, considering the far-reaching area under his command, General Carleton held firm against both hostile Indians and rebel Texans. As the tide turned against the Confederates, many of their soldiers deserted to the North for want of food, which farmers would not sell for Confederate money. Hunger also tamed the mighty Navajos.

NOTES ON CHAPTER THIRTEEN

1. Hildreth, *Dragoon Campaigns to the Rocky Mountains.*

2. Carson was succeeded by W. F. Arny as agent. G. W. Leihy was appointed to the Superintendency, serving until 1866. When G. W. Dent, brother-in-law of General Grant, was sent to replace him, he found Leihy and a clerk killed by the Apaches.

3. See Keleher, *Turmoil in New Mexico;* Waldrip, "New Mexico During the Civil War" *(New Mexico Historical Review,* July, 1953); Walker, "Causes of the Confederate Invasion of New Mexico" *(New Mexico Historical Review,* Vol. VIII).

4. See Crimmins, "Battle of Valverde" *(New Mexico Historical Review,* Vol. VII).

5. See Santee, "Battle of La Glorieta" *(New Mexico Historical Review,* Vol. VI).

6. Cowles, "Genealogy." See letter from Frank M. Wynkoop to Colonel Calvin D. Cowles.

7. Heitman, *Historical Register and Dictionary of the United States Army.*

8. General Canby was killed by Indians while attending a council with the Klamath and Modoc at Klamath Lake, Oregon, near the site of Fremont's camp.

Brigadier General (1863-1865)

Yet he is called a heathen
Who always lived with God.
CHARLES RUSSELL

THE NAVAJO NATION was scattered far through a broken sand-rock desert and, unlike other tribes of the Southwest, had never accepted Christianity. "The land is one of unearthly grandeur where natural rocks take the shapes of towers, temples, palaces and fortresses of mountainous height, blazing scarlet in color, and on one side lies the Painted Desert where sands refract light like a colossal rainbow."[1] They were a clean, proud, and handsome people who had turned to agriculture and made the desert blossom in the few fertile stretches along streams hidden deep in chasms and ravines. They raised immense herds of sheep to furnish wool for artistic and beautifully woven blankets that were their chief articles of trade.

Three expeditions directed against them had failed to bring the Navajos from their fearsome canyons. The treaty Colonel A. W. Doniphan had reluctantly obtained from them in 1846 was soon disregarded. They had been warring with the Mexicans and Pueblos since ancient times and did not think it was any business of the United States to interfere. With the discovery of gold in Arizona, bringing in a wave of immigrants, the Navajo forays had become increasingly more bold and bloody.

In spite of their lawlessness, Carson had always held this tribe in admiration. In a report dated August 31, 1858, he had written: "As Indians generally learn

the vices and not the virtues of civilized men, they
will become a degraded tribe, instead of being as
they are now, the most noble and virtuous tribe within our territory. Humanity as well as our desire to
benefit the Indian race demands that they be removed
as far as practicable from the settlements."

Kit had long advocated the reservation policy drawn
up by Edward Beale, setting apart special lands for the
various tribes, as the only just solution to the Indian
problem. They had to be cared for or they would be
annihilated, for nothing has ever stayed the white
man's ambition. Early in 1863, General Carleton
and Colonel Carson planned a campaign to force the
Navajos into submission by systematically destroying
their crops and driving off their sheep. It was Carleton's dream to place the mighty tribe in a spot known
as the Bosque Redondo ("Round Grove"), where
the California Column had built Fort Sumner on
the Pecos River. Though only a row of low adobe
barracks with a parade ground and corral, Carleton
called it "the handsomest and most picturesque in
the country."

In October, 1862, Colonel Carson had been ordered
to Fort Stanton, which had been abandoned with
Lynde's surrender of Fort Fillmore and was later
burned by the rebels. Carson reported:

I found the post a mass of ruins; all floors and windows burnt
even walls damaged so that I have hardly any hope to see my
command under better shelter this winter than the Sibley
tent affords. Roofed and made serviceable a commissary and
quartermasters store room. Hostile Indians all around and
orders to chastise them besides watching the rebels of the
Pecos, for the greater part of my command will be constantly
engaged upon active service protecting the public herds. How
then can I repair this post, I mean repair it sufficiently to

give protection against the winter, usually severe in this part of the country. . . . Horses in poor condition, many perfectly worthless. Less than fifteen days supply of corn. The grass is very scarce. The hay to be furnished is in coarse bottom grass fifteen miles distant.

Manuelita, a chieftain of the Mescalero Apaches, came voluntarily to Carson's camp to say he wished to be at peace with the white man and would fight Confederates or any other enemy of the United States. "When the moon is nearly gone, he will go to Santa Fe with the principal chiefs to make a treaty with Collins. They are destitute of clothing and it might be well to furnish them a small supply for the present time," wrote Carson to Headquarters. But before the right time of the moon arrived, one of Carson's officers, Captain James Graydon, met and attacked a band of thirty Mescaleros and among the eleven slain was Chief Manuelita. At Carson's insistence, Carleton ordered the seventeen mules, captured by Graydon, returned with an apology to the Apaches, whose faith in the integrity of the United States was badly shaken.

While at Fort Stanton, Colonel Carson was put to the severe test of dealing with a revolt among his cavalrymen, instigated by an officer who objected to the one Negro in his regiment and urged his whole company to desert to the Confederates. In the midst of this discontent, Dr. J. M. Whitlock, a close friend of Carson, arrived at the fort. The doctor had published an article condemning Captain Graydon for his treatment of the Indians, accusing him of inviting several Apaches to drink Mescal wine until intoxicated, then coldly shooting them down. When Whitlock refused to retract, Graydon challenged him to a duel. Both men were wounded on the first shot and Paddy Graydon was killed on the second. When the captain fell, the men of his command turned on Dr. Whitlock and massacred him. His body was rolled into a ditch and pierced by a hundred bayonet thrusts as the company passed by. At this point, Colonel Carson arrived on the scene and ordered the entire company to disarm. Order was maintained by Kit's firm command of the situation and the belligerents eventually were restored to duty.[6]

Constantly by Carson's side from the start of the war was his devoted aide, Captain Albert H. Pfeiffer, a graduate of the Stockholm Military Institute. Pfeiffer had married a beautiful Spanish girl named Antonita. Her wedding gown, handmade at the convent, was said to be the loveliest ever seen in Santa Fe. Before leaving on the Navajo campaign, Captain Pfeiffer and his wife had gone, with two servants and a six-man escort, to enjoy a short leave at the desert spa, Hot Springs. While the captain was relaxing in the steaming bath, a band of Apaches suddenly rode up and killed the lovely Antonita. Without waiting to dress, Pfeiffer rode after the Indians and was shot by an arrow which he pulled through his leg, leaving him lame for the rest of his life. After the tragedy Carson took Pfeiffer's small son, who was his godchild, to live with Josefa and the children at Taos. Pfeiffer, recklessly vowing vengeance on the Apaches, became known for his daring as "the soldier who always receives a wound but comes out alive."

Kit was sent to Taos to enlist a hundred Utes for the campaign. He wanted the Utes because they were "very brave, fine shots, fine trailers, uncommonly energetic in the field and Navajos entertain a great dread of them." Headquarters for the campaign were set up at Las Lunas on the Rio del Norte, with sixteen officers and 290 men answering the muster call.

It was a strange aggregation, most of them without uniforms, and what few there were, were handmade by the soldiers' wives from whatever material was available. All-blue uniforms had not yet arrived for the officers and some units were still in gray. Carson noted in his report that the New Mexico Volunteers had not yet received "one single cent of their pay due them for 12 Or 13 months, neither have they been furnished by the government with their allowance for clothing."

The troops were divided into several parties, each taking only a little sugar, flour, coffee and salt, depending on "beef or sheep on the hoof" for their food. Kit sent them out with the warning that the only way to hunt Indians is to move silently or accomplish nothing. The volunteers made a clean sweep of the canyon-crossed country, driving before them great herds of sheep. They lived off the Navajos' pumpkins, melons, and beans, and took grain for their animals, destroying or caching the rest to force the Navajos to emigrate or go hungry. Thousands of fine peach trees were cut down, a large number, by mistake, belonging to the peaceful Hopis. It was not without regret and admiration for the primitive farmer that had made them flourish in that arid land.[2]

It was a difficult campaign. Constant rain soaked the soldiers' packs and midday sun was often past endurance. There were all-night marches without a halt in search of water over barren trails pitted with prairie-dog holes and no sign that anyone had traveled over them in months. Perilous canyon walls were ascended with courage and "an awful lot of profanity in English, Dutch and Spanish." Wild roses were found growing by cool springs deep in the chasms and more than one dragoon wrote home that their sweetness had not been wasted on the desert air. The young men carved their names in foot-square letters on the smooth sand rock, the same as Navajo youths, centuries before, had drawn figures of men and animals to record the history of their people.

After evening mess, Carson would pull up his camp chair to listen to the reports from his men as they sat around him in a semicircle, smoking, and drinking coffee (black soup). Kit preferred a brier pipe but most of his officers smoked the more fashionable Meerschaums. A game of draw poker usually followed with a can of fruit, a chicken, or some lemonade sugar for stakes. Lieutenant Nelson Thomasson, a nephew of former Governor Meriweather, in telling these experiences, said Colonel Carson did not want to hear discussions of religion and theology. Whenever the conversation turned in that direction, he would turn his back and puff hard on his pipe until the subject was changed. "He was a believer in pure religion. Man was his creed. Man must never do anything in the daytime that would make him repent thereof when night came."[3]

The men of his command idolized the "Little Colonel" and begged him to tell of his experiences and exciting adventures as they lay feet to the fire wrapped in their blankets. He was modest but, to please them, he would often respond with much gesturing and expressions of rare droll humor. A favorite story told of the time he was chased by a horde of wild Comanches until his horse fell from sheer exhaustion. Losing his rifle in the fall, he pulled out his skinning knife and ran into a large fissure in the rock with the Indians in hot pursuit. The split in the rock narrowed until he found himself wedged in with an Indian screaming at his very heels. As he swung at his assailant, his knife hit the rock and broke off at the hilt just as the Comanche reached out for his scalp. At this point Kit would pause and puff on his pipe while the listeners waited breathlessly. "Then, what happened?" was the cry. "Well," Kit drawled, "then the Indian killed me!"[4]

The main body of the Navajo had come together at the sound of the war drum and took refuge in the spectacular Canyon de Chelly which, from ancient times, had been their impregnable stronghold. The sheer walls of red sandstone rose a thousand feet above a river bed which was strangely dry during the day but sometimes ran six inches deep at night. As the white men entered the hitherto unpenetrated chasm, the Navajos made a brave attempt to hold them off. Double guard was posted at night but there was little sleep with the demoniacal yelling of the Indians trying to stampede the herds. After a few shots in the air, the noise would stop only to begin again with triple strength, then die away. The Indians rolled huge stones down from the great heights above and clambered like mountain goats over the rocky ledges to let their useless arrows fly and fall below. "It was much like a bull trying to butt off a locomotive," wrote one dragoon.[5]

On this first excursion into the forbidden canyon, there was little shooting. Only one soldier was killed, Major Cummings, who had rushed ahead of his command into a dog-leg cañoncito to be hit by an arrow. The sadness felt by the loss of this popular officer was somewhat overshadowed by the arrival of an express from Fort Defiance, telling of the capture of Vicksburg by the Union forces six weeks before. Though far from that part of the conflict, the news caused great

excitement among the men camped deep in the gro-
tesque chasm of the Southwestern desert.

After months of scouring the country and scorching the earth, Carson moved his forces to Fort Defiance, recently renamed Fort Canby, where he found
twenty-seven Navajos waiting for him. They were
completely destitute and almost naked. They had
attacked a wagon train, killed the wagon master, and
had butchered one of the mules for food, yet Carson's
great heart suffered for their plight. With the destruction of their grain by Carson's command, they had
been left without food of any description. Only the
unusual growth of the piñon "berry" had kept them
from starvation. The desperate Indians had not even
built fires in the severe weather for fear of being captured.

Fort Canby was a much more pleasant post than
bleak Fort Stanton but the men were hardly settled
in their quarters when Kit received a letter from
Carleton suggesting that it would be wise to take
another look at Canyon de Chelly before closing the
campaign. Early in January Carson led his men from
the comfortable fort into the winter's deepest snow
to carry out the order. As they trudged through the
heavy winter, the soldiers sang a marching song com-
posed by one of their company.

> Come dress your ranks, my gallant souls, a-standing
>   in a row,
> Kit Carson he is waiting to march against the foe,
> At night we march to Moqui o'er lofty hills of snow,
> To meet and crush the savage foe
>   Johnny Navajo!
> O Johnny Navajo! O Johnny Navajo!
> We'll first chastize, then civilize,
>   Bold Johnny Navajo![7]

Winter campaigning called for much ingenuity, especially when bedding down to sleep in a blizzard.
Each man carried two blankets under his saddle and
his greatcoat across the pommel. His first concern was
to keep one blanket dry. As two men usually slept
together for warmth, one blanket was spread on the
ground, then both greatcoats were put down and
covered with the two horse blankets and topped off
with the other bed blanket. In his way, each would
have a dry blanket in the morning to put next to
his horse with the wet blanket next to the saddle,
which was his pillow. A light snowfall added warmth
and all were tired enough to sleep soundly.[8]

Reaching the Canyon de Chelly for the final sweep,
Carson sent a divided force on both sides above while
Captain Pfeiffer's party passed completely through the
chasm; all parties met at the far end. Only a few
Indians were found to resist and nearly a hundred
were brought out as captives.

It was a victory almost without bloodshed, with no
battle in the entire campaign. In the end the proud
chiefs of the Navajos bowed to Carson and after a
talk and a smoke, agreed that peace would be "good
medicine." Most of the tribe came in at the bidding
of their chieftains, accepting the tragic loss of their
freedom with a steady, unblinking gaze. Those who
refused to leave the lands of their gods were finally
driven in by hunger. Some volunteered to fight the
Texans and Kit suggested to Carleton that if they
"be allowed to cripple the enemy, consistent with
rules of warfare," they could be valuable auxiliaries.

"Conquest was a necessity and it was well that this
was entrusted to gentle, just, wise and heroic Carson,"
wrote General Carleton in a glowing report of the

success of the campaign to Adjutant General Lorenzo
Thomas.

The operation of the troops during the severe weather has
been of the most praiseworthy character, crowned with unparalleled success. The first time any troops . . . have been
able to pass through the Cañon de Chelly which for its great
depth, length and perpendicular walls and its labyrinthian
character has been regarded by eminent geologists as the
most remarkable fissure on the face of the globe. . . . It is
reserved for Col. Carson to be the first to succeed. . . . I request the government will favorably notice that officer and
give him substantial reward for the crowning act in a long
life spent in various capacities in the service of his country.

Having no other choice, the Navajos left their vault-
ed red canyons, their silver and turquoise "sky stones,"
and the gods of their fathers, and came by the thousands to the Bosque Redondo which Carleton had
pictured as a Garden of Eden for them. He ordered
peach, apple and apricot trees to be planted, "before
the frosty nights are done," and asked Washington to
send plows, garden seeds, and clothing at once. Five
thousand had been expected but when the final count
was made there were more nearly eight thousand
Navajos to care for.

When a month passed without any word of supplies, Carleton in desperation begged the Adjutant
General to cut the red tape and send the food so
urgently needed. Carson moved into Fort Sumner
"to give the counsel they so much need at this time
to start farms and commence their new life." Most
of Carleton's time was spent drafting frantic appeals
to Washington without any concrete results. Tele-
grams, sent in answer, got no farther than Denver
where they lay undelivered in the post office. Every
day Carleton sent long letters, written with the hope

that some would get through. "For Pity's sake, if not moved by other consideration, let us as a great nation for once treat the Indian as he deserves to be treated."

Washington, busy with the crucial last year of the Civil War, did give some thought to the far-off Southwest. By executive order, January 15, 1864, a tract of land forty miles square, with Fort Sumner in the center, was established as a reservation for the Navajos. A vessel, sent out with substantial supplies, arrived in April, after seventy days at sea, at the mouth of the Colorado River, still hundreds of desert miles from the Bosque.

Carson faced the situation squarely and together with Carleton, reassured the Indians of the good intent of the government to care for them. Miles of *acequias* were dug to bring water to thousands of acres of virgin land, turned by hands that had never before touched a plow. Crops with the earliest yield were sown, wheat to be followed by beans on the same ground. General Carleton personally wrote out recipes for nutritious soups to be made from the scarce supply of meat, vegetables, and flour, to be rationed equally to men, women, and children until the crops matured.

By April, enough progress had been made for Carson to write Carleton asking to be sent to some post where he could have his family near him. "My children are small and need my presence to look after their education. I have been with them only fifteen days in over a year and now that the war is successfully terminated and peace and security given New Mexico, my service can easily be dispensed with and my children have the next claim on my time and attention. I certainly cannot remain away from my family much longer and I hope you will not ask me to." Carson was still at Fort Sumner in June and on the twenty-fifth of that month he sent in his resignation to Carleton. It was returned for further consideration and tendered again in September. But in spite of his personal feeling, Kit Carson stayed with the army.

During that summer of 1864, reports had drifted in that the tribes of the Plains were uniting in a last desperate drive to wipe out the white invader and once again have the freedom of their hunting grounds. The Comanches, Kiowas, Arapahos, Cheyennes, and remnants of the Apache nation began a wave of terror, called the bloodiest era of the West. Wagons were attacked and destroyed with savage fury, women and children taken captive, ranches pillaged, and horse and cattle herds stolen. Not even the military posts escaped the embittered vengeance. Fearing the rampage might spread into New Mexico and hinder the war effort, Carleton asked Carson to plan an expedition against the Comanches and Kiowas who were known to be in winter quarters somewhere on the Canadian River. "Give those Indians a good drubbing," wrote Carleton to Carson, "and should you get among the buffaloes, you can stay out if necessary a much longer time than you otherwise would."

Kit turned the command of Fort Sumner over to General Crocker, who was ordered to plant five thousand trees along the *acequias* to shade the water, strengthen the banks, and eventually supply fuel when the mesquite roots had been consumed. "Pray have every plow running, and every spade, shovel and pick employed in enlarging acequias, in opening new ones and grubbing out roots where land must be ploughed and in spading up for cultivation."

Once again Kit called on his friendly Utes to enlist in a campaign against their traditional enemies of the Plains. There were but a few precious days with Josefa and the children he had yearned to see, then he was off on another perilous assignment. Carleton had said he wanted more than a patched-up, injudicious peace with the troublesome tribes and hoped Carson would be able to "teach them a wholesome lesson they will not soon forget. . . . Your knowledge of the haunts of the Indians of the Plains and the great confidence the Ute Indians have in you as a friend and leader, point to yourself as the most fitting person to organize, direct and bring this enterprise to a successful issue." So wrote Carleton to Carson on October 18, 1864, on the eve of departure for what was to be Kit Carson's last Indian fight.

General Carleton had his hands full trying to feed thousands of Navajos, plan a campaign against the unruly Indians of the Plains, and protect New Mexico from the Texans. He did not expect trouble from the South but said he would not be surprised by it and hesitated to express an opinion lest he be considered an alarmist. As most of the Regulars were needed in the East, Carleton had to rely for the most part on the volunteers with only two companies of regular troops scattered over a great stretch of territory. Confederate prisoners of war helped to fill out the rolls, volunteering for frontier duty rather than be shot or sent home to starve. These "reverse English volunteers," also called "galvanized soldiers," made good frontier fighters.

In the meantime the Union forces had succeeded in getting a toe hold in Texas and General Nathaniel Banks straightway wrote Carleton to send reinforcements to Brownsville if possible. The best the dis-

traught General Carleton could do was to send con-
gratulations explaining: "It is out of my power to
send troops out of New Mexico because of the Indians and the lack of transportation over 700 miles of
nearly a desert from the Rio Grande to San Antonio."

Worst of all, Carleton had to worry about the
criticism he was receiving from Washington over the
Navajo reservation. He feared Congress might have
the Navajos returned. "If this formidable tribe should
block the road to Arizona, the progress of the Territory would be retarded a quarter of a century,"
wrote Carleton to the commander of Fort Whipple.
Carleton was accused of planning to starve the Navajos
when in fact he was desperately trying to find food
for the underestimated number. The Indians were
wise enough to know he did not have to go to the
trouble of bringing them together if he wished to kill
them. Some New Mexicans claimed that the Navajo
reservation had taken some of the best grassland that
should have been left for the settlers. Nobody was
happy about the arrangement.

Colonel Kit Carson took the field in October with
a command of 14 officers, 72 Indians and 320 enlisted men—most of them mounted—with two small
howitzers on prairie carriages, 27 wagons, and a spring-
wagon ambulance. The Utes were given "old and
worn rifles, powder and ball and a blanket apiece."
Rations issued were: "1¼ lbs. of beef and 1 lb. of
bread-stuff and the necessary salt." The plan was for
Major General Blount to move from Fort Larned,
Kansas, with a force to join Carson on the Palo Duro
in the Texas Panhandle.

With fine weather and fair grass, the company made
good progress through country familiar to Kit. Pass-

ing the scene of the White massacre, they camped at
Wheel Gulch—a large stand of cottonwoods where the
Mexicans came for wood to repair the large solid
wheels of their *carretas*. The only unpleasant part
of the trek was the infernal noise of the war dance
which the Utes kept up all night long every night.

Arriving at Fort Bascom, they found a company of
licensed traders preparing to take their wagons into
Indian territory. As hostilities were likely to begin
at any time, Carson ordered them to remain at the
fort. The traders managed to slip past the pickets
and not only warned the Indians that Colonel Carson's company was approaching but sold them arms
and ammunition to use against them. Kit led his
men on and when they were about two days' march
from General Blount's force, the Ute spies, far in
advance, suddenly located the hostile village. Kit's
company was resting at Mule Spring when, to the
surprise of everyone, several of the Utes suddenly
sprang to their feet exclaiming that the encampment
had been found. It seemed impossible that they could
have received any communication from the scouts who
were at least two miles away and barely visible in the
waning light. Without questioning the Utes, Carson
gave orders to saddle up and start on after dark along
the river without smoking or talking. Seventy-five men
and one officer were left to guard the supply wagons.

The trail was discovered about midnight. All dismounted and stood holding their horses in the chill
night air until ordered to mount and move on at
daybreak. Kit revealed to Captain Pfeiffer that he
had had a dream the night before of a battle with
cannon fire and bloodshed—a premonition of what was
about to happen. The Ute warriors, riding ahead,
presented a queer sight wrapped in buffalo robes

with their knees drawn up to their chins. At the sound of a war cry from one of the advance scouts, they threw the robes from their bodies, paint-streaked and naked to the breechclout, and plunged their ponies into the icy water.

The Kiowas, taken completely by surprise, fled the village at the first warning cry, following their old Chief To-Hausan up the little stream, now called Carson Creek, to warn the next village. Carson's men pursued them through coarse river grass growing so tall their horses were almost hidden and so rough that the cannon carriages overturned to cause delay. In the distance could be seen the white lodges of another village looking so much like an army encampment that Kit wondered if Sibley's men had arrived to foster the uprising. Their location was about forty miles from the future town of Amarillo, Texas, near the crumbling ruins of the old adobe fort William Bent had built years before for trade with the Plains Indians who were afraid to come to the big fort. Carson knew the country as well as his own back yard.

As they rode in to attack, Kit threw his greatcoat into the bushes to lighten his load, intending to pick it up on the way back. But this time, instead of running, the Indians rode out in waves with a dozen or more chiefs leading small skirmishing bands and outnumbering the white men ten to one. Quickly sizing up the situation, Carson ordered his men to take refuge behind the Adobe Walls which would provide protection for the horses as well as serve as an emergency hospital base. When, after some effort, the howitzers were rolled up and fired, the Indians turned back to their village. Soon, not an Indian was to be seen though five hundred lodges were in plain view of the Adobe Walls.

The first danger having passed, Kit ordered a recess. Neither men nor mules had eaten since the night before. The mules were loosened from the cannon carriages, watered, and picketed out to graze on the lush uncropped grass while the men opened their knapsacks to bring out the despised hardtack. Almost at once the Indians started pouring out of the lodges to be reinforced by more hundreds coming over the rimming hills. They rode singly, scattering smartly to avoid being a massed target for the cannon. The howitzers, rolled hastily into position, did little damage as most of the balls were effectively dodged. One horse was hit, the cannon ball going completely through the animal before it exploded. Two braves rode in to rescue the rider, each grabbing an arm and dragging him off at full speed so he would not be scalped and thus deprived of any hope of reaching the happy hunting ground.

The Indians rode with superb savage grace, the bodies of their horses as well as their own garishly painted with vermilion and yellow ochre. Feathers and fox tails floated wildly in the wind and the air hummed with whirring arrows. The white men could only hide in the grass and try to pick off as many as possible of the colorful warriors as they rode by, yelling and screaming out their defiance. The battle kept up all through the day with one note of comedy. Every time the army bugle sounded, an Indian bugler blew the opposite call. He was so expert that Kit thought he must surely be a white man, possibly a rebel.

As the battle dragged on without a chance to make an attack, Carson ordered columns formed for a retreat. Fearing for the safety of the supply wagons, he hoped to be well on the way before the Indians renewed the attack. Not attempting to follow the rules of warfare, Carson ordered the cannon to the rear. The Indians, following at a distance, fired the grass which, luckily, burned too slowly to cause any trouble in the orderly retreat of Carson and his company.

In the village they had bypassed earlier they found a store of material stolen from emigrant trains and express wagons, even some cavalry helmets and belts. In their hurried flight the Indians had left behind an old spring wagon ambulance Major Sedgwick had given to the Kiowa Chief Little Mountain several years before. The old chieftain had used it to ride proudly about his prairie domain with two boys riding the horses because he had never learned to drive. After salvaging as much as could be carried, including a buffalo robe to replace Carson's lost greatcoat, the march proceeded. They had gone only a short distance when a shout of joy went up at the sight of their supply wagons approaching. The officer in charge had ordered them forward with the sound of the cannon. After thirty hours of fighting and marching, the men were ravenously hungry and nearly exhausted from fatigue. A hearty breakfast of wild turkey and roast antelope was gulped down in full view of the Indians watching from a distance. Before resuming the march, Kit allowed his men to rest a full day without any disturbance whatever.

Only two soldiers and one Ute had been killed. The Indians' loss was estimated to be about a hundred killed and fifty wounded. Several of Carson's men were wounded—one casualty, a Mexican boy bitten by a rattlesnake. With a minimum of loss and bloodshed on both sides, the expedition had served its purpose by breaking up the coalition of the tribes that had scourged the Plains. With a less cautious and understanding commander, the battle of Adobe Walls might have been more disastrous than the better known battle of the Little Big Horn. Kit gave all credit to the howitzers that covered the retreat. General Carleton, who had expected this campaign to be only exploratory leading to a final all-out war, called it a decisive victory and wrote Carson a congratulatory letter in his usual ornate style. "This brilliant affair adds another green leaf to the laurel wreathe which you have so nobly won in the service of your country."

The hostile tribes of the Plains were subdued one by one, the mighty Sioux and Cheyenne, victims of irresponsible men with military authority. Some years before, the Eastern press had played up the story of Lieutenant Grattan's tragic mistake at Fort Laramie and demanded that Sioux Chief Bear be hanged as a criminal. The chief was spared that indignity by dying, but over eighty of his people were killed in a ruthless massacre of reprisal. But that was almost insignificant compared to the fate awaiting the Cheyenne.

Carson's trusted friend, Colonel Wynkoop, was replaced as commander of Fort Lyon (Bent's Fort) by Major Scott Anthony, who was expected to be more firm in dealing with the Indians. Colonel Chivington, the hero of La Glorieta, had resigned his commission but was still in command of the Colorado Firsts when a letter was sent to him by General S. R. Curtis, from headquarters at Fort Leavenworth, saying he wanted no peace until the Indians had suffered more. The Cheyennes had been quiet, assured by William Bent, who still wielded great influence over the tribe, that they could hunt safely as long as they kept the flag flying and remained peaceful. About the time Colonel Carson was returning from his encounter at Adobe Walls, Chivington offered up prayers as he always did before an attack, then swooped down on the sleeping Cheyenne village at Sand Creek about forty miles above Bent's. Almost a thousand men, women and children were routed from their lodges and either shot trying to escape or died hopelessly trapped. Even babes in the arms of their mothers were not spared as Chivington reminded his men that "nits make lice."

In his report to General Curtis, Chivington gave the cold figures of 900 to 1000 Cheyennes, forming a battle line "resolved to do us all the injury possible before losing their lives." In six hours, 500 to 600 were left dead and scattered over six miles, 550 ponies and mules captured, all lodges destroyed, 8 soldiers dead, 10 wounded, 2 died later. "Exceedingly regretful that the command could not have pressed the Indians farther." Chivington was angered at the conduct of one of his captains who had made "the ill advised statement that he thanked God he had killed no Indians, proving him more in sympathy with the Indians than the Whites. . . . On every hand the evidence was clear that no lick had been struck amiss."

The only prisoners taken were three small children, later shown as curiosities between the acts of a play in a theater in Denver. Chivington, proudly displaying his collection of scalps, went back to Ohio to run for Congress. When public opinion forced him to withdraw, he accepted a job as coroner and escaped court-martial only by mustering out of service before being brought to trial for what has been called the most unjustifiable crime in the annals of America.

Carson was shocked and indignant that Chivington, a man of the Church, could heartlessly massacre the friendlies and shoot down squaws with babies in their arms, ". . . and you call them civilized men and the Indians savages." By sobering contrast, Chivington's wanton massacre points up Carson's great wisdom in dealing with the hostile Kiowas and Comanches at Adobe Walls where a show of force accomplished the desired effect with small loss of life.[9]

Jim Bridger, back in the mountains after attempting to settle on his farm, agreed with Kit and Blackfoot Smith—the government interpreter who was in the Cheyenne camp when the attack was made—that there would be fearful reprisals. The frenzied Cheyennes raged through the country, burning, razing, destroying wantonly. Fort Rankin at Julesburg, Colorado, was attacked and pillaged, the telegraph line wrecked and the stage-line stations burned out. Charles Bent, the half-Cheyenne son of William, who had been educated in the East, returned to his mother's people to become a desperado with a price on his head, even threatening his father's life. In the final accounting, probably many more white men were killed because of Chivington than Cheyennes at Sand Creek.

With the coming of spring, the devastating raids were renewed with more vicious attacks on the expresses and wagon freights along the Cimarron route. Carson took some men into the hostile territory in an effort to find a solution. "In my opinion," wrote Carleton, "your consultation and rifle with the Indians of the Plains will stop the war." He stressed "promptness in getting into the saddle and a disposition to move quick . . . each man with his little bag of flour,

a little salt and coffee and not hampered by packs.
. . . Have arms in their hands the last thing at night
and the first thing in the morning . . . see that they
are ready to fight. If they fear us, they will behave.
. . . They must not think to stop the commerce of
the Plains."

Kit had hardly set up camp at Cold Springs to
await the arrival of the express his men were to escort to Santa Fe when he received this message: "Turn
over your command to Maj. Pfeiffer and report at
once to Headquarters. A Congressional Investigation
Committee is here to inquire into Indian matters and
your testimony will doubtless be required." Kit made
the long ride back, irritated at what seemed interference with men doing their best, at risk of life itself,
to quell the rioting red men and keep the lines of
communication and transportation open.

The mail service was unpredictable, delivery depending at times on the slimmest chance. An express
package brought to Santa Fe was found to have been
opened and a letter taken out. An explanation was
asked with this reply: "The missing communication
from the express package was probably taken out by
Col. Carson while en route to Santa Fe. The express-
man had orders to give him a letter from the package
if he should meet the Col. on the road."

As the time of service of the volunteers was about
to run out, General Carleton was greatly concerned
about replacements. In his difficult position, it was
reassuring for him to have Carson's promise not to
leave him. "It gratifies me to learn that you will not
leave the service while I am here. . . . A good deal
of my good fortune in Indian matters here, in fact
all with reference to Navajo, Mescalero Apache and

Kiowa, is due to you and it affords me pleasure to acknowledge the value of your service."

Back in the East, the presses rolled off angry protests about the expense and the treatment of the Indians. It was even suggested that Carleton face court-martial. After the experience of Fremont, it was inconceivable to Carson that another great and respected friend should be required to face that ordeal. The reservation at the Bosque turned out to be a great heartache for both Carleton and Carson, though no two men of the West were more sincerely devoted to the welfare of the Indian. Unfortunately, by an order from Washington, a number of Apaches were placed with the Navajos and inevitable intertribal disputes arose. They had not reckoned with such enemies as beetles, bugs, storms, floods, and drouth. There was the stark tragedy of three thousand acres of corn in tassel being attacked by cutworms that destroyed the entire crop. The wheat was nearly ready for harvest when an unprecedented rainstorm beat it down and over half was lost. Hail and severe frost destroyed the whole bean crop that would have furnished food enough for two years. The pumpkin yield was good but it was discovered that the Indians were selling the produce instead of storing it. This brought an order forbidding anyone "to buy a single article of food animate or inanimate from the Indians on the reservation." A reporter for the *Santa Fe Gazette* wrote of that calamitous year of 1865: "Properly to describe the misery . . . a man ought to write with tears instead of ink."

The head chief of the Comanches came voluntarily to Carleton to seek peace. "He has returned to get some of his principal men when he will come back in the last quarter of the moon. . . . Then I shall go down to see them and if possible come to some under-standing with them. If you get back in time, I wish you to go with me," wrote Carleton to Carson, now in command of Fort Union and soon to leave for Fort Lyon to make a deposition on the Chivington affair.

The greatest honor of his life came to Christopher Kit Carson on March 13, 1865, when he was brevet-ted Brigadier General of the Army and cited "for gallantry in the Battle of Val Verde and for his con-duct and long and meritorious service in New Mexico." It was doubly sweet to taste such reward, remember-ing the heartbreaking refusal of a lieutenancy in 1848. The rank of general did not in any way change Kit Carson, the man. One day one of his soldiers at Fort Union apologized for addressing him as Colonel in-stead of General Carson. Kit smiled to put the man at ease and said, "Oh, call me Kit and be done with it!" Carson's men loved him for his modesty and consideration but also respected his firmness. His twinkling eyes could blaze like a rattlesnake's at in-justice and the gentle voice was capable of intense pathos. "I do not like a hostile Red Skin any more than you do and when they are hostile, I have fit 'em—fout 'em—and I expect to fight 'em hard as any man. That's my business. But I never drew a bead on a squaw or papoose and I despise a man who would."[10]

When the news reached Fort Union that the War between the States had ended with Lee's surrender, "the whole prairie rang with shouts of joy." Com-munications were so slow that there were still clashes between Rebel and Union forces several weeks after the word had been dispatched to the Southwest from far-off Virginia, April 9, 1865. The end of the war did not make much difference to the military command in New Mexico for the Indians were still on the rampage along the Santa Fe Trail and the weekly stage run over the wild strip to the Cimarron was a harrowing experience. As reported by Colonel James A. Meline, "The Cimarron still remains almost in its primitive isolation and seclusion. Maps have done nothing for it and we find it difficult to locate ourselves day by day when we halt."[11] Again, Carson was called to go into that region and talk with the chiefs of the warring tribes "to impress them of their folly of continuing their bad course" and, at the same time, select a suitable location for a post to protect the trail.

Carleton favored building several small posts rather than a few large ones since the Indians were scattered far and hidden in secret mountain haunts. In midsummer of 1865, Carson left Fort Union with three companies of New Mexico and California Cavalry under his command. Riding about 130 miles to the east, they set up a camp half a mile off the trail at a spot called Cedar Bluffs in the barren Oklahoma Panhandle. A small city of white tents was erected near a little stream known as the Nameless and the men were soon at work cutting and hauling limestone blocks to construct a permanent fort to be named Fort Nichols.

There were, in addition to the soldiers, ten Indian scouts, two squaws, two laundresses—wives of Mexican soldiers who were paid a dollar a month for their services—and two officers' wives, one the twenty-year-old bride of Lieutenant R. D. Russell. Marian Russell was completely charmed by General Carson, especially by his tender regard for his wife, "Little Jo," as he called her. "He wore shyness before his face like a veil . . . in his eyes an infinite capacity for tenderness . . . his laughter, a short sharp bark."[12]

Carson was most solicitous of the women's welfare, warning them not to go farther than a few yards from the camp in that open Indian country. He arranged for the Russells to have one of the first dugouts for their quarters. The only piece of furniture was a folding table. Stumps served for chairs and a split log covered with branches and straw was a not-too-uncomfortable bed. White cloth covered the windows and a blanket was hung for a door. All cooking was done in a Dutch oven set in the fireplace. The houses were half-dugouts, built four feet underground and four above, surrounded by rock walls and a deep moat to give an imposing picture of strength. Strict military discipline was observed at all times. Through the torrid summer, Carson and his men always appeared with their uniforms properly buttoned. Only those on scouting duty were allowed to wear soft cotton blouses.

Work on the fort progressed rapidly, though Carson himself did little supervising. The strain of the war had left him tired and the old injury sustained in the fall from his horse had developed into an annoying bronchial condition. During the last year, an army ambulance had been placed at his disposal to relieve the strain of traveling. To endure the oppressive summer heat, Carson spent much of the time in his tent with the sides rolled up, resting on a bed that was nothing more than a number of poles laid across four forked sticks stuck in the ground. One day, during a sudden windstorm, the tent collapsed and the General, unable to extricate himself, was forced to call out for help.

The mere presence of soldiers building so pretentious a fortress seemed to discourage the half-barbarous Indians of the prairies in their wave of terror. Travel on the trail, almost abandoned during the war, began to roll again. In the flat country, great clouds of dust could be seen long before the wagons came within sight of Carson's camp. Some trains had as many as five hundred wagons with great herds of livestock and the whips of the bullwhackers cracked like gunshots in the still air.

Fort Nichols was never finished. Early in September Carson was suddenly called to Fort Union, leaving Major Pfeiffer in command. The project was abandoned by the end of the month, leaving large haystacks and piles of cut stone to stand untouched for many years to come. The fort had served its purpose in opening the Santa Fe Trail to regular traffic.

Carson, William Bent, and General Jesse Leavenworth were ordered to meet with the chiefs of the Sioux, Cheyennes, and Arapahos on October 16, 1865, at Bluff Creek, forty miles south of the Little Arkansas.[18] There the troops of the United States were censured for unpardonable behavior and formal apologies were offered to the Indians for the treatment their tribes had suffered. Assurance was given that they would be free again to roam and live as they once had in the territory between the Black Hills and the Rockies to the Yellowstone. It was an unenforceable treaty, prematurely drawn up by men sincerely trying to right a grievous wrong but destined to be disregarded whenever inconvenient, forcing the tribes to accept life on the reservations.

The meeting offered the opportunity for a long-delayed visit between Carson and William Bent. William had leased his new fort to the government for the duration of the war and now that hostilities had ceased, he demanded payment or possession. More years of fruitless wrangling were in store for him.

After the council meeting, Carson was ordered to headquarters in St. Louis to report on the Indian situation, escorted by fifty Kansas volunteers returning home from service in New Mexico. In St. Louis Kit renewed acquaintance with General William T. Sherman, who was making an inspection tour of Indian agencies to report to the Department of the Interior. Kit invited Sherman to be a guest in his home when he came to Taos. Dramatic incident seemed to follow Kit Carson like a shadow wherever he went. He lost all his luggage in the fire that destroyed the Planters Hotel but luckily escaped injury to himself. When the hearing was finished, Carson returned to assume command of Fort Union on December 8, 1865.

It was particularly gratifying to Kit to be assigned a post where he could be near his family. Josefa and the children remained at Taos, only a few hours away. When word was received that General Sherman would arrive, Kit sent the boys into the mountains to bring back saplings and branches to place along the plaza in a feeble effort to dress up the drab and treeless village. After Sherman's visit, the friendship between the two generals was even more firmly cemented. The outspoken Sherman made no secret of the fact that he heartily disliked the Plains. As for establishing more scattered outposts "that would not be worth a Confederate note," he said he would suggest selling the land back to Mexico for the $15,000,000 the United States had paid for it and lending them the greenbacks to pay for it.

Many soldiers, discharged from the service at the end of the war, stayed to work on the railroad that had pushed steadily westward in spite of war and Indians who pulled out the rails, burned the ties, and ambushed the section crews. The course through the mountains, that Fremont had sought in vain, was mapped by Grenville Dodge, a close friend of President Lincoln. He discovered the canyon, found to be the most direct passage, by watching a party of Indians ride into it. The former Pony Express boy, William F. Cody, was employed by the railroad company to supply meat for the working crews, thereby winning the nickname, "Buffalo Bill." Bill Cody held Kit Carson in the highest respect and to show his regard for him, later named his only son Kit Carson Cody. Fremont had invested heavily in the transcontinental railroad and ultimately lost his entire fortune. Kit, who had probed the rocky barrier with Fremont, followed the progress of the rail line with intense interest but the golden spike that would join East to West would not be driven in his lifetime.[14]

NOTES ON CHAPTER FOURTEEN

1. From an unidentified newspaper clipping.

2. Report of Captain Thompson, First Cavalry, New Mexico Volunteers, to Major Julius Shaw, August 12, 1864, tells of the complete destruction of hundreds of trees by a company of 24 enlisted men, 2 volunteers and 1 Indian guide. Lost no men, 1 mule, and saw no Indians.

3. Thomasson, "Recollection of Kit Carson" (Speech before the Loyal Legion of U.S., State of Illinois, 1928). Library of Congress.

4. See Sabin, *Kit Carson Days.*

5. From the diary of an unnamed officer of Company B, First New Mexico Volunteers (manuscript, Ritch Collection, Henry E. Huntington Library, San Marino, California).

6. See *History of New Mexico* published at Los Angeles, 1907; Keleher, *Turmoil in New Mexico.*

7. Printed in *Rio Abato Press,* December 8, 1863. See Keleher, *Turmoil in New Mexico.*

8. See Rodenbough, *From Everglade to Cañon with the Second Dragoons.*

9. Ellis, *Life of Kit Carson.*

10. Ellis, *Life of Kit Carson.*

11. Meline, *Two Thousand Miles on Horseback.*

12. See Marian (Sloan) Russell, *Land of Enchantment.*

13. Near the site of Wichita, Kansas.

14. The transcontinental railroad was completed May 10, 1869, at Promontory Point, Utah.

CHAPTER FIFTEEN

Trail's End (1866-1868)

In his time and country, a great
power for good. . . . My one wish is
that in the life hereafter,
I may mix with him again.

COL. JAMES F. MELINE
*Two Thousand Miles on
Horseback*

NOW THAT THE war was over and the hostile tribes pacified, uppermost in Kit Carson's mind was the welfare of his family. Before being relieved of command in New Mexico, General Carleton had suggested that Carson could add to his income by taking over the sutler store at Fort Union. Though the offer was attractive to him, Kit feared his knowledge of trading was not extensive enough to undertake so large a business as the post at Fort Union demanded and asked to be given a smaller post. This led to Carson's assignment to Fort Garland, the most important post in the mountain area, eighty miles north of Taos, in the heart of Ute territory. It was hoped that sullen tribe could be judiciously controlled by the man who knew them best, their former agent, Kit Carson.

He arrived May 6, 1866, with his handsome wife, their five children and the motherless son of Major Pfeiffer, and moved into the commander's quarters which became at once an open house for everyone Indian or white, officer or volunteer, settler or passer-by.

Fort Garland, built eight years before to replace Fort Massachusetts, which had been abandoned after the bloody Christmas Day massacre by Blanco's men, was situated above the fertile San Luis Valley, a less dangerous location in the open. The fort commanded a spectacular view of heavily forested mountains rising tier upon tier to imposing snow-crusted peaks—a region teeming with game for the soldiers' favorite pastime of hunting. Constructed of rough adobe and logs chinked with mud, the fort was a rectangle of flat one-story buildings facing a large parade ground entirely enclosed by a ditch with water boxes at each corner carrying ever-cold water from the mountain snows. It was a complete village in itself with blacksmith shop, laundry, bakery, tailor shop, storehouse, trader's store, and chapel. Only the officers' quarters had board floors and whitewashed walls.

Several officers had brought their families from the East to enliven the drab frontier post and settlers from the valley, now numbering in the thousands, joined in the social life it offered. There was little strict formality with so unmilitary a commander as General Carson, who spent every leisure hour romping with his children who ran about the grounds like a small tribe of untamed savages, completely adored by their father.

Kit Carson, at fifty-five, was "a rather stout, talkative, not very noticeable man—his hair well silvered —face full and florid with breadth and openness of brow—his quick blue eye caught everything at a glance, beaming with benevolence and kindliness and blazing with anger when aroused—full square jaw that shut tight as Grant's or Sherman's—nothing of the swashbuckler or border ruffian about him—gentle, soft-voiced and sympathetic." So General James F. Rusling described him, adding that he wore a mustache and occasionally leaned on a cane.[1]

The restless Utes had been stirring up trouble against the orders of their Chief Ouray (The Arrow), a most remarkable Indian, greatly admired and respected by both Carleton and Carson as a strong friend. Ouray had been to Washington and talked with President Lincoln in an effort to solve the problems of his people. As soon as the Utes learned that Carson was stationed at Fort Garland, they began streaming into the fort expecting their "Kitty" to feed and care for them as he had for so many years as their agent. Many were almost without rations and in a pitiable state. He gave them whatever supplies could be spared from the fort and requested additional goods from the Indian agent, whose duty it was to look after the tribe. The commanding general could often be found sitting on the ground with a group of Utes gathered around him conversing animatedly in their language of sign and pantomime. With Ouray's help, Carson succeeded in proving to the Utes that he remained their firm friend and convinced them that the government policy toward them was in their best interest.

Not long after coming to Fort Garland, General Carson, through his secretary, Luke Cahill, wrote a rather pathetic letter to Senator L. F. Foster explaining why he was seeking the sutlership of Fort Garland.

Allow me to state that having entered the service by appointment of the President, July 25, 1861, after having served five years I can truthfully say I shall leave poorer than when I entered it. . . . During this time my family has increased and it behooves me now to make some preparation for their subsistence and education. . . . The post at Ft. Garland is small and the business would not require more than my own supervision and would probably be the means of comfortably supporting myself and family. . . .

The request was denied because of a new ruling separating the sutlership from the military.

Late in September of that year 1866, General Sherman arrived at Fort Garland with a delegation to confer with Carson and the Ute chiefs, hoping to

induce the tribe to accept life on a reservation. Sherman, making the tour of military posts by army ambulance with only two staff officers and a teamster,
had not seen a single hostile Indian in crossing 1,200
miles.

The meeting between Sherman and Carson at Fort
Garland was preparatory to a large council to be held
a few days later on the Rio Grande, thirty miles from
Fort Garland. After long and excited discussions in
the Ute dialect, liberally punctuated with English profanity the Indians had picked up from the soldiers,
the chiefs were quieted with promises of food. They
reluctantly agreed to a treaty permitting a road to
be built across their lands but warned that the young
braves of the tribe were skeptical about moving to a
reservation unless their enemies, the Cheyennes and
Comanches, agreed first. With skilled diplomacy, the
chiefs told the white men that they could not guaran-
tee to restrain their youths. At this, Sherman jumped
up shouting, "If another white man is scalped, it will
be impossible to hold mine in!" He was greatly impressed with the Indians' deep regard for Carson.
"Those redskins think Kit twice as big a man as me,"
he remarked later to Colonel Rusling, "why, his integrity is simply perfect."

The two generals held further conferences with
Chief Ouray in Carson's office facing the parade
grounds. It was a colorful scene with dragoons in dark
blue gold-trimmed coats, sky-blue trousers with yellow
stripes and sashes, and high hats with gold eagles and
cockades. Carson, in dress uniform, was seated at his
deerskin-covered desk in front of a deerhoof gunrack
holding a small arsenal. A fine mounted elk's head
looked down from a place above the brightly burning
fireplace. A huge bear rug partly covered the rough

board floor. Chief Ouray, impressive in painted deerskins and beaded moccasins, his sleek braids bound
at the ends with silver ornaments, held in his hand an
ornately decorated peace pipe. Rumpled, red-haired
Sherman, with far less poise, waited impatiently to
hear Kit's interpretation of his unhurried conversation with the principal man of the nation that was
being asked to surrender. All the while the Carson
children ran about the room "half-clad and boisterous,
as wild and untrained as a brood of Mexican mustangs," according to General Sherman.[2]

Later he asked Kit what he was doing about the
education of his children. "It has caused me much
anxiety," Kit told him. "I never had much education
myself and I fear I have not done right by my children." Sherman told him that among the honors he
had received was a scholarship to the college at South
Bend, Indiana, and suggested that it might be shared
by two of the boys for five years each. Kit thanked
him for the generous offer and said he would give it
consideration.

The grand council of the tribes was considered a
success. A village of three hundred or more white
wigwams was set up with as much regularity as
city streets. It took on the appearance of a carni-
val fair with squaws decked out in glittering beaded
sacques and bright feathers and the men in every
kind of dress from old army uniforms with discarded
plumed artillery hats to narrow breechclouts. Handsome Ouray rode about the camp with impressive
dignity without whip or spur while the young boys
rode their spirited ponies at breakneck speed back
and forth over the mile-long road from their village
to the military encampment. The soldiers came to
the Indian village to trade for souvenirs to take home

to the East and found that the red man could drive a shrewd bargain.

The council opened with the traditional calumet ceremony, each man sitting in the circle taking several puffs on the pipe. Carson was interpreter while Sherman, smoking his own brier, walked around with his hands stuffed deep into his pockets, pausing only to listen intently whenever Carson spoke. Chief Ouray, accompanied by his principal warrior, Shavano (Blue Flower), proved to be an astute statesman and convinced his people that they must find a way to live in peace with the white man. After the treaty was signed, presents were distributed and three fine beeves, provided by the Indian agency, were roasted to celebrate the occasion. Of Chief Ouray and Shavano, it has been said: "No ruler and his greatest general ever accomplished more with what they had to deal with."

The agreement reached with the Utes did not mean an end of all trouble in their region for the next month, Chief Eaneache of the Muauache Utes, who had opposed Ouray's dealing with the white men, took his band on the warpath against the settlers. A detachment of cavalry was sent from the fort to round up the offenders and thereafter a vigilant peace was maintained. Kit found that the most effective way to deal with the recalcitrant ones was to keep them close to the fort with promises of food.

One evening during an hour of leisure, Kit came upon Captain A. W. Archibald reading the familiar words from Sir Walter Scott's *The Lady of the Lake:* "The stag at eve had drunk his fill." He asked to hear the entire poem and was so impressed by this beautiful expression of the world of nature he knew and loved that he requested to hear it read many times and learned to quote some of the stanzas from memory. After most of a lifetime spent in a harsh and sometimes cruel world, Kit Carson, beneath the unpolished exterior, retained an almost childlike eagerness and curiosity. "He stored away a wealth of knowledge in his retentive mind that few of his compeers could equal," wrote one of his men.[3]

Conscious of the handicap of his limited education, Kit was determined even so late in his career to improve himself. For years he had studied to improve his reading and writing with the help of Chipita, as he affectionately called Josefa. Since she knew only Spanish, Kit was more proficient in that language than English. He might at times hesitate in choosing the right word in English but he spoke Spanish, French, and many Indian languages fluently. Realizing the responsibility of his position and desiring the respect as well as the affection of his men, Carson spent many hours at Fort Garland in serious study with some of the officers of his staff.

The robust good health Kit had enjoyed most of his life was due, he said, to his abstinence and the fact that he had sowed all his wild oats before he was twenty-one. "He was not a drinker, nor was he a teetotaler," according to Robert Lowery, who served under Carson at Fort Union, and told of seeing him enjoy a bowl of hot punch with his friends at Maxwell's. His failing health worried Kit and since he would not be entitled to a pension or half pay when leaving the service, he was greatly concerned about the welfare of his family. Another daughter, named Estafana (Stella), was born to Josefa in December, 1866, the day before Kit's fifty-seventh birthday.

After the sutlership of Fort Garland was denied him, Kit decided to seek the Superintendency of Indian Affairs in the territory of Colorado, a position soon to be separated from the governorship. Josefa had suggested that rather than raise their family in a frontier army post, they should plan to settle, after his retirement from service, in the new town Tom Boggs was building on the Purgatoire in Colorado. While stationed at Fort Union, Kit had visited St. Vrain at his ranch near Mora and bought from him two tracts of land adjoining the land Tom Boggs had claimed for his wife Rumalda when the vast St. Vrain-Vigil estate had been partitioned by government order in 1860. Kit loved that region he had once roamed as hunter for Bent's Fort and it would be an ideal location from which to direct Indian affairs if he should be fortunate enough to receive the appointment.

Carson sent the following letter, dated December 16, 1866, to General J. C. McFerran in Washington:

... It is my intention to settle on the Purgatoire and as this is in Colorado Territory, it may lead to my obtaining a position that would in every way suit me, I mean the Indian Superintendency for Colorado. . . . My new home will be, comparatively speaking, in the midst of the Indians and with my knowledge of their character and a determination to act with justice, I think I could perform the duties with success for myself and credit to the government. . . . At my time of life, I have no desire to come to Washington as I am satisfied my interests will not suffer from delay or neglect. . . . Should the government decide on removing the Utes westward, it becomes a matter of grave importance that one conversant with them and their character should be Supt. . . .

On receiving the letter, General McFerran, with the help of Lieutenant Nelson Thomasson, circulated a petition among Carson's many friends in Washington —members of Congress, army officers, officials of the Bureau of Indian Affairs, dragoons and soldiers who had served under him. All wrote glowing tributes recommending Carson's appointment. A telegram, short and to the point, was sent to the Secretary of the Interior: "Kit Carson ought to be Supt. of Ind. Aff. in N. M. (signed) W. T. Sherman, General." Then followed a year of waiting before Kit would know if his request would be granted.

Going ahead with plans to retire, Kit rode across country to Boggsville, five miles upriver from Fort Lyon, where Tom Boggs had finished building three rows of adobe houses on the high ground above the river. Kit decided one of these would be adequate for his family until he could build on the acres he had bought from Ceran. Stopping at Fort Lyon, Carson happened to be present when Wild Bill Hickok rode in with a prisoner. Hickok, driving steers to La Junta with a dozen other cow hands, met a posse from Las Vegas trailing two Mexican outlaws. Riding well in advance of the others, Wild Bill came upon the bandits resting before their campfire. Without hesitating, he spurred his horse into the center of the camp. By the time the posse arrived, one bad man was dead and the other wounded and tied with a lariat. Kit congratulated Hickok and told him he knew of no other man in the West who could equal his courage and fearlessness. This tribute from the man he idolized was considered by Wild Bill Hickok to be the greatest honor ever to come to him.[4]

During the summer, when the Utes were quiet, Kit made a business trip to Maxwell's. The estate had been partitioned in the great land shuffle of 1860, at which time William Bent had brought suit against Lucien to settle the claims of the heirs of Charles Bent. Though Kit had testified against his old partner, Maxwell, this did not sever their friendship. The suit was settled for a mere $18,000. Twenty-five hundred acres of the ranch had been deeded to Dick Wootton to build a toll road over Raton Pass and squatters had pre-empted considerable acreage. Lucien saw the great inheritance he hoped to pass on to his son, Pete, slipping away piece by piece.

While Kit was visiting the ranch, Lucien and some of the soldiers stationed at the Rayado decided to fire a rusty old howitzer to celebrate the Fourth of July. The blast blew off a captain's arm and blinded one eye, and Maxwell's thumb was shattered. A sergeant rode fifty miles to Fort Union to bring the nearest surgeon, pushing his horse so hard that the animal fell dead at the door of the doctor's quarters. The captain lived and Lucien's wound seemed of small consequence. However, an infection developed later and Carson took his old friend in a state of delirious fever by coach to Fort Union. The surgeon waited until the heat of the day had cooled to amputate, with Kit holding an oil lamp. Without benefit of opiate, Maxwell mercifully fell into a dead faint but completely recovered.[5]

This probably was Kit Carson's last visit to the Rayado where his happiest years had been spent. Maxwell, speculating in bank and railroad stocks, lost most of his great fortune. He purchased Fort Sumner after the Navajos were allowed to return to their homelands and Carleton's "Eden" had reverted to a plow-torn wasteland. Lucien drove some nine thousand cattle from the Rayado to Fort Sumner where he lived in the officers' quarters until his death in 1875. (The outlaw, Billy the Kid, was killed in a bedroom of this house in July, 1881.)

Carson remained in command of Fort Garland until November 22, 1867, when he was mustered out of

service at Santa Fe, terminating four decades of un-
selfish and unequalled service to the West. A reporter
for the *Santa Fe Gazette* described him at that time
as very young looking for his fifty-eight years. "He
wore the Brigadier-General's uniform in a careless,
half-Indian way, measured his words as if his life depended on expressing himself in proper shape. Sometimes he would stop in conversation, as if to recall
a word, and, naturally, I would suggest one, but with
the greatest indifference, he would pass my aid unnoticed and using some strong Saxon phrase of his
own, finish the subject, oblivious to any remarks,
questions or conversations around him."[6]

By the end of the year, the Carson family and some
of their possessions were moved into their new home
at Boggsville, next door to the trading post of John
Hough. A few miles distant was the large ranch of
William Bent, where Kit visited often to reminisce.
Bent's son George called on Kit and bought from him
the horse Carson had ridden at the battle of Adobe
Walls. The horse carried scars on his back, not from
arrow or gunpowder, but from wounds where the skin
had come off after having been saddled for four days.
Earlier that year, William had brought back from St.
Louis a very young bride, the part-Blackfoot former
Miss Adaline Harney.

William Bent was disgusted over the treatment he
had received on his futile trip to Washington and objected to government regulations of transportation on
the trail. When an order was issued requiring wagon
freights to leave Missouri in April instead of May
as they had always done, William ordered his wagoners to obey the letter of the law by driving a few
miles from Westport, setting up camp, and waiting
a month until there was good grass. Unfortunately,

William Bent was not destined to see his business affairs settled satisfactorily during the two years of life left to him.

While waiting for the expected word of his appointment, Kit prepared to rest and enjoy the first freedom from duty he had known in many years. His oldest son was sixteen, the age Kit had reached when he ran away to the West. The children were all healthy, handsome and happy in their new surroundings. Josefa expected to add another child in the spring. The pine-linteled doorway of the house looked to the west where on clear days Kit could see the outlines of the Spanish Peaks. Nearby ran the trappers' favorite stream, the Purgatoire—named by the Spaniards "El Rio de las Animas Perdidas en Purgatorio (The River of Souls Lost in Purgatory) "—but called the Picketwire by most mountaineers. Here Kit looked forward to a quieter life that would restore his failing health.

In January of 1868 the appointment he sought came through on the death of Colonel A. B. Norton at Santa Fe. General McFerran happened to meet General U. S. Grant, his classmate at West Point, as Grant was leaving his office and showed him the petition for Carson's appointment to the superintendency. Glancing at the imposing list of names, Grant ordered his aide, Major Leit, to forward the commission to Carson. It was a rare sentimental gesture for a well-loved comrade whose days of service were drawing to a close.

Some of the Ute chiefs were still dissatisfied with the terms of their treaty and nothing would pacify them until they had gone to Washington to see the Great White Father. After much consideration, General Carson consented to accompany a delegation to the capital in February so that the Utes might put their grievances before the authorities. At the same time Kit could seek medical help for himself. Kit went by stage to Fort Hays, Kansas, while Governor Hunt, of Colorado, Ouray, and the other chiefs boarded the train at Cheyenne, the western terminal of the railroad, to meet Kit in St. Louis. The party was joined there by General Albert Gallatin Boone, a grandson of Daniel Boone, recently appointed Special Commissioner of Indians.

Though wan and weak after the taxing trip, Carson was able to join his old friends, Fremont, Carleton, and others, in a heartwarming reunion in Washington. Distressed to see Carson looking so thin and ill, Fremont sent word to Jessie at their home on the Hudson to meet Kit when he came to New York for consultation and, if possible, persuade him to go to their home for a rest. Mrs. Fremont left word at the Metropolitan Hotel that she would be waiting to hear from him at the home of a friend on Madison Square.

I was thinking [wrote Jessie Fremont later] how strange it was that my first and this my last meeting with this unlettered but true knight and gentleman, should be framed in by libraries, when the door opened and my poor Carson came in, holding the hand of my boy and resting on his sturdy shoulder.

He ought not have come out, but it would not have been Carson had he let me go to him. "No, you couldn't have done that—I'm alive yet." But he was exhausted and had to rest before he could talk. . . . It had pleased him to find the father's face repeated in the son. The youngster had gone up himself to Carson's room to find him and in answer to his knock . . . entered to several Indians and found Carson lying down. . . .

Before he could speak, Carson exclaimed, "My boy, I know you! You are a Fremont!" and so introduced him to the Chiefs. . . . Bringing his Indians through on the night train, he had gone at once to Dr. Sayre. . . . He wanted to get home, return his Indians to their people and die among his own people. If Dr. Sayre could help him do this, he expected no more for he felt he was near death. . . . With a gentle smile of amusement, Carson added, "And the Doctor said I must not do any drinking!"

"I must take the Chiefs to Boston. . . . Then we go home, straight. My wife must see me. . . . If I died here, it would kill her. I must get home. I think I can do it." His will was concentrated in the order to avoid excitement. He told me all this simply, choking the signs of distress. I could not entirely keep back. "Now don't. You must help me get home." And so he went his way and I saw him no more.[7]

When doctors in Boston could offer no encouragement, Kit started the fatiguing journey home. The chiefs were solicitous of his comfort but the once-vigorous traveler was forced to rest a week in Denver before the stage ride home. This was particularly distressing to Kit for Josefa's time was drawing near and he wanted to be home with the children. His eyes grew misty when he saw her waiting to greet him at La Junta. Words faltered as he tried to express his gratitude for having been given the strength to complete his mission and return safely to her.

It was now the first week of April and Kit hoped with the coming of warmer days and a long period of rest to regain his strength. Five days after their return to Boggsville, Josefa gave birth to a daughter who was named Josefita. Ten days later, without any warning, Kit received the cruelest blow of his lifetime when Josefa, his beautiful beloved, suddenly died.

He suppressed his great sorrow in concern for the children who soon would be orphaned, but the fighting will to live was gone. Remorse and a sense of failure shook him when he realized, after a lifetime of service, how little would be left for his family. In this upsurge of emotion, the aneurism in his throat developed rapidly. Colonel Henry R. Tilton, the Assistant Surgeon-General at Fort Lyon, came daily to attend the sick man. When the rushing spring floods made the fording of the river too difficult, Carson was moved into Colonel Tilton's own quarters at Fort Lyon.

A pile of blankets and buffalo robes in the corner of the room served as a bed for "The General," as the soldiers called him, and everything possible was tried to make the patient comfortable. He asked to be informed of the progress of his condition and wanted to know what he might expect to happen. Colonel Tilton frankly told him the tumor might choke him to death or rupture into a hemorrhage at any time. Kit thanked the doctor, apologizing for the trouble he was causing. "If it weren't for this," he said, pointing to his throat, "I might live to be a hundred."

"Though he knew he was doomed, he lived bravely, sweetly and unpretentious as ever," wrote John Hough's son, Emerson (author of *The Covered Wagon*). Carson was pleased when the young cavalrymen came from the barracks to visit him and Colonel Tilton read passages from Dr. DeWitt C. Peters' book of Carson's life, published ten years earlier. Kit listened intently as though reliving the great excitement, occasionally commenting on some adventure. Once he shook his head, remarking that Peters had "laid it on a little too thick." Having only contempt for braggarts and shams, Kit did not care to hear his own remarkable feats of courage enlarged upon. "I could not imagine," wrote Dr. Tilton later, "the quiet, modest retiring little man had done so much."[8]

On May 5, Kit asked one of the soldiers to write a letter to his nephew Aloysius Scheurich of Taos.

This last letter Carson was to send told how trying the days had been since the misfortune of losing his wife but he believed his health was improving. "I expect to be on the other side of the mountains by the end of the month . . . to avoid the heat during the summer months. . . ." Aloys and Teresina came at once from Taos to be with him and help care for the children at the Boggs' home.

With the help of Colonel Tilton, Carson drew up a will listing the following property: "Cattle from one to a hundred, seven yokes of steers, two ore wagons, four horses and one carriage, house and lot in Taos (to be sold for not less than $1000 or rented), furniture at Taos (to be sold), two or three pieces of land lying in the valley of Taos (to be rented), and money due from Maxwell for cattle sold." The will was filed in Pueblo County, Colorado Territory, May 15, 1868. Thomas and Rumalda Boggs were named guardians of the seven Carson children.

May 23 was a fresh, rain-washed spring day and Kit's spirits seemed brighter. He had slept well in a half-sitting position that was more comfortable and was more talkative than usual. Toward the middle of the afternoon, he asked Aloys to fix him a steak—a good piece of buffalo—and he would like some chili. He ate with relish, then asked for his pipes, which had been denied him. He chose the brier Fremont had given him, pressed the bowl full of fragrant leaf and took several deep draughts. It was as though he had decided there was no need to postpone his his last great adventure. "Concluded to attack, done so." Clear-minded, determined and resourceful to the last moment. The final spasm came quickly and with the words: "Doctor, Compadres, Adios!" Kit Carson's cavalcade of days was ended.

General Penrose, commander of Fort Lyon, ordered the flag lowered and arranged for "Holy Joe" Collins, the post chaplain, to conduct the last rites for "The General." Three fifers and three drummers from the infantry played the somber march, three volleys were fired by the cavalry and three by the infantry, and the guns of the fort sounded each minute during the simple service. After taps, a muffled drum roll and a final salute from the weeping boys who loved him, Kit Carson—the greatest Westerner of all—was taken to lie beside Josefa in a garden at Boggsville, his rough pine casket lined with the wedding dress of a captain's wife and decorated with the only flowers that could be found—those from the women's hats. (The following year, Captain Smith Simpson, to fulfill Carson's last request, took the bodies of Kit and Josefa to lie in a little burial plot not far from their home in Taos.) [9]

The news of Carson's death was printed in the first issue of the *Pueblo Chieftain* and flashed east by telegraph. Jessie Fremont, hearing the long-expected last news of their devoted friend, opened her journal to write these lines:

> Fleet foot in the forest
> Sage head in the cumber
> Red hand in the foray
> How sound is thy slumber?

NOTES ON CHAPTER FIFTEEN

1. Rusling, *Across America.*
2. Sherman, *Memoirs.*
3. See Sabin, *Kit Carson Days.*
4. See Eisele, *The Real Wild Bill Hickok;* Wilstach, *Wild Bill Hickok, Prince of Pistoleers.*

5. Inman, *The Old Santa Fe Trail.*
6. See Keleher, *Turmoil in New Mexico.*
7. Fremont, Jessie Benton, *The Will and the Way Stories.*
8. Tilton, *The Last Days of Kit Carson.*
9. See *Colorado Magazine,* Vol. V, "Death and Last Will of Kit Carson," by Albert W. Thompson.

Bibliography

ABBOTT, J. S. C. *Christopher Carson, Familiarly Known as Kit Carson.* New York, 1873.

ALTER, J. CECIL. *James Bridger, Trapper, Frontiersman, Scout and Guide.* Salt Lake City, 1925.

BANCROFT, HUBERT HOWE. *History of California.* San Francisco, 1890.

BASHFORD, HUBERT, and WAGNER, HARR. *A Man Unafraid; The Story of John Charles Fremont.* San Francisco, 1927.

BECKWOURTH, JAMES P. *Life and Adventures of James P. Beckwourth.* Edited by Bernard DeVoto. New York, 1931.

BENNETT, JAMES. *Overland Journey to California.* New Harmony, Indiana, 1906.

BENNETT, JAMES A. *Forts and Forays* [the diary of] *a Dragoon in New Mexico, 1850-1856.* Edited by Clinton E. Brooks and Frank D. Reeves. Albuquerque, New Mexico, 1948.

BENTON, THOMAS HART. *Thirty Years' View.* New York, 1856.

BIDWELL, JOHN. *Echoes of the Past About California.* Edited by Milo Milton Quaife. Chicago, 1928.

BIGELOW, JOHN. *Memoir of the Life and Public Services of John Charles Fremont.* New York, 1856.

BONSAL, STEPHEN. *Edward Fitzgerald Beale, a Pioneer in the Path of Empire.* New York, 1912.

BRADLEY, GLENN D. *Winning the Southwest.* Chicago, 1912.

BRANDON, WILLIAM. *The Men and the Mountain.* New York, 1955.

BREWERTON, COL. GEORGE D. *Overland with Kit Carson.* Edited by Stallo Vinton. New York, 1930.

BROWN, JENNIE B. *Fort Hall on the Oregon Trail.* Caldwell, Idaho, 1932.

BRYANT, EDWIN. *What I Saw in California.* New York, 1848.

BURDETT, CHARLES. *The Life and Adventures of Christopher Carson.* Philadelphia, 1860.

BURT, STRUTHERS. *Powder River.* New York, 1938.

CARSON, CHRISTOPHER. *Kit Carson's Autobiography.* Edited by Milo Milton Quaife. Chicago, 1935.

———. *Kit Carson's Own Story of His Life, as dictated to Col. and Mrs. D. C. Peters about 1856-57, and never before published.* Edited by Blanche C. Grant. Taos, New Mexico, 1926.

CHASE, LUCIAN B. *History of the Polk Administration.* New York, 1850.

CHEETHAM, FRANCIS T. *Kit Carson.* Taos, New Mexico, 1926.

CHITTENDEN, HIRAM M. *The American Fur Trade of the Far West.* New York, 1935.

——. *Yellowstone National Park, Historical and Descriptive.* Revised by Eleanor Chittenden Cress and Isabelle F. Story. Stanford University, California, 1933.

CLELAND, ROBERT G. *A History of California: The American Period.* New York, 1922.

——. *From Wilderness to Empire.* New York, 1944.

——. *This Reckless Breed of Men; the Trappers and Fur Traders of the Southwest.* New York, 1950.

CLYMAN, JAMES. *James Clyman, American Frontiersman, 1792-1881.* Edited by Charles L. Camp. San Francisco, 1928.

CODY, WILLIAM F. *Story of the Wild West.* Philadelphia, 1888.

COLLINS, LEWIS. *History of Kentucky.* Louisville, 1877.

CONRAD, HOWARD L. *"Uncle Dick" Wootton.* Chicago, 1890.

COOKE, PHILIP ST. GEORGE. *Scenes and Adventures in the Army; or, Romance of Military Life.* Philadelphia, 1857.

——. *The Conquest of New Mexico and California.* New York, 1878.

——; WHITING, WILLIAM HENRY CHASE; and AUBRY, FRANCOIS XAVIER. *Exploring Southwestern Trails, 1846-1854.* Edited by Ralph P. Bieber and Averam B. Bender. ("Southwest Historical Series," Vol. VII.) Glendale, California, 1938.

CORLE, EDWIN. *The Gila.* New York, 1951.

COUTANT, C. G. *History of Fort Bridger.* Laramie, 1899.

COWLES, COL. CALVIN D. "Genealogy of Five Allied Families." Manuscript, Rare Books, The Library of Congress.

CUTTS, JAMES M. *The Conquest of California and New Mexico.* Philadelphia, 1847.

DALE, EDWARD EVERETT. *The Indians of the Southwest.* Norman, Oklahoma, 1949.

DANA, JULIAN. *The Sacramento.* New York, 1938.

DELLENBAUGH, FREDERICK S. *Fremont and '49.* New York, 1914.

DEVOTO, BERNARD. *Across the Wide Missouri.* Boston, 1947.

——. *The Year of Decision: 1846.* Boston, 1943.

DICK, EVERETT. *Vanguards of the Frontier.* New York, 1941.

DODGE, COL. RICHARD IRVING. *The Plains of the Great West and their Inhabitants.* New York, 1877.

DUFFUS, ROBERT L. *The Santa Fe Trail.* New York, 1930.

EASTON, JEANETTE. *Narcissa Whitman.* New York, 1941.

EELLS, MYRON. *Father Eells.* Boston, 1894.

——. *Marcus Whitman, Pathfinder and Patriot.* Seattle, 1909.

EISELE, WILBERT E. *The Real Wild Bill Hickok.* Denver, 1931.

ELLIS, EDWARD S. *Life of Kit Carson.* New York, 1899.

ELLSWORTH, HENRY L. *Washington Irving on the Prairie.* Edited by Stanley T. Williams and Barbara D. Simison. New York, 1937.

EMORY, LIEUT. COL. WILLIAM H. *Notes of a Military Reconnoissance, from Fort Leavenworth, in Missouri, to San Diego, in California.* (House Ex. Doc. No. 41, 30th Cong., 1st Sess.) Washington, 1848. Also includes Lieut. J. W. Abert's journal, Col. Philip St. George Cooke's report of the Mormon Battalion from Santa Fe, New Mexico, to San Diego, Upper California, Capt. A. R. Johnson's journal, and other reports.

ESTERGREEN, MARION. *The Real Kit Carson.* Taos, New Mexico, 1955.

EYRE, ALICE. *The Famous Fremonts and their America.* Santa Ana, California, 1948.

FAVOUR, ALPHEUS H. *Old Bill Williams, Mountain Man.* Chapel Hill, North Carolina, 1936.

FERGUSSON, ERNA. *New Mexico; a Pageant of Three Peoples.* New York, 1951.

——. *Our Southwest.* New York, 1940.

FERRIS, WARREN A. *Life in the Rocky Mountains.* Edited by Paul C. Phillips. Denver, 1940.

FREMONT, JESSIE BENTON. *Far-West Sketches.* Boston, 1890.

——. *The Will and the Way Stories.* Boston, 1891.

FREMONT, JOHN CHARLES. *Memoirs of My Life.* Chicago, 1887.

——. *Narratives of Exploration and Adventure.* Edited by Allan Nevins. New York, 1956.

——. *Report of the Exploring Expedition to the Rocky Mountains in the Year 1842, and to Oregon and North California in the Years 1843-'44.* Washington, 1845.

——. *The Exploring Expedition to the Rocky Mountains, Oregon and California.* Buffalo, 1854.

FULLER, GEORGE. *A History of the Pacific Northwest.* New York, 1931.

GARRARD, LEWIS H. *Wah-to-yah and the Taos Trail.* New edition, with introduction by A. B. Guthrie, Jr. Norman, Oklahoma, 1955.

GHENT, W. J. *The Early Far West.* New York, 1931.

——. *The Road to Oregon.* New York, 1929.

GOODWIN, CARDINAL. *John Charles Fremont.* Stanford University, California, 1930.

GRANT, BLANCHE. *When Old Trails Were New; The Story of Taos.* New York, 1934.

GRAY, WILLIAM HENRY. *A History of Oregon.* Portland, 1871.

GREELEY, HORACE. *Overland Journey from New York to San Francisco in the Summer of 1859.* New York, 1860.

GREGG, JOSIAH. *Commerce of the Prairies.* Edited by Reuben Gold Thwaites. Cleveland, 1905.

——. Edited by Max L. Moorhead. Norman, Oklahoma, 1954.

——. *Diary and Letters.* Edited by Maurice Garland Fulton. Norman, Oklahoma, 1941.

GRIFFIN, DR. JOHN STROTHER. *A Doctor Comes to California; the Diary of* [the] *Assistant Surgeon with Kearny's Dragoons, 1846-1847.* San Francisco, 1943.

GRINNELL, GEORGE BIRD. *Beyond the Old Frontier; Adventures of Indian Fighters, Hunters, and Fur Traders.* New York, 1913.

——. *The Fighting Cheyennes.* New York, 1915.

HAFEN, LEROY R. *The Overland Mail, 1849-1869.* Cleveland, Ohio, 1926.

—— and GHENT, W. J. *Broken Hand, the Life Story of Thomas Fitzpatrick, Chief of the Mountain Men.* Denver, 1931.

—— and YOUNG, FRANCIS MARION. *Fort Laramie and the Pageant of the West, 1834-1890.* Glendale, California, 1938.

HEITMAN, FRANCIS B. *Historical Register and Dictionary of the United States Army.* Washington, 1903.

HEWETT, EDGAR L. *Kit Carson, He Led the Way.* (Papers of the School of American Research, Archaeological Institute of America, printed by Carson Memorial Foundation, Taos, New Mexico, by permission of the Museum of New Mexico, Santa Fe.)

HILDRETH, JAMES S. *Dragoon Campaigns to the Rocky Mountains.* New York, 1836.

HOBBS, CAPT. JAMES. *Wild Life in the Far West.* Hartford, 1872.

HOLBROOK, STEWART H. *The Columbia River.* New York, 1956.

HOOPES, ALBAN W. *Indian Affairs and their Administration, with Special Reference to the Far West, 1849-1860.* Philadelphia, 1932.

HOUCK, LOUIS. *History of Missouri.* Chicago, 1908.

HOUGH, EMERSON. *The Way to the West.* Indianapolis, 1903.

HULBERT, ARCHER B., ed. *Southwest on the Turquoise Trail; the First Diaries* (Becknell, Sibley, Wetmore, Armijo) *of the Road to Santa Fe.* Denver, 1933.

IDE, WILLIAM B. *Who Conquered California?* Edited by Simeon Ide. Claremont, New Hampshire, 1880.

INMAN, COL. HENRY H. *The Great Salt Lake Trail.* New York, 1898.

——. *The Old Santa Fe Trail.* New York, 1898.

JACKSON, W. TURRENTINE. *Wagon Roads West; a Study of Federal Road Surveys and Construction in the Trans-Mississippi West, 1846-49.* Berkeley, California, 1952.

JAMES, GEORGE WHARTON. *Fremont in California.* San Francisco, 1903.

KEARNY, THOMAS. *The Mexican War and the Conquest of California.* San Francisco, 1929.

KELEHER, WILLIAM A. *The Maxwell Land Grant: A New Mexico Item.* Santa Fe, 1942.

——. *Turmoil in New Mexico.* Santa Fe, 1952.

KELLY, CHARLES. *Salt Desert Trails.* Salt Lake City, 1930.

LAUT, AGNES C. *The Fur Trade of America.* New York, 1921.

LAVENDER, DAVID. *Bent's Fort.* New York, 1954.

LEONARD, ZENAS. *Narrative of the Adventures of Zenas Leonard.* Edited by Milo Milton Quaife. Chicago, 1934.

LEVENS, HENRY C., and DRAKE, NATHANIEL. *History of Cooper County, Missouri.* St. Louis, 1876.

——. *History of Howard and Cooper Counties, Missouri.* St. Louis, 1883.

LEWIS, OSCAR. *California in 1846.* San Francisco, 1934.

MACK, EFFIE MONA, and SAWYER, BYRD WALL. *Our State: Nevada.* Caldwell, Idaho, 1940.

McWILLIAMS, CAREY. *Southern California Country.* New York, 1946.

MARY LOYOLA, SISTER. *American Occupation of New Mexico, 1821-1852.* Santa Fe, 1937.

MELINE, JAMES F. *Two Thousand Miles on Horseback.* New York, 1867.

MILLER, ALFRED JACOB. *The West of Alfred Jacob Miller.* Norman, Oklahoma, 1951.

MOODY, MARSHALL D. "Kit Carson, Agent to the Indians in New Mexico, 1853-1856." Paper presented to the faculty of the Department of History, the American University. (*New Mexico Historical Review,* Vol. XXVIII.)

MORGAN, DALE L. *The Great Salt Lake.* Indianapolis, 1947.

——. *The Humboldt, Highroad to the West.* New York, 1943.

MUMEY, NOLIE. *Old Forts and Trading Posts.* Denver, 1956.

NEVINS, ALLAN. *Fremont, Pathmarker of the West.* New York, 1937.

PALMER, ROSE A. *The North American Indians.* ("Smithsonian Scientific Series," Vol. IV.) New York, 1938.

PANCOAST, CHARLES E. *A Quaker Forty-Niner.* Edited by Anna Paschall Hannum. Philadelphia, 1930.

PARKER, SAMUEL. *A Journey Beyond the Rocky Mountains in 1835, 1836, and 1837.* Edinburgh, 1841.

PETERS, DEWITT C. *The Life and Adventures of Kit Carson, the Nestor of the Rocky Mountains.* Boston, 1858.

PETTIS, CAPT. GEORGE HENRY. *Kit Carson's Fight with the Comanche and Kiowa Indians, at the Adobe Walls on the Canadian River.* Providence, 1878.

PHILLIPS, CATHERINE COFFIN. *Jessie Benton Fremont, a Woman who Made History.* San Francisco, 1935.

PIKE, ALBERT. *Prose Sketches and Poems, Written in the Western Country.* Boston, 1834.

POLK, JAMES KNOX. *Polk; the Diary of a President, 1845-1849.* Edited by Allan Nevins. New York, 1929.

PREUSS, CHARLES. *Exploring with Fremont; the Private Diaries of Charles Preuss, Cartographer for John C. Fremont on His First, Second, and Fourth Expeditions to the Far West.* Edited by Erwin G. and Elizabeth K. Gudde. Norman, Oklahoma, 1958.

QUAIFE, MILO MILTON, ed. *Diary of James Knox Polk.* Chicago, 1910.

REVERE, JOSEPH W. *A Tour of Duty in California.* Boston, 1849.

———. *Keel and Saddle.* Boston, 1872.

RICHARDSON, MARVIN. *The Whitman Mission.* Walla Walla, Washington, 1940.

RICHARDSON, RUPERT N., and RISTER, CARL COKE. *The Greater Southwest.* Glendale, California, 1934.

RISTER, CARL COKE. *The Southwestern Frontier, 1865-1881.* Cleveland, 1928.

RODENBOUGH, THEOPHILUS FRANCIS. *From Everglade to Cañon with the Second Dragoons (Second United States Cavalry); an Authentic Account of Service in Florida, Mexico, Virginia, and the Indian Country.* New York, 1875.

ROOT, FRANK A., and CONNELLEY, WILLIAM ELSEY. *The Overland Stage to California; Personal Reminiscences and Authentic History of the Great Overland Stage Line and Pony Express from the Missouri River to the Pacific Ocean.* Topeka, Kansas, 1901.

RUSLING, JAMES F. *Across America; or, The Great West and the Pacific Coast.* New York, 1874.

RUSSELL, MARIAN SLOAN. *Land of Enchantment; Memoirs Along the Santa Fe Trail.* Edited by Garnet M. Brayer. Evanston, Illinois, 1954.

RUSSELL, OSBORNE. *Journal of a Trapper; or, Nine Years in the Rocky Mountains, 1834-1843.* Boise, Idaho, 1921.

RUXTON, GEORGE F. *Life in the Far West.* Edited by LeRoy R. Hafen, with a foreword by Mae Reed Porter. Norman, Oklahoma, 1951.

———. *Ruxton of the Rockies;* collected by Clyde and Mae Reed Porter. Edited by LeRoy R. Hafen. Norman, Oklahoma, 1950.

SABIN, EDWIN L. *Kit Carson Days.* Chicago, 1914.

———. Revised ed. with new matter. New York, 1935.

SAGE, RUFUS B. *Rocky Mountain Life; or, Startling Scenes and Perilous Adventures in the Far West.* Dayton, Ohio, 1841.

———. *Scenes in the Rocky Mountains and in Oregon, California, New Mexico, Texas, and the Grand Prairies.* Philadelphia, 1846.

SCHERER, JAMES A. B. *Thirty-First Star.* New York, 1942.

SELL, HENRY BLACKMAN, and WEYBRIGHT, VICTOR. *Buffalo Bill and the Wild West.* New York, 1955.

SHERMAN, GEN. WILLIAM T. *Memoirs.* New York, 1891.

SIBLEY, GEORGE CHAMPLIN. *The Road to Santa Fe; the Journal and Diaries of George Champlin Sibley.* Albuquerque, New Mexico, 1952.

SMITH, HENRY NASH. *Virgin Land; the American West as Symbol and Myth.* Cambridge, Massachusetts, 1950.

SMITH, JUSTIN. *The War with Mexico.* New York, 1919.

SMITH, T. BERRY. *History of Howard and Chariton Counties, Missouri.* Topeka, Kansas, 1923.

STEWART, SIR WILLIAM DRUMMOND. *Altowan: or, Incidents of Life and Adventure in the Rocky Mountains.* New York, 1846.

———. *Edward Warren.* London, 1854.

STONE, IRVING. *Men to Match My Mountains; the Opening of the Far West, 1840-1900.* New York, 1956.

SUTTER, JOHANN AUGUST. *Diary.* Edited by Douglas Watson. San Francisco, 1932.

TALBOT, THEODORE. *The Journals of Theodore Talbot, 1843 and 1849-52; with the Fremont Expedition of 1843 and with the First Military Company in Oregon Territory, 1849-1852.* Edited by Charles H. Carey. Portland, Oregon, 1931.

TILTON, HENRY REMSEN. *The Last Days of Kit Carson.* Grand Forks, North Dakota, 1939.

TWITCHELL, RALPH EMERSON. *Spanish Archives of New Mexico,* Vol. I. Cedar Rapids, Iowa, 1914.

———. *The History of the Military Occupation of New Mexico.* Denver, 1909.

———. *The Leading Facts of New Mexico History.* Cedar Rapids, Iowa, 1911.

UPHAM, CHARLES W. *Life, Explorations and Public Services of John Charles Fremont.* Boston, 1856.

VESTAL, STANLEY. *Kit Carson, the Happy Warrior of the Old West.* Boston, 1928.

———. *Warpath and Council Fire; the Plains Indians' Struggle for Survival in War and in Diplomacy, 1851-1891.* New York, 1948.

VICTOR, FRANCES FULLER. *The River of the West* (life of Joe Meek). Hartford, 1870.

WALDO, WILLIAM. "Recall of a Septuagenarian." Paper printed by the Missouri Historical Society, 1880. Reprinted in *Glimpses of the Past,* Vol. V (1938).

WEBB, WALTER PRESCOTT. *The Great Plains.* Boston, 1931.

WILCOX, CADMUS M. *History of the Mexican War.* Washington, 1892.

WILLIAMS, ALBERT N. *Rocky Mountain Country.* New York, 1950.

WILLIAMS, ANN (WEST). *Narcissa and Marcus Whitman; Martyrs on the Oregon Trail.* New York, 1954.

WILLIAMS, CHAUNCEY P. *Lone Elk: The Life Story of Bill Williams, Trapper and Guide of the Far West.* Denver, 1935.

WILSTACH, FRANK J. *Wild Bill Hickok, the Prince of Pistoleers.* New York, 1934.

WOODWARD, ARTHUR. *Lances at San Pascual.* San Francisco, 1948.

YOUNG, OTIS E. *The First Military Escort on the Santa Fe Trail, 1829; from the Journal and Reports of Major Bennet Riley and Lieutenant Philip St. George Cooke.* Glendale, California, 1952.

HISTORICAL SOCIETY PUBLICATIONS

History of the Arkansas Valley

California Historical Society
   Kit Carson in California. Article by Charles L. Camp. San Francisco, 1922.

Historical Society of Southern California

State Historical Society of Colorado
   Bent's Fort on the Arkansas, by James T. Forrest. Denver, 1954
   Old Fort Garland, by James T. Forrest. Denver, 1954
   Colorado Magazine

Kansas Historical Quarterly

Mississippi Valley Historical Review

Missouri Historical Review

New Mexico Historical Review

Oregon Historical Quarterly

Southwestern Historical Quarterly

Great Southwest Magazine

Boggsville Committee
   Boggsville, by C. W. Hurd. Las Animas, Colorado, 1957

Numerous letters, documents, records, narratives, periodicals and newspapers examined at The Library of Congress; The National Archives—Department of the Interior, Bureau of Indian Affairs, Department of Old Army; The Henry E. Huntington Library, San Marino, California; The Archives of New Mexico, Santa Fe.